24 / 7

*Time and Temporality in
the Network Society*

Edited by Robert Hassan and
Ronald E. Purser

STANFORD BUSINESS BOOKS
An Imprint of Stanford University Press
Stanford, California
2007

Stanford University Press
Stanford, California

Printed in the United States of America on acid-free, archival-quality paper

Library of Congress Cataloging-in-Publication Data

24/7 : time and temporality in the network society / edited by Robert Hassan and
Ronald E. Purser.
    p. cm.
  Includes bibliographical references and index.
  ISBN 978-0-8047-5196-4 (cloth : alk. paper)--ISBN 978-0-8047-5197-1 (pbk. : alk. paper)
  1. Time--Sociological aspects. 2. Information society. 3. Information technology-
-Social aspects. 4. Computers and civilization. I. Hassan, Robert, 1959- II. Purser,
Ronald E., 1956- III. Title: Twenty-four seven.

HM656.A14 2007
303.48'33--dc22   2007007539

Designed by Bruce Lundquist

Typeset at Stanford University Press in 10/14 Minion

Special discounts for bulk quantities of Stanford Business Books are available to
corporations, professional associations, and other organizations. For details and
discount information, contact the special sales department of Stanford University
Press. Tel: (650) 736-1783, Fax: (650) 736-1784

To Paul

&

To Theo, Camille, and Kate

Contents

Foreword

REVOLUTIONARY SOCIAL CHANGES have a habit of sneaking up on us. They are easy to detect from a temporal distance but much harder to identify while they are happening, and we are inescapably implicated in the processes of change and their effects. It is difficult, for example, to notice the threshold when a novelty becomes pervasive and begins to restructure the way things are done at the widest possible societal level. The subject matter of this book addresses just such a situation. It deals with communication and information technologies that have become an integral part of almost every contemporary institutional practice in the industrialized world and beyond, and it seeks to understand this change in relation to the much older and slower, if equally pervasive, processes of global change associated with the social relations, technologies, and economies of time.

To achieve its task, the collection of essays draws on the combined expertise of the two editors in both these areas of investigation. The editors, in turn, have assembled an interdisciplinary panel of international academics whose individual knowledge bases complement each other and who have produced an extraordinarily rich body of work. Their contributions illuminate both the relation between networked time and information technology and its sociocultural and socioeconomic time-space distantiated effects. Looking at the issues in the round, the collection of chapters offers its readers an almost holographic perspective on social relations within the network society, dealing, on the one hand, with the temporal relations of acceleration and, on the other, with nonstop activity in the sphere of work, communication, consumption, and profit creation.

Methodologically the book is a treatise in explication. It renders explicit what forms a largely taken-for-granted feature of the socioeconomic practices that structure our everyday existence. It foregrounds issues that have invaded our lives almost unnoticed until social and cultural scientists, historians, and philosophers awoke to the resultant contradictions that began to pull their routine assumptions and unquestioned frameworks of meaning into bizarre shapes, jolting everyone into the unaccustomed temporal realm of networks. Where we used to deal with space, materiality, and quantity, we are now required to encompass time, virtuality, and networked processes. Yet the latter is not replacing the former but operates in contexts of everyday materiality and spatial linearity. Information Communication Technology (ICT) temporality is embedded and functioning within social contexts of clock time that are continuing to play their dominant role and have *not* evaporated with the event of ICT time. This means, for example, that the control of time, afforded most prominently through clock time, and the loss of control through ICTs have to be understood with reference and in relation to each other. This requires a new temporal imagination and an approach to the social that leaves behind the world of either-or choices and moves toward the realm of temporal multiplicity. Complexity rather than simplicity is the order of the day and demands from researchers new strategies that transcend the dualisms of old.

To encompass that complexity, some of the authors of this collection begin to unravel the historically distinct temporal logic of the network society. In the course of this work they show how this logic enframes not just understanding but also daily practice at the personal and collective level, acting as both unbounded opportunity and restricting framework that delimits room for maneuvering in every sphere of social life.

If we understand the temporal relations of industrial society as a steady development toward increase of control, commodification, and colonization, we begin to realize that with networked information and communication technologies operating at or near the speed of light, control and commodification have begun to implode whilst the colonization of time and space has risen to previously unknown heights and depths. On the one hand, ICT provides the potential to be connected anywhere, anytime; on the other hand, it affords the capacity to be everywhere at once and nowhere in particular. This places users of ICT in the realm if not quite of the gods then at least of angels.

ICT time, we need to appreciate further, departs significantly from the established clock-time norm. It is globally networked rather than globally zoned. It is instantaneous rather than durational and causal. It is simultaneous rather than sequential, marked by a chronoscopic temporality rather than spatially constituted clock time. This raises problems for time control: with instantaneity (which means processes without a gap between cause and effect in the linear chain of events) there can be no interception, no intervening action. With simultaneity (which means action that is happening at the same time and is dispersed across space) there can be no certainty over effects. That is to say, when there is no durational gap for establishing difference and change, when there is no discernible sequence, and when the speeds involved operate outside the capacity of the conscious mind, then the control achieved over clock-time processes is rendered inoperable. A similar effect applies to the relation between clock time and money: when there is no longer a gap that can be spatialized and quantified, the commodification of time becomes difficult if not impossible. As this book shows, new strategies need to be and are established for creation of both profit and political action.

The contributions to this collection analyze these processes and critically evaluate associated debates. Together they provide important insights and create a much-needed window on a largely unquestioned aspect of our lives that seems to operate beyond our influence. By bringing together such a breadth of expertise in one volume, the editors have opened up for discussion and academic scrutiny an important contemporary development that impacts sociocultural existence almost anywhere on this planet. I wish readers much enjoyment and intellectual challenge.

Barbara Adam
Cardiff, July 2006

Contributors

BEN AGGER teaches in the Department of Sociology at the University of Texas at Arlington, where he also directs the Center for Theory. He writes in the areas of critical theory, cultural studies, and media / Internet studies. Among his recent books are *Postponing the Postmodern* (Lanham, MD: Rowman and Littlefield, 2002); *The Virtual Self* (Malden, MA: Blackwell, 2004); and *Speeding Up Fast Capitalism* (Boulder, CO: Paradigm, 2004). He is working on a book on the 1960s (*The Sixties at Forty*) and, with Beth Anne Shelton, a book on the family and childhood (*Fast Families, Virtual Children*). He also edits the journal *Fast Capitalism* (www.fastcapitalism.com).

MIKE CRANG is a reader in geography at Durham University. Since he obtained his doctorate, he has worked on issues of temporality and social memory and is interested in the conceptual and empirical relationships of space and time. He has been the coeditor of the journal *Time & Society* since 1997 and has written several papers and essays on space and time (putting together an edited collection, *Thinking Space* [London: Routledge, 2000], with Nigel Thrift). He has also worked on urban information and communication technologies, publishing several papers and an edited collection (*Virtual Geographies* [London: Routledge, 1999], with Phil Crang and Jon May). He has recently been working on an ESRC-funded project, "Multispeed cities and the logistics of daily life in an information age," and previously on a British Academy project on Singapore as an Intelligent Island.

ROBERT HASSAN is an Australian Research Council Senior Fellow in media and communications at the Media and Communications Program at the University of Melbourne. He has written numerous articles on the subjects of information technology and time. His books include *The Chronoscopic Society* (New York: Lang, 2003); *Media, Politics, and the Network Society* (Maidenhead: Open University Press, 2004); *The New Media in Theory Reader* (with Julian Thomas) (Oxford: Oxford University Press, 2006); and *Empire of Speed* (in press). He is currently writing *The Political Economy of Information*. With Carmen Leccardi, he is editor of *Time & Society*.

THOMAS HYLLAND ERIKSEN is Professor of Social Anthropology at the University of Oslo and at the Free University of Amsterdam. He is formerly a Senior Research Fellow at the International Institute of Peace Research and has served as editor of the cultural journal *Samtiden (Our Times)*; the book series Anthropology, Culture, and Society (Pluto Press); and the *Norwegian Journal of Anthropology*. He has published numerous books, including *Tyranny of the Moment: Fast and Slow Time in the Information Age* (London: Pluto, 2001); *Ethnicity and Nationalism* (London: Pluto, 1993 / 2002); and *Engaging Anthropology: The Case for a Public Presence* (Oxford: Berg, 2006). His academic writings span such topics as ethnicity, identity politics, nationalism, anthropological theory, and minority issues. He has also written about evolution and selfishness and is currently writing a book on globalization and one on rubbish.

CARMEN LECCARDI is Professor of Cultural Sociology at the University of Milan-Bicocca, Italy. She has published widely on the topics of time, youth, and gender and has a special interest in the issue of the future and planning in a risk society. During 2000 and 2001 she was one of a small group of youth-research experts whom the European Commission asked to take part in its White Paper consultation process, developing a strategy for young people across Europe. A former member of the Council of the International Society for the Study of Time, since 1999 she has been coeditor of the journal *Time & Society*. Her latest books include *Il tempo nella società* (Time in Society) (Milan: Baldini

Castoldi Dalai, 2006); and *A New Youth? Young People, Generations, and Family Life* (coedited with Elisabetta Ruspini) (Aldershot: Ashgate, 2006).

GEERT LOVINK is a media theorist, net critic, and author of *Dark Fiber* (Cambridge, MA: MIT Press, 2002); *Uncanny Networks* (Cambridge, MA: MIT Press, 2002); and *My First Recession* (Rotterdam: V2/NAi, 2003). He is a member of the Adilkno collective (Cracking the Movement, The Media Archive) and cofounder of Internet projects such as The Digital City, Nettime, Fibreculture, and Incommunicado. He holds a PhD from the University of Melbourne and in 2003 was postdoc at the Centre for Critical and Cultural Studies, University of Queensland. In 2004 he founded the Institute of Network Cultures as a part of his newly created job in Amsterdam as professor at Interactive Media (Hogeschool van Amsterdam) and associate professor in the Media and Culture Department, University of Amsterdam. From 2005 to 2006 he was a fellow at the Wissenschaftkolleg, the Berlin Institute for Advanced Study. Web archive: www.laudanum.net/geert. Blog: www.networkcultures.org/geert.

DAVID R. LOY is Besl Professor of Religion, Ethics, and Society at Xavier University in Cincinnati. His books include *Nonduality: A Study in Comparative Philosophy* (New Haven, CT: Yale University Press, 1988); *Lack and Transcendence: The Problem of Death and Life in Psychotherapy, Existentialism, and Buddhism* (Atlantic Highlands, NJ: Humanities Press, 1996); *A Buddhist History of the West: Studies in Lack* (Albany: State University of New York Press, 2002); and *The Great Awakening: A Buddhist Social Theory* (Boston: Wisdom, 2003). He is a longtime student of Zen and is qualified as a Zen sensei (teacher) in the Sanbo Kyodan lineage.

ADRIAN MACKENZIE teaches at the Institute for Cultural Research, Lancaster University. His research is in the area of technology, science, and culture using approaches from cultural studies, social studies of technology, and critical theory. He has published several monographs on technology, including *Transductions: Bodies and Machines at Speed* (London: Continuum, 2002); and *Cutting Code: Software and Sociality* (New York: Peter Lang, 2006); as well as a range of articles on technology, digital media, science, and culture.

ANDREW MURPHIE is a Senior Lecturer in the School of Media, Film, and
Theatre, University of New South Wales, Australia. He has published
on the work of Gilles Deleuze and Félix Guattari, cultural theory, virtual media, network ecologies, and popular music. He is the coauthor
with John Potts of *Culture and Technology* (New York: Palgrave, 2003);
and editor of the *Fibreculture Journal* (http://journal.fibreculture.
org/). His current research focuses on the cultural politics of models
of cognition, perception, and life; media ecologies; electronic music;
and performance technologies. His recent online publications include
"Differential Life, Perception and the Nervous Elements: Whitehead, Bergson, and Virno on the Technics of Living," in *Culture Machine* (2005); and "The Mutation of 'Cognition' and the Fracturing of
Modernity: Cognitive Technics, Extended Mind, and Cultural Crisis,"
in *Scan* (2005).

JACK PETRANKER, MA University of California at Berkeley, JD Yale Law
School, is founder and director of the Center for Creative Inquiry
and the author of *When It Rains, Does Space Get Wet?* (Berkeley, CA:
Dharma, 2006). A former dean of the Nyingma Institute in Berkeley,
California, he teaches at the institute and offers programs and work-
shops on three continents. His research interests include first-person
methodologies in consciousness studies, the lived significance of time
and space, creative inquiry in the classroom, prospects for transforming the legal profession, and the new forms of human experience generated by technological knowledge. He is an active member of the
California Bar.

RONALD E. PURSER is Professor of Management in the College of Business
at San Francisco State University, past division chair of the Organization Development and Change (ODC) division of the Academy of
Management, and cofounder of the International Network for Time in
Management and Organizations (INTiMO). He has chaired sympo-
sia on time and organizations at the Academy of Management meetings and was guest editor of a special issue of the *Journal of Managerial
Psychology* on "Timescapes in Management." Dr. Purser's articles on
time have appeared in such outlets as the *Journal of Applied Behavioral
Science*; *Research in Organizational Change and Development*; *Making
Time* (Oxford: Oxford University Press, 2002); and *In Search of Time*

(Palermo: Fabio Orlando Editore, 2005). He is a member of the International Society for the Study of Time.

HANS RÄMÖ is Associate Professor in the School of Business at Stockholm University. His recent research interests include temporal and spatial factors of management and organization, project management, organizational trust, food industry, health care and environmental management, and philosophy and sociology of science. He has published a number of articles, including in the journal *Time & Society*, as well as book chapters.

IDA H. J. SABELIS is Assistant Professor in the Department of Culture, Organization, and Management at Free University in Amsterdam. Her research focuses on time in organizations, temporal compression and acceleration, and identity processes in contemporary organizational life. She is book review editor for *Time & Society*; associate editor of the serial *Gender, Work, and Organization* (Oxford: Blackwell, 1994–); editor for the Dutch journal *Filosofie in Bedrijf* (Philosophy of Organization); and is an active member of the Tutzing Time Ecology Project (Germany), INTiMO (International Network of Time Studies in Management and Organization), and the ISST (International Society for the Study of Time).

DARREN TOFTS is Associate Professor of Media and Communications, Swinburne University of Technology, Melbourne. He is the author (with artist Murray McKeich) of *Memory Trade: A Prehistory of Cyberculture* (Sydney: Interface Books, 1998); *Parallax: Essays on Art, Culture, and Technology* (Sydney: Interface Books, 1999); and editor (with Annemarie Jonson and Alessio Cavallaro) of *Prefiguring Cyberculture: An Intellectual History* (Sydney: Power Publications / MIT Press, 2003). His most recent book is *Interzone: Media Arts in Australia* (Melbourne: Thames and Hudson, 2005). He is a member of the editorial boards of *Postmodern Culture, Continuum, fibreculture journal, Rhizomes,* and *RealTime*.

24 / 7

Introduction

Robert Hassan and Ronald E. Purser

C AN A SET OF NUMBERS be a buzzword or a neologism? Although *24/7* offers no answer to this particular question, the specific arrangement of numbers, used typically to signify twenty-four hours a day for every day of the week, does seem to us appropriate for what it is we are trying to convey and for what the essays in this volume grapple with: our experience of time in the network society.

First it seems worthwhile, no matter how appropriate or taken for granted the term *24/7* may seem, to try to define or explain what it means. The designation turns out to be of uncertain provenance. Google wasn't much help to us in trying to clear things up. With characteristic overkill it located some 171,000,000 pages of possible relevance (in 0.17 seconds). After sifting through the first ten results, however, we were already discouraged. Predictably, perhaps, most of the results were related to media companies who for one reason or another had *24/7* in either their company name or as an indication of the time frame in which they promise to deliver their product or service. The only exception to this commercial rule was *24/7 Prayer* (www.24-7prayer.com), which offers "non-stop prayer across the nations."

The next near-to-hand alternative source of information on the term was from Wikipedia.com. This is a rapidly growing online encyclopedia for which anyone can write up the definition to any term or construct an explanation for any subject. Wikipedia currently has more than one million entries, among which a definition for *24/7* was duly found: "In commerce and industry, it identifies a service that will be present regardless of current time or day, as might be offered by a supermarket, ATM, gas station, diner or restaurant, concierge service or manned datacenter." This is a disappointingly empty description. There is no sense of connectivity, of digital networks, of speed, of compressed time, and no sense of the fact that more and more of our "24/7" life is being *colonized* by the blandishments and the demands of "commerce and industry." Crucially, there is no sense that the goods and services that exist in the supermarket through to the datacenter are part of a flowing and ever-accelerating networked and globalized life where the time of the clock no longer schedules and meters our individual and collective existence in as predictable a fashion as it once did.

As theorists of time, we as editors envisage something of much stronger import in 24/7, something more fully centered around the ideas that reflect a changing relationship with time. The stark entry in the Web site Dictionary. com offers a definition that comes closer to how we perceive the term. It says, simply, "continuously; unceasingly." These words suggest that 24/7 has more to do with individuals and societies being *driven* or pushed by a systemic temporal logic, as opposed to the mere availability of everything at our fingertips; things to be pulled toward us to satisfy our needs and whims at any "time" we want. At another level this definition indicates something more deeply *temporal* that goes beyond the mere designation of the hours and the days.

The emergence of the networked society has seen a revolution in the temporal dynamics of both our personal lives and society as a whole. The evidence is everywhere if we care to look and reflect. For example, if we consider the Wikipedia example a bit more closely, the fact that services are available "regardless of the current time of day" says something about what is now *expected* of people in a temporal sense. In order to be *flexible* and *efficient* (two buzzwords closely related to 24/7), we may find ourselves working on a networked computer at midnight, communicating with someone half a world away, then stopping for a break to go to the local all-night supermarket to buy milk for the coffee we need to stay awake. This colonization of the night by industry is, of course, as old as the introduction of shift-working. What is different today, however, is that networked globalization pulls millions of people into the orbit of the "24/7" life, where what the clock on the wall says becomes secondary to the demands of "flexible accumulation." The old-fashioned notion of "shift-work" (a specific time and place) is giving way to the imperatives of "flexibility" and "efficiency" (any time, any place). The temporal bound-

ary of the weekend, similarly, morphs into becoming just another couple of workdays, where the computer, cell phone, PDA, and so on connect us to the "normal" concerns of the working week. To borrow a term from the purveyors of broadband computer services, 24/7 means to be "always on"—always connected or connectable—and always available to work or to consume.

The changing relationship with time that we experience through living and working in the 24/7 networked society is becoming increasingly documented. As the following examples in this introduction show, however, it is usually from a perspective on time that does not actually grasp or help reveal the important issues contained in a deeper level of temporal analysis. For example, at the empirical level of sociology Juliet B. Schor informed us in the early 1990s of something we intuitively knew when she wrote that workers in the United States were "starved for time" and that society more generally suffered from what she termed a "time-squeeze" (Schor 1992, 1993). There are not enough hours in the day, in other words, to enable us to do all the things we need to do. This was bad news, even if it was old news. From the French cultural theorist Paul Virilio, however, the tidings are even worse. Networked information systems, he argues, have brought us to such a point of acceleration (real time) that we experience a "loss of orientation" in the world. Cyberspace, or the "real time" of "instantaneous, globalized information flows," is driving humanity toward what Virilio sees as a "dictatorship of speed" (Virilio 1995).

Schor and Virilio both write about time—but at a surface level. Schor's sociological work is derived from tables and statistics that she interprets at a conventional level of analysis. This approach portrays people as feeling anxious or stressed about "not enough time in the day" and is connected to structural changes in the nature of work. This finding is true enough, but Schor's analysis remains on the surface level of describing and defining time. And in Virilio's theory-based perspective cyberspace is propelling us all to an unknown and uncertain future, a future in which machines "choke the senses" with the speed at which they bombard us with information. Speed is central to his thesis, but the profound connection of *speed to time*—and how high-speed networked technology has affected our relationship with time—is not explained. We are at a loss, in other words, to understand why speed has become so central (and so problematic) in society, other than as an effect of computerization.

There is truth and there is intellectual value in both of these arguments. If, however, we are to understand the nature of the network society, then a deeper understanding of time is required. Schor and Virilio point to something that most of us recognize intuitively: our relationship with time has changed over the last quarter-century. This, not unconnectedly, as we will see, is the period of time that has seen unprecedented spatiotemporal transformation through the growth and spread of neoliberal globalization and the revolution in information and communication technologies. So as a precursor to the chapters that follow, let us look more closely at the subject of time and develop a tentative framework of analysis to help us understand (and possibly have some control over) the changing "timescapes" (Adam 2004) we encounter and experience in the network society.

About Time

The question of time is a rather odd one. Time's passage, to paraphrase J. T. Fraser (2003, 15), is both intimately familiar and strangely elusive. For many people in everyday social life, time tends to be viewed as something that just "is," a backdrop to our being in the world and something we deal with almost without conscious thought. As we will see, its elusiveness was perhaps too easily "solved" by accepting the clock as the reification of time's passage. This acceptance has left a debilitating legacy as far as how theorists in the social sciences—in politics, economics, sociology, and so on—have dealt with the subject of time. This is evident in the one-dimensional treatment of time by social scientists such as Schor and the more elliptical perspective from social theorists such as Virilio.

The tide seems to be turning, however, in this respect. Journals such as *Time & Society*, *KronoScope*, and others have become intellectual poles of attraction for a growing academic interest in the nature of time—an interest that looks to disparate thinkers such as Schor and Virilio for either guidance or evidence of where more work needs to be done.

Much more focused and reflective thinking has been done within the humanities into the nature of time. And this philosophical literature constitutes the foundation for the critical thinking on time that has been making inroads into the mainstream of social science, helping to transform the discipline with the added emphasis on time. In respect of the foundational thinkers on time, we need to begin with two who wrote during the late nineteenth century and well into the twentieth and opened up profound insights onto the subject: Henri Bergson and Edmund Husserl.

Bergson's philosophy was aligned with a countertendency to the Enlightenment that included (most notably) Sade, Schopenhauer, and Nietzsche. He was concerned, along with others such as Alfred North Whitehead, to create an alternative metaphysics to that generated by the overly mechanistic and scientistic view generated by strict rationality. Bergson's fields of inquiry, consequently, were concerned with those subtle and hard-to-pin-down areas that escape rationality's forensic gaze, such as irrationality, becoming, memory, and intuition.

Our day-to-day perception of what constitutes time, according to Bergson, comes to us courtesy of the Enlightenment and its creation of the physical sciences. This view apprehends time mathematically, as a series of fixed states that can be separated out and measured. Alternatively, he argued that time is not something that can be wholly understood by numbers but is something lived (internal, not external) and having duration—*durée*. For example, he notes in his *Time and Free Will* that durée "forms both the past and the present states into an organic whole, as happens when we recall the notes of a tune, melting, so to speak, into one another" (Bergson 1913 / 2001). Time, for Bergson, was a state of becoming and a process of living duration. Intuitions of the "indeterminate" states of time were central to Bergson's philosophy. In *The Creative Mind: An Introduction to Metaphysics* Bergson described intuition as "thinking in duration," a process that reflected the flow of reality (Bergson 1946). Conceptual thinking and intuition were a necessary combination to perceive and understand the flow of temporality. Time, then, is not made understandable through a simple rationality that taxonomizes, calculates, divides, measures, and dissects. According to Bergson time is indivisible and flows. This fluidity is accessible and may be intuited as a lived reality. The value of Bergson's work is that he sought to separate out the qualitative temporality of the lived durée, the temporality of experience, intuition, memory, and consciousness from that of the quantitative temporality of a rationalized time based on science, measurement, and invariant rhythms. Such a perspective opened up a way of explaining another, more evanescent and nonrational, aspect of time that most of us experience (the way in which our experience of time does not easily fit with the ticking of seconds through minutes and hours) but have difficulty in reconciling with the mathematical ordering of duration that classical science takes as the measure of temporal reality.

Husserl was an almost exact contemporary of Bergson, and, indeed, their works share certain features that serve to complement each other and take the perspective on time to a higher synthesis. Husserl is the founder of phenomenology, a philosophy that takes intuitive experience of phenomena as its starting point and tries to extract the fundamental features of experiences and the essence of what we experience. Like Bergson's durée, Husserl's phenomenology is opposed to Enlightenment-derived concepts of objectivism and positivism. His philosophical system was thus a descriptive analysis of subjective processes that may be described as the intuitive study of essence.

Again, like Bergson, Husserl did not accept the idea that time could be perceived (measured and categorized) as a series of successive nows. He argued that the essence of time is derived from our subjective experience of time (Husserl 1964). In other words, the essence of time is how we perceive it, not as a universal and absolute process as Newtonian-based thinking would have it. As Scott Lash writes, "Husserl enjoins us to begin not with the thought or the 'I think,' but with the 'I experience'" (Lash 2002, 102). Time also needs to be understood as having certain subjective qualities, what Bruno Latour (1993, 172) has termed the "feel of time." In contrast to scientistic conventions, Husserl conceived of the present as a "living present," a flowing present, a "now" in which impressions and perceptions stretch the mode of being through memory and expectations (retentions and protentions). "Immanent contents," he explains in *The Phenomenology of Internal Time Consciousness*, "are what they are only in so far as during their 'actual' duration they refer ahead to something futural and back to something past. . . . [W]e have retentions of the preceding and pretensions of the coming phases of precisely this content" (Husserl 1964, 110).

Like Bergson, Husserl utilizes the metaphor of music to make his point on the durational and flowing nature of temporal experience. Memory and expectation, the stretching of the lived present into the past and the future, are central to the process of listening to music or playing it. Each note has a musical quality that depends on the location of the note in a whole flowing sequence of notes, the lived present, where the music is perceived. The isolated note does not have the same quality. As part of a flow of notes, the previous note retains its presence without actually becoming present. Similarly, with speech, or text, the word or sentence comes alive only when the preceding words are retained in the present and the future words, the "coming phrases" (the expectation of future words), make the speech or text comprehensible. The past and the future dimensions of time are always in some sense in the present in Husserl's subjective experience of time.

Time Barriers

There have been, historically, some very deep social, political, and scientific currents that have militated against such holistic and flexible interpretations of time gaining intellectual and popular currency. If philosophy has helped us gain some insight into our relationship with time, it has been a limited achievement. Unfortunately, as a discipline philosophy speaks mainly to itself, to the community of philosophers, so its ideas and concepts tend to have little purchase on the wider world—unless, that is, they have a direct and measurable application. An example today would be the philosophy of human rights that develops moral and legal norms in the context of (what seems to be) a growing international culture of legal, political, and social abuse. The perspectives on time given to us through such thinkers as Bergson and Husserl, however, remain marginal to how people in everyday life develop an understanding of, and relationship to, time.

So far as the promotion of a nuanced and complex understanding of time and temporality goes, the social sciences have a similar story to tell in terms of their net effect on society—but from somewhat different (though not unrelated) causes. As noted previously, the major social science disciplines of sociology, politics, economics, and history have traditionally tended to view time through a particularly narrow and uncomplicated lens. As disciplines they have developed, in general, in the traditions of the Enlightenment. Like the natural and physical sciences, their formative base and their foundational thinkers were reflective of a time when the tenets of modernity, of Reason, of rationality, of positivism and objectivism were taken as unquestionable truths. Indeed, the whole motivation of an Enlightenment-based modernity was to uncover these "hidden" truths in the social and natural worlds.

The social science understanding of time, like the natural and physical science understanding of time, was shaped by these dogmas. What this meant was that, deriving from the ideas of Newton, a towering figure of the burgeoning seventeenth-century modernity and a believer that mathematics and numbers were the key to making sense of the world, time was something external, like the movement of the planets in space, and, like these, was a dynamic that had to be quantified and measured in order to be properly understood (Adam 2004).

From the beginnings of the modern period the mechanical clock was harnessed to the task of "rationalizing" time for an increasingly rational society. This process was strengthened immeasurably by growing industrialization.

Capitalism and the industry that it spawned and the human society that made it possible required the organizational power of the clock. Orientation around a clock-based perspective on what constituted time was therefore a vital ingredient in the industrialization process (Thompson 1993; Thrift 1996; Weber 1989).

Moving out of the feudalism that had endured for a thousand years and more across early modern Europe, and in Britain especially, the shift to a clock-time-based economy was immensely significant. Change was everywhere, and as Nigel Thrift has argued, "Of these changes, by far the most important was the calculation of time economy allowing for the intensification of work practices" (1996, 196). Work, everyday life, the running of the economy, and the philosophical and political foundations of the era all rested increasingly on a specific and narrow perspective of what time was—and that was represented through the external and rigidly mathematical time expressed on a clock face. Over the decades, over the centuries, and over many generations individuals and cultures were born into this form of time-reckoning, to the point that we did not think about time or the nature of duration because the clock measured, organized, and proportioned it for us. No longer were human societies in complex and partially autonomous relationship with a diversity of temporalities. With the coming of the rational society and capitalist industrialism that was driven by the clock, all we had to do was to synchronize with its rhythm.

The culture of inquiry that formed the social sciences as a way to understand the social world left this clock-based domination and this perception of time relatively unchallenged for more than two hundred years. The study of time dwelled in the margins of disciplinary inquiry because, after all, what was there to question? Time had become self-evident and made real in the general sense. Clocks metered social life and their ubiquity grew to the point where their logic and rhythm seeped into our consciousness and suffused our cultures. Even Einstein's 1905 theory of relativity (where time is relative), which blew the Newtonian view (where time is absolute) out of the water, barely dented the modernist assumptions we had internalized regarding how we viewed time.

In the latter part of the twentieth century, deep economic and social currents of change were flowing. Notwithstanding the general refusal to view time as relative and to see the clock as simply a technological artifact, theorists began to reflect on the nature of time in the context of changing global circumstances. What were these changing circumstances? The model of industrialization based on the weighty eighteenth-century canon, what Jean-

François Lyotard (1979) called the "grand narratives" of modernity, had, by the last quarter of the twentieth century, developed into its full maturity. Indeed, as David Harvey (1989) pointed out, the system of Fordism, which was modernity at its most developed industrial and social form, had become rigid, sclerotic, and was sunk into deep economic and social crises. The shift to a postmodernity, for Harvey, was underpinned by the transition from an economic and social system based on Fordism to one based on flexible accumulation. The "resolution" to the worldwide economic and social crises of the 1970s is still being played out today. It is a dual-process that encompasses economic, political, and social transformation on an unprecedented scale. Harvey didn't name it in his book because the terms had not yet entered common currency in the late 1980s, but the twin dynamics he described as propelling these changes, these "resolutions," were neoliberal globalization and the revolution in information and communication technologies (ICTs).

In the turbulent and change-filled years and decades that followed the 1970s dénouement of Fordism, neoliberal globalization and the ICT revolution constituted a mutually implicating dynamic that ended a whole way of life in the Anglo-American Western economies in particular, a logic that spread across the rest of the world more generally. It was a way of being, of thinking and seeing (a weltanschauung), that can readily be described (and recognized) as modern. The sureties of progress, of predictability, of the idea of a discernible past and a future that looked positive—the lived realities of modernity's "grand narratives," in other words, were swept away by wave after wave of neoliberal globalization and the insertion of networked ICTs into every nook and cranny of social life.

As the stories we told ourselves no longer made the same sense, and as the routines we had built into our lives no longer seemed appropriate (not fast enough or "productive" enough), and as the shape of the real world no longer reflected what we had been brought up to believe was worthwhile and enduring, profound ontological and epistemological questions began to emerge. The innumerable existential and practical dilemmas that the new world had furnished—for academics, for artists, for anyone who would stop and reflect on his or her condition—were neatly summed up by Michael Hardt and Antonio Negri when they observed, "At the end of modernity reappear the unresolved problems of its beginnings" (2006, 237).

The "unresolved problem" that concerns us here is our individual, social, and cultural relationship with time. The global earthquake that was neoliberal globalization and the revolution in ICTs shook up the complacency regarding the nature of time. What Jack Petranker in this volume calls the "objective time . . . of the measured-out grid," that is to say the time of the clock, became a form of time reckoning that ceased to be "natural" and implicit. The time of the clock became, if not problematic, at least more explicit in the daily lives of people and institutions. The "time-space compression" that David Harvey saw to be such an important factor in the shift toward a postmodernity threw the artificial nature of the clock into stark relief. The emergence of communicative networks that stretched across time and space revealed that clock time is not an absolute backdrop against which we synchronize and "tell" the time but a human construction that has very little to do with time other than as an inflexible way of measuring duration.

Information networks, of course, act as another form of artificial temporality. Through them humans now create a *virtual* time and space. Networks may be seen as a kind of temporal ecology outside the centripetal force of clock time. People from any point on the globe can communicate in something approaching "real time" through video or email, voice, and so on, creating a temporal context where what the local time of the clock reads is of no importance. It is here that the implicit nature of time that sustained us through the long phase of modernity became explicit in the postmodern networked society—increasingly so as networks and computers became so prevalent throughout the entire social composition. These networks constitute what Castells famously termed a space of "flows" that produce a "timeless time" (1996, 469). Indeed, Castells was one of the first to appreciate the significance of exponentially increasing interconnectivity and set about laying out its scope in the vast canvas that was his three-volume work *The Information Age: Economy, Society, and Culture* (1996, 1997, 1998). In the first volume Castells captured the essence of the network society: "The new economy is organized around global networks of capital, management, and information, whose access to technological know-how is at the roots of productivity and competitiveness. There is not, sociologically and economically, such a thing as a global capitalist class. But there is an integrated, global capital network, whose movements and variable logic ultimately determine economies and influence societies" (1996, 473). Irrespective of one's views on Castells's theorization, what he, David Harvey, and others such as Anthony Giddens (1990) were expressing were technologically and ideologically driven real-world changes that were transforming the ways in which we perceived time. Indeed, terms such as *instantaneity, real time*, and 24/7 quickly entered the social and technical lexicon to describe the kinds of time the network society generated, its greatly increased tempo, and its totalizing logic.

The meter of clock time that drove the industrial revolution is now being compressed and accelerated by the infinitely more rapid time-loaded functions of high-speed computerization. Computers now run at such fast speeds that engineers have had to devise new time fractions to measure them. The "second," which is the fastest time fraction in the regime of clock time, is archaically slow as a time frame to measure computer-processing speeds. Notwithstanding our historic inability to properly synchronize with the time of the clock, however, computer-processing speeds are now measured in nanoseconds (one billionth of a second) and picoseconds (one trillionth). Time, literally, has speeded up. These new superfast time frames are far too rapid for us to comprehend, let alone cognitively perceive. Like the superfast picture of the bullet piercing the balloon, these are "invisible" moments that we can only capture mechanistically and mathematically. Such a quantum leap in technological acceleration represents a shift from chronological to *chronoscopic* time (Purser 2002).

Yet this is how ICTs are "entimed"; this is the "limit acceleration" of the network society; and this is the "compression" of time in the shifting from the time frame of the chronologic to the chronoscopic. Networking is key to this shift. This "new social morphology" stemming from the "diffusion" of the network logic, as Castells describes it, is indeed modifying "the operation and outcomes in processes of production, experience, power, and culture" (Castells 1996, 469). And to this list we can add time. Humans, through their ever-increasing use of networked PCs, PDAs, cell phones, voicemail, faxes, pagers, computer games, and so on, are creating an accelerated temporal ecology (an experience of time) that is entirely unprecedented. It is a temporality that is based on clock time, but it is a clock time that has been massively compressed within the ecology of the network and has exploded into a million different time fractions, as many time fractions as there are users with ICT applications.

Network Timescapes

Academic interest in bringing time in from the margins of the social sciences—much of this interest building on the philosophical legacies of Bergson and Husserl—began to develop momentum during the 1980s. Barbara

Adam (1988) laid the groundwork for the emerging field of time studies when she developed a body of work underpinned by the idea that there exists an intricate diversity of times in the social world. Helga Nowotny (1989) employed the German term *Eigenzeiten*, or "a time in everything," to emphasize a similar point, that we move through innumerable temporal realms, both social and natural, objective and subjective, and that we need to understand these realms more clearly in order to have a more complete framework through which to analyze social dynamics.

As a way of theorizing the temporal complexity of the world, Adam (1998) developed the concept of "timescapes" to argue that our temporal world is immensely complex, almost uncomprehendingly so. Adam's theory of timescapes may be seen as the intricate intersecting of the rhythms, beats, sequences, beginnings and ends, growth and decay, birth and death, night and day, seasonality, memory, and so on that constitute the embedded temporality that is part of everything—the eons it takes for a lump of quartz to reduce to sand, the birth and death of a civilization, the lifetimes or minutes that permeate a memory or dream, or the life span of the fruit fly.

We are unavoidably immersed and implicated in these constantly shifting timescapes. Think of sitting in a park while reading a book, looking up occasionally to watch children play football. It could be any imaginable context, really. Innumerable timescapes are connecting, breaking, and reconnecting—and we are barely conscious of it. If we become conscious of the temporal context, become what Ida Sabelis (2002) calls "time aware," we can understand that, for example, the temporal experiences of the playing children are different from ours. For them it could be a feeling of time moving fast or slow. They could be bored or excited, tired or full of energy; they could be fully focused on the present, or be anticipating the end of the game, or be thinking back to mistakes they had made, or be remembering periods of good play they had contributed to the game. At some level of consciousness the child could be experiencing all or some of these sensations, and they feed into the creation and the experience of time.

Sitting in that imaginary park, countless relationships with time are occurring all around. For example, by concentrating on the book, we can enter another time. We can be "immersed" in the temporality of its narrative, become part of it and its imagery, its scenarios and the issues it conjures up. Looking up from the book to the trees that are around us, we can see ancient branches move slowly in the breeze, marking their time in its variable strength; or we can look down and watch the short stalks of grass vibrate at a much faster tempo in the same wind. What emerges from this consciously connecting with the temporal ecology of which we are a part are the Bergsonian times of experience, of memory, of intuition, and so on that we discussed earlier. We are a central part of this temporal diversity, and we bring to it (and take from it) our own context of being in time. In the form of the subjective person, the timescapes we connect with in our everyday life ripple out endlessly through the complex myriad of the social, natural, and objective worlds—and ripple back in again to touch us. Our context touches that of others to create another connection, another context, another ring in the outward and inward rippling of time, or timescape.

It is impossible to carry this temporal complexity in all its growing fullness into practical life; we can't *think* about this stuff all the time, in other words. This is part of the reason, perhaps, for the human compulsion to order and control time, to rationalize it to make it manipulable and predictable so that our lives appear more stable. What we can do is to use a pared-back version of viewing the world through timescapes to become "time aware," to have at the forefront of one's mind the temporal dimensions, making the implicit explicit as a matter of course. This is a habit of mind to be acquired and developed, much as many Buddhists do, who view time very much differently from the conception derived from Western industrialism; or even as people in some Latin countries do in the cliché that contains a grain of truth in that these cultures have traditionally proved resistant to the rigid temporality of the clock (Wilson 2004).

In many respects the network society is a vast, technologically sustained global timescape that we create and share; and through it we transform the world and ourselves. Furthermore, we do so at an ever-increasing pace. Social acceleration through ICTs has changed forever the ways in which most of us work. Indeed, it has changed the very nature of work, which tends now toward "immaterial" forms such as ideas and services, software and information. The network society annihilates space (and clock time) and has brought time (and speed) as a legitimate dimension of social inquiry to the fore in the work of many thinkers in recent years (Gleick 1999; Klein 2004; Lash 2002; Rifkin 2001; Thrift and May 2001; Virilio 1995).

This growing awareness of the role and potential of time in its new technologically oriented forms has been the motivation behind the present collection, which is intended to highlight the kind of theorization that "time awareness" brings to the network context. This is a timescape that is disordered. It is dominated by capitalism and the market yet does not function on the predictability afforded by the clock. As such, it very much constitutes a new temporal and spatial problematic—for the postmodern and postindustrial "project" of capitalism as much as for theorists who seek to understand its dynamics.

Overview of the Chapters

This volume contains a variety of scholarly explorations and provocative essays on time and temporality in the network society. Given the ubiquity of networks and the massive temporal changes occurring on a global scale, the compilation is timely in itself. But it is also defined by its omissions of both people and subject matter. We prefer, however, to see these "silences" as suggestive of topics for future exploration and research in the field of time studies. The contributions to follow come from such disparate fields as media and communications, cultural studies, geography, neuroscience, sociology, anthropology, religion, and management. They reflect the original perspectives of eminent scholars from Europe, Australia, and North America. Although these interdisciplinary contributions address a wide range of themes, they nonetheless share a common thread in providing a deeper and more critical understanding of the temporal dynamics of digital networks and the impact these are having on our changing temporal ecology.

Part 1, Time in the Network Society, acts as a mise-en-scène for the volume by providing a sweeping historical, sociological, and technological overview of the temporal transformations that have resulted from the emergence of information and communication technologies. The first chapter, "New Temporal Perspectives in the 'High-Speed Society,'" by Carmen Leccardi, analyzes the dynamics of acceleration in modern capitalistic society, culminating in what Leccardi describes as a "detemporalized present." Leccardi argues that the forces of temporal acceleration—social acceleration, technological innovation, and the accelerated rhythms of daily life—are rapidly leading to a loss of present space for reflective action that has a temporal connection to the past and future. The implications of such a loss are personal, cultural, and political: widespread alienation from time degrades democratic civil society, resulting in historical amnesia, a lack of personal responsibility for the future, and pervasive existential angst. According to Leccardi a new way of envisioning time is already underway through the antiglobalization movement, which is ironically empowered through the very proliferation of ICTs. Resistance to such forces of temporal compression is possible as these social movements penetrate everyday life, raising awareness of the links between space, time, and values.

Robert Hassan argues in "Network Time" that the convergence of neoliberal globalization and the "revolution" in information and communication technologies has created a new form of technologically generated time, the time of the network, which is a qualitatively and quantitatively different time from that of the clock. It is a new experience of time that is the defining characteristic of our twenty-first-century postmodernity. Network time, he argues, is very much a time of "potentiality." High-speed postmodern society is a society in flux, where no direction or control is apparent. Echoing Leccardi, however, Hassan shows that individuals and groups are able to create the contexts for the time of the network in ways that were impossible with the "outside" and abstract time of the clock. In this sense the network and network time represent modes of political action where democratic forms of communication may be generated to replace the institutional forms of "modern" liberal democracy made moribund by neoliberal globalization. In other words, human control over temporal processes is possible in network time in ways that were impossible through the mechanical time of the clock.

In "Speed = Distance / Time: Chronotopographies of Action" Mike Crang presents a valuable analysis of changing temporalities in society that are byproducts of the information technology revolution. Locating the major shifts in space and time as understood by key temporal theorists, Crang suggests that such space-time shifts are more complex than commonly thought, requiring a conceptual approach that better captures the effects of ICTs on the spatial and temporal fabric of our daily lives. Crang shows how the flexibility of location and the timing of activities are mutually interactive dimensions, and he provides a unique conceptual framework that incorporates the complexity of real-time technologies.

In a highly original perspective Adrian Mackenzie, in "Protocols and the Irreducible Traces of Embodiment: The Viterbi Algorithm and the Mosaic of Machine Time," takes the idea of control further and deeper into the logic of computing itself, not into the rigid binary code that constitutes the core of computing but into the algorithmic logic that is "attached" to computer-based technologies. He seeks to soften the hard edges of machine time by "finding middle ground between the temporality of technologies . . . and the temporal flows of subjective experience." Mackenzie argues that algorithms in general, and in the Viterbi algorithm that he uses as an example, may be "judged as embodying singular applications of human individual or collective intelligence." The algorithm, in other words, brings the deadening logic of ones and zeros—the basis of binary code—to life. The software that algorithms make possible gives expression to "a new kind of substance, halfway between matter and mind," which undermines the mere "repetition" that is at the heart of abstract machine logic. This idea follows in an important way from Hassan's essay in that Mackenzie's thesis leads to the conclusion that the mechanical clock *entimes* according to a preset and invariable rhythm, whereas the computer-based time of the network is a "microworld" that is *entimed* by the "irreducible traces" of human intervention and the potentially unlimited experiences of duration that these may generate.

In Part 2 the contributions turn toward the digitalization of various forms of media and communications to examine how these changes are radically altering our temporal perceptions. From cyberculture to digital cinema the authors explore the temporal implications of digitalization on aesthetics, memory, and our cultural sense of duration and rhythm. Darren Tofts kicks off this section with an apropos cultural study of the cult classic film *The Matrix*. In "Truth at Twelve Thousand Frames per Second: *The Matrix* and Time-Image Cinema" Tofts shows how the film's signature bullet photography, designed for the DVD's ability to pause an image, represents a convergence of gaming and interactive video to form a kind of virtual or immersive cinema. Tofts proposes that *The Matrix* is the perfect illustration of Gilles Deleuze's concept of the time-image, which represents a greater emphasis on the spectacle of the shot, the image. This chapter illustrates how the translation of commercial cinema releases to DVD changes our conventional way of watching film as one continuous image. With the advent of digital media, watching film as separate events taken out of sequence is now an option. Drawing on the works of Deleuze and Bergson, the author helps us to better understand the time-image as the interplay between the virtual and the actual, an artistic articulation of a new economy of distributed networks, convergent media, and immersive technologies.

In his chapter, "The Fallen Present: Time in the Mix," Andrew Murphie provides a cogent and in-depth analysis of how human thinking processes are being impacted by real-time network technologies. According to Murphie our very notion of the "present moment" has been redefined by network technologies to such an extent that it has "fallen" and that we are constantly falling into this present—which is "a fall away from historical purpose or future hope." His chapter continues the trope on the "political" nature of time by articulating the need for an "ontogenetic politics of cognition," which can shed light on how network culture is reforming our sense of what constitutes "the present" and its connection to the past and future. Murphie argues that such changes wrought by networked technologies require a reconceptualization of politics, a "neuropolitics" that takes account of both macro- and microcognitive processes.

Thomas Hylland Eriksen, in "Stacking and Continuity: On Temporal Regimes in Popular Culture," notes a fundamental change in our culture from the relatively slow and linear to the fast and momentary, where socially shared routines for distinguishing between wanted and unwanted information are severely lacking. Contrasting the MP3 player to the CD, and the Web to the book, along with examples from rhythmic music, Eriksen argues that information society emerges as cascades of decontextualized signs that are randomly connected to each other. Such acceleration and exponential growth of information leads to what he describes as "vertical stacking." Given the limits on the time we have available, information is compressed and stacked in time spans that become shorter and shorter, leaving little opportunity for internal integration. Eriksen warns us that vertical stacking threatens internal development in postmodern culture because it becomes increasingly difficult to create narratives, developmental sequences, and continuity.

In Part 3, Temporal Presence, attention shifts to the deeper existential and ontological questions concerning human consciousness of time within the context of network technologies. While the three authors in this section approach such questions in their own unique way, each challenges conventional wisdom regarding our potential for "being in time" within our 24/7, networked society. In network societies what we lack is not information but the capacity for sustaining undivided human attention. For example, "fast parents" struggle in a 24/7 world to be more temporally present with their children—what is colloquially referred to as "quality time." It is in this section that our very sense of "temporal presence" in the network society is examined from a critical perspective.

Geert Lovink begins the section by exploring the time regimes of Internet users. His chapter, "Indifference of the Networked Presence: On Time

Management of the Self," explores how the real challenge of being wired and online is not "time management" but time and media indifference. By media indifference, Lovink is referring to how users passively accept the architecture of various media at the expense of wasting large chunks of time on nonessential tasks. He concludes by proposing new ideas for overcoming the binary opposition between lived time and machine time, fashioning a self-styled approach to Internet use.

In "The Presence of Others: Network Experience as an Antidote to the Subjectivity of Time" Jack Petranker explores an optimistic vision of network technologies as offering possibilities for new forms of temporal presence that are life enhancing rather than debilitating. Petranker's chapter challenges the chorus of critics that have focused on the isolating and alienating tendencies of network technologies (e.g., Virilio's "telepresence") by exploring the phenomenological experience of feeling the presence of others at a distance—what he calls a "temporality of presence." Accessing temporal presence requires an understanding of time that is not divided into objective and subjective dimensions. When time is divided, according to Petranker, we are isolated from our own experience of presence, and the horror of such a loss comes back to haunt us in what seems to be an inexorable momentum—what Petranker refers to as "Frankentime." Rather than unknowingly adapting ourselves to the monstrous mode of temporality that Frankentime dictates, Petranker proposes that we can change our way of knowing time and reclaim an intimacy of presence. Network time generates new opportunities for presence if we can engage the media by embodying new forms of temporality.

Drawing from the Buddhist tradition, as well as from his firsthand experience as a Zen student and teacher, David Loy calls into question the claims that the digital revolution is extending consciousness by simulating a "timeless time." In "CyberLack" Loy argues that the root of human suffering is due to a repression of "groundlessness," a core inner feeling of lack and compulsive need to fill the existential void in an attempt to make ourselves real. The temporality of cybertime and our 24/7 society is reflective of how we attempt to resolve our existential sense of lack. Loy's chapter juxtaposes the "timeless time" of network technology against the experience of "timeless time" as described by Dōgen, a thirteenth-century Japanese Zen master, and illustrates how the latter supports a nondual experience of time while the former merely leads to further alienation. Cybertime, Loy argues, achieves instantaneity by speeding things up, but it fails to liberate us from our sense of lack because we are still ridden with the delusion of being trapped in an external and dualistic objective temporality.

The contributions in Part 4, Time in the Network Economy, focus on the temporal upheavals occurring in organizations, management, and the political economy as a result of the ICT revolution. From a variety of perspectives—critical social theory, organizational behavior, and management theory—the authors examine the temporality of global networks that are linked to the flow of capital and information. Focusing on the temporal dimensions of organizational life and socioeconomic relations, the chapters wrestle with such issues as the colonization of time by "fast capitalism," challenges of establishing trust in virtual organizations, and the coping strategies of executives who must deal with the demands of real-time network technologies.

Ben Agger opens this final section by tracing the historical socioeconomic dynamics of capitalism and by examining how such dynamics have amounted to what he refers to as "time theft." In "Time Robbers, Time Rebels: Limits to Fast Capital" Agger argues that recent developments due to the ICT revolution have intensified the magnitude of this time theft, in effect robbing people of the time and space for authentically recreating themselves. Fast capitalism, or what Agger refers to as the "total administration of time," has colonized even our leisure activities—breeding mass discontent that is instrumental for rampant consumerism. Drawing from the work of the Frankfurt School, Agger proposes a new political agenda of resistance based on a "slowmodernity" enacted through our everyday lives by becoming a "time rebel."

In the next chapter Hans Rämö is concerned with how ICT-based networks influence the formation of trust in organizations. In "Finding Time and Place for Trust in ICT Network Organizations" Rämö engages in a spatiotemporal analysis of various forms of trust in network-based organizations by focusing on the dimensions of time/timing and space/place. His chapter presents a new theoretical matrix for understanding trust in networked organizations and suggests the conditions necessary for the emergence of trust in ICT network settings.

Drawing on ethnographic studies of corporations and academic settings, Ida Sabelis, in "The Clock-Time Paradox: Time Regimes in the Network Society," examines contemporary patterns of time use among executives and academics who have come to rely increasingly on ICTs in their daily work. Her research study is focused on identifying the unintended effects of network technology on the boundaries between organizational and private life and between work and family, as well as on the impact of temporal compression on issues related to professional and personal identities. Sabelis maintains that time regimes are essentially patterns of time use that are pervaded by values and norms that remain mostly invisible and implicit in studies of labor, organization, and management. In organizations time regimes act as *zeitgebers*, or temporal markers, that conceal the norms surrounding performance expectations embedded in applications of various network technologies.

As editors it has been our intention that the following chapters confront the "temporal problematic" of our networked postmodernity. Our intention is to present a wide range of interpretations and diverse opinions regarding the transformed nature of social / technological time. Our new relationship with time is only gradually becoming understood in all its social, economic, political, and geographic dimensions, so much more reading, writing, thinking, talking, and listening need to be done across a whole range of areas in the humanities and social sciences. The works contained here can serve, we trust, as another layer for the foundation of a new temporal ontology through which to interpret (and thus maybe have some agency and control over) the new world that digital networks have created and the (literally) "new times" that are being created with every network connection.

References

Adam, Barbara. 1988. The social versus the natural: A traditional distinction re-examined. In *The rhythms of society*, ed. M. Young and T. Schuller, 181–193. London: Routledge.

———. 1998. *Timescapes of modernity: The environment and invisible hazards.* London: Routledge.

———. 2004. *Time.* Cambridge, MA: Polity.

Bergson, Henri. 1913 / 2001. *Time and free will: An essay on the immediate data of consciousness.* Repr. Mineola, NY: Dover.

———. 1946. *The creative mind: An introduction to metaphysics.* New York: Kensington.

Castells, Manuel. 1996. *The rise of the network society.* Vol. 1 of *The information age: Economy, society, and culture.* Oxford: Blackwell.

———. 1997. *The power of identity.* Vol. 2 of *The information age: Economy, society, and culture.* Oxford: Blackwell.

———. 1998. *End of millennium.* Vol. 3 of *The information age: Economy, society, and culture.* Oxford: Blackwell.

Giddens, Anthony. 1990. *The consequences of modernity.* Cambridge, UK: Polity.

Gleick, James. 1999. *Faster: The acceleration of just about everything.* New York: Abacus.

Hardt, Michael, and Antonio Negri. 2006. *Multitude: War and democracy in an age of empire.* New York: Penguin.

Harvey, David. 1983. *The limits to capital.* Oxford: Blackwell.

————. 1989. *The condition of postmodernity.* Oxford: Blackwell.

Husserl, Edmund. 1964. *The phenomenology of internal time consciousness.* Trans. J. S. Churchill. The Hague: Martinus Nijhoff.

Klein, Olivier. 2004. Social perception of time, distance and high-speed transportation. *Time & Society* 13 (2/3): 245–263.

Lash, Scott. 2002. *Critique of information.* London: Sage.

Latour, Bruno. 1993. *We have never been modern.* Trans. Catherine Porter. New York: Harvester Wheatsheaf.

Lyotard, Jean-François. 1979. *The postmodern condition: A report on knowledge.* Manchester: Manchester University Press.

Nowotny, Helga. 1989. *Eigenzeit: Entstehung und Strukturierung eines Zeitgefühls.* Frankfurt am Main: Suhrkamp Verlag.

Purser, Ronald E. 2002. Contested presents: Critical perspectives on "real-time" management. In *Making time: Time and management in modern organizations,* ed. Richard Whipp, Barbara Adam, and Ida Sabelis, 155–167. Oxford: Oxford University Press.

Rifkin, Jeremy. 2001. *The age of access.* London: Penguin.

Sabelis, Ida. 2002. *Managers' times.* Amsterdam: Bee's Books.

Schor, Juliet B. 1993. *The overworked American.* New York: Basic Books.

Schor, Juliet B., and Laura Leete-Guy. 1992. The great American time-squeeze. Briefing paper, Economic Policy Institute.

Thompson, E. P. 1993. Time, work-discipline, and industrial capitalism. In *Customs in common: Studies in traditional popular culture,* 352–403. London: New Press. Orig. pub. in *Past and Present* 38 (1967): 56–97.

Thrift, Nigel. 1996. *Spatial formations.* London: Sage.

Thrift, Nigel, and Jon May, eds. 2001. *Timespace: Geographies of temporality.* London: Routledge.

Virilio, Paul. 1995. Speed and information: Cyberspace alarm! *CTheory* (Aug. 27): www.ctheory.net/text_file.asp?pick=72 (accessed Jan. 25, 2007).

Weber, Max. 1989. *The protestant ethic and the spirit of capitalism.* Trans. Talcott Parsons. London: Unwin Hyman.

Wilson, P. W. 2004. *Romance of the calendar: How man has measured time through the ages.* London: Kessinger.

1 TIME IN THE NETWORK SOCIETY

1 New Temporal Perspectives in the "High-Speed Society"

Carmen Leccardi

SOCIAL ACCELERATION is certainly not a unique phenomenon of our times. According to Reinhard Koselleck (1986, 283) the modern era is characterized by "the acceleration of change which erodes experience, meaning a "shortening of the time lapses which allow a homogenous experience." Koselleck states that since the mid-eighteenth century, "before the technicisation of communication and information, acceleration has become a specific experience of time" (289). From the beginning of the nineteenth century, the general feeling that time "slips away" is already widespread, and "what used to proceed at walking pace is now galloping" (Arndt, quoted in Koselleck 1986, 283). This process, which goes hand in hand with the attrition of tradition, radically redefines the relation between the past, the present, and the future: the past seems to be an increasingly distant dimension, whereas the future takes on the characteristics of a challenge. The "newness" is, for its part, the feature that connotes the present.[1]

The spectacular technological innovation that took place from the mid-nineteenth century until World War I—ranging from the gas engine to the advantages derived from the application of the laws of electromagnetism (from electrical power to the construction of electrical engines, from the invention of the telephone to that of the telegraph) up to the invention of cinema and the precipitous development of railway transport—shaped this new zeitgeist (Kern 1983). While the hitherto unknown modes of thinking about space and time spread in physics as well as in psychology, in the arts as much as in music, the collective experience of time and space underwent a profound transformation (Berman 1983). The consequence of a rising speed in the circulation of goods, people, and information, as well as the shortening of distances between places, signifies an intensified rhythm of life (Stein 2001).

It must be stressed that this acceleration process serves in the first instance the demands of capitalism for greater speed in the circulation of capital and information (Catalano 1999). As Marx (1857–1858 / 1953) observed in the mid-nineteenth century, reducing the time used in movement is, for capital, an essential condition for the affirmation of its own hegemony. The progressive standardization of time imposed by the development of rail transport (Bartky 1989)—which culminated in 1913, when time was synchronized worldwide through the Eiffel Tower in Paris—attests to the progressive subjugation of space by time.

Thus, if social acceleration is a process at least two hundred years old, are we justified in claiming that today it has taken on explosive characteristics to the extent of becoming a specific feature of the globalization era? Is the massive and penetrating flow of new information technology sufficient to make us speak of an "acceleration society" (Gleick 1999)?[2]

In a structured analysis of social acceleration Hartmut Rosa (2003) identifies three "motors" of acceleration. The first, the economic, expresses fundamentally the capitalist need to save time on the basis of equivalence between time and profit and, more generally, on the basis of identification between growth, on the one hand, and the acceleration of production and productivity, on the other hand. The second is cultural and sees in the acceleration of the rhythm of life a certification of the ideals of constant change inherent to modernity and, more specifically, the secular answer to the problem of death. The more life span is a nontranscendent and time-limited resource, the more the need to open oneself to the greatest possible quantity of experiences in the (limited) lapse of time existentially possible—a need with which social acceleration seems to be particularly in harmony—becomes important. Finally the third, the structural "motor," refers to the acceleration of the rhythms of change as a consequence of the specific differentiation of modern society. In a scenario identifying the future with growing social complexity and contingency, the most rational experience of time on the societal level becomes sustained change and acceleration. This is due to the permanent increase of systemic options created by the increasing social complexity with which only an acceleration selection process is able to deal.

If these are the forces that, according to Rosa, stimulate social acceleration, one also has to distinguish between the different analytical levels at its heart. The first level is, of course, that of technological acceleration and the extraordinary process of time-space compression it generates (Harvey 1990). The new information and communication technology, for instance, fundamentally redefines the experience of space but also manipulates time, to the extent of destroying it as a historical dimension. In the scenario of the informational economy (Castells 2000), as a consequence of the spread of these technologies, time is transformed, as I will undertake to illustrate later, into a simultaneous and concurrently eternal entity. Also the acceleration of the process of social change, related both to productive and reproductive institutions, from work to family, contribute to the contemporary positive valuation of speed. If the generational change constituted one parameter of the rhythms of change during the "first modernity," in the contemporary modernity every generation is forced to confront a multitude of processes of change, traversing and transforming everyday scenarios. This acceleration of the rhythms of transformation has clear consequences on, among others, the life of institutions—by undermining the foundations of their stability—as well as on the construction of individual biographies (Bauman 2001).

Finally, there is the acceleration of the rhythm of life. This aspect refers in a literary sense to the temporal compression of our daily actions. It denotes the process according to which the quantity of actions contained in a lapse of time tends to increase. The obsession with the lack of time (Paolucci 1986) serves as a corollary to this type of acceleration—an obsession that, one could say, constitutes one of the pillars of contemporary experience—itself inseparable from the *burnout* condition of psychophysical stress (Balbo 1991). All of these give everyday life ambivalent aspects. While the range of possibilities of action grows and expands its horizons, the temporal pressure in the end weakens its quality. In more general terms the tension between interior rhythms and social rhythms is the distinctive sign of this form of acceleration.

Rosa emphasizes that when one looks at the whole of these dimensions, a paradox becomes obvious. While the process of acceleration spreads—by reducing the time necessary for communication, transport, production—the feeling of a lack of time increases, meaning that the time saved through technology has been swallowed up by the process of social acceleration. Consequently the vision of the "acceleration society" as a social form emerges, where "technological acceleration and the growing scarcity of time (i.e., an acceleration of the 'pace of life') occur simultaneously" (Rosa 2003, 10), where, in other words, the progression of the sensation of a lack of time surpasses the possible positive outcomes (of time savings) of acceleration.

Among the many aspects of the "acceleration society" that could throw light on the present, here I would like to dwell above all on its passage from the present as a strategic dimension of action to the present as detemporalized instantaneity.

A Detemporalized Present?

The transfer refers to two stages of the acceleration process: the first well identified in the conceptual proposition of David Harvey at the end of the 1980s (Harvey 1990) by the term "time-space compression"; the second connected to the *Gegenwartsschrumpfung* (reduction / contraction of the present), a concept proposed by the German philosopher Hermann Lübbe (1998) less than ten years later. As we all know, with the expression of the "time-space compression" Harvey intended to designate the collapse of time horizons and spatial barriers. This process, stimulated by the acceleration of the rhythm of life induced by capitalism, questions not only a way to represent time and space, where one constitutes the measure of the other, but more generally redefines the coordinates through which we represent the world: "As space appears to shrink to a 'global village' of telecommunications and a 'spaceship earth' of economic and ecological interdependencies . . . and as time horizons shorten to the point where the present is all there is (the world of the schizophrenic), so we have to learn to cope with an overwhelming sense of *compression* of our spatial and temporal worlds" (Harvey 1990, 240).

In the representation of the world that is shrinking through human action—by increasing above all the speed of transport, human beings annihilate space through time[3]—lies what Castoriadis (1987) defined as the "capitalist imaginary": the domination of nature through the unlimited expansion of (rational) control of the world. This imaginative world is fed by the philosophical concept, dating from the Enlightenment, of the future as a time to curb and control in accord with a world vision where (social) progress takes the place of (spiritual) perfection.

Gegenwartsschrumpfung (reduction / contraction of the present) is where human willpower and rationality replace divine greatness. I consider it particularly important to keep in mind the trajectory that leads to this "shrinking map of the world," to use the expression of Harvey (1990, 241). It is indeed the natural evolution of the modern concept of the "open future" (Koselleck 1986) that removes the future from the double influence of God and nature and ties it to human decisions matured in the present. The present is here completely shaped by the idea of the future (it is the time that *prepares* the future). An increasingly "futuristic" universe replaces the "backward-looking" one that preceded the French Revolution. As Krzysztof Pomian (1981, 108) writes, the "centre of gravity of time and, along with it, individual and collective behaviour" moves toward the future. What is unheard of, original, what is still unknown, what *innovates*—in economical, technical, or scientific terms—becomes significant and marginalizes what tends to reproduce things that have already existed. The movement, the continuous and accelerated transformation of the social environment, arranges things in a way that anticipations prevail over habit and expectations over memory.

This particular vision of time is the basis of the process leading to time-space compression. Through the acceleration of social life in all its different forms, progress (a synonym for the "modern era," as designated by Koselleck) can be constructed by recovering the "delay of reason." More precisely, as Nowotny (1994) stresses, the partnership of quantification and acceleration of time, placed into a historical horizon constructed around the concept of linearity, forms the foundations of the capitalist process of accumulation. On the other hand, the acceleration of time takes on itself the task of bringing near the open future and individual existence, transforming the idea of universal progression into individual life span (Blumenberg 1986). As a consequence, starting from the Enlightenment, the *need of time* becomes a trait of Western societies, as does pride in the conquest of the future.

From the mid-twentieth century onward the dominating vision of the future as an open field of possibilities tends to fade away little by little. A constellation of elements helps to explain this dwindling belief in the future as a time of progress: from the loss of finalistic orientations of history to the enormous extension of the field of possibilities linked to the rapid development of information and communication technology, from the threat of an imminent ecological / nuclear catastrophe to present-day international terrorism.[4] The diffuse contemporary feeling of living in an era of uncontrollable risks and equally important uncertainties (Beck 1999) can be interpreted on a general level as a signal of this transformed experience of the future. Social acceleration leads, for its part, away from the concept of an open future: the future withdraws to the present and wears out before even being born.

The present becomes "all there is," transforming itself in the dimension that Agnes Heller (1999, 7) defines as the "absolute present." In temporal scenes redefined by time-space compression this present appears as the only temporal dimension that is available for the definition of choice, an existential horizon that includes and replaces future and past. To be more precise: even if the reference to the future can still constitute a routine for social systems, as well as for individuals, it is, in fact, the present that is associated with the concept of potential governability and controllability, which the "first modernity" linked to the future.

When the accelerated sequence of social changes, chained to the speed of technological innovation, ties itself to the acceleration of the rhythms of life in a globalized space, the temporal dimension of the present will also contract (Lübbe 1998). In this case a *loss* of the present as a space of choice and of reflexive action occurs. The present seems no longer to be time open to experience (inasmuch as the mutilation of the temporal horizons of the past and the future allows it) but rather precarious time, in the sense that Bourdieu (1998) conferred on this term. That is to say, the present seems a time when not only forms of rational anticipation appear impracticable but when the idea of "hold" on the world vanishes. In other words the loss of control extends from the future to the present. The grounds of this difficulty are constituted in its fragmentation into a multitude of segments without reciprocal relations, of simple detemporalized surfaces. The contraction/reduction of the present makes the present as temporal aggregate disappear and reduces its existence to a cloud of moving (but not ordered) particles.

In his analysis of the "network society" Castells refers to this characterization of time in relation to the spread of what he calls the "paradigm of information technologies" (Castells 2000, 460), closely linked, for its part, with the dominance of the "space of flows." In this context acceleration produces a temporal compression up to the point where an actual *disappearance of time as a process* (ibid., 464) occurs. This detemporalized time is what remains as ultimate outcome of the acceleration processes in economic, political, and cultural life. To sum up, it can be stated that this type of time creates the conditions for a drying up of the dimension of the present as a space for meaningful action. In fact, with the disappearance of "temporal time" comes the disappearance of the possibility of creative intervention in the world. In this scenario the problem moves from the redefinition of the concept of temporal continuity, which the "absolute present" brings into play, toward a global re-definition of temporality, pushed inevitably toward inertia by the violence of speed (Virilio 2000).

But what could be the *lines of resistance* against the destructuration of the temporal experience linked to this expansion of speed? We know that in so-cieties change is never exclusively the result of social / natural processes and events but always that of the relation between these processes and these events and their interpretation by individuals and groups. The possibility of recon-ceptualizing problems could thus be considered a preliminary condition for giving them a direction. In other words, an acceleration of the conceptual innovation could play a strategic role in the building of pockets of resistance against the "detemporalization" of time accompanying the contemporary process of social acceleration (Leccardi 2003).

Resisting the "Detemporalization of Time": The Role of the Antiglobalization Movements

I would like to stress here the strategic role played by the movement against the neoliberal globalization within these pockets of resistance.[5] This "move-ment of movements" actually brings back into discussion the temporal and spatial order of globalized societies: their "time without time," based on simultaneity, as well as on their "space without place," dried up from experi-ence (Giaccardi and Magatti 2003). This time and this space are functional to the creation of transnational and transcontinental networks and flows of economic activities and the concurrent new and dramatic forms of inequality that accompany them.

The movement critical of globalization suggests, in fact, an alternative vi-sion of time and space, within a conceptual horizon on solid ethical-political foundations, based on a sense of universal responsibility: for the protection of the environment, for new forms of shared democracy, for the reduction of imbalances in the distribution of wealth, for a different solidarity (Archibugi 2003; Archibugi and Held 1995). It sketches the methods of "active resistance" to the global present we live in and the global decontextualized space to which it is linked. Its critique, notably of the sovereignty of the market, penetrates the sphere of everyday life by explaining its forms of "ordinary domination"

(Martuccelli 2001) and by suggesting its rebuilding on the basis of a redefinition of the link between space, time, and values.

It actively opposes the "detemporalized" vision of time and the underlying abstract conception of space, and it suggests a reevaluation of the lived dimensions of space and time and their subsequent torsion in a historical and political sense. On this basis the global and deterritorialized space can be transformed into a global democratic space; its unlimited and rootless opening can become the basis of a new type of cosmopolitanism, a democratic cosmopolitanism nourished by global interdependencies and the confrontation of cultures typical of our time (Archibugi, Held, and Köhler 1998; Beck 2006; Melucci 2000). In a context of social relations "without territory"—a context made possible by contemporary economical, technological, and cultural processes—this cosmopolitanism reestablishes the idea of a public sphere and creates new forms of global citizenship. In the world-risk society, where the borders between public and private, political and nonpolitical have become blurred and political institutions seem to be in a profound crisis, interest in direct participation, in civic initiatives and forms of nontraditional collective action, is growing. With "politics" and "political institutions" no longer coinciding, the sphere of everyday life tends to politicize more and more. This renaissance of political subjectivity, closely linked to the expressions of twentieth- and twenty-first-century cosmopolitanism, materializes in and through everyday life. Everyday life is not only the arena where these unconventional forms of engagement are expressed, but it is also the privileged dimension through which the world becomes meaningful (Jedlowski and Leccardi 2003).

In the context of rediscovered political subjectivity, the new communication and information technologies present themselves as perfect "global" tools to stimulate the growth and consolidation of this democratic space-time. Individuals and groups, even those spatially distant, can share perspectives, mobilize civic resources, promote opinion forming, and elaborate a direct response to social and political institutions whose credibility is declining. In this sense the Internet, the "net of nets," has proven to be the ideal environment for the growth of the "movement of movements": for the spread of information, for networking and mobilization, for activities that aim at reconquering the idea of shaping the future (Diani 2001; Poster 1997; Webster 2001).

The challenge launched by the social movement critical of globalization concerns, at the same time, through the democratic appropriation of global space, the dominant conception of time. The strategic character of their battle for a cosmopolitan democracy capable of redefining dimensions such as citizenship, sovereignty, and political community derives, in fact, mostly from their capacity to keep together cosmopolitanism and reference to temporality (Cwerner 2000). This cosmopolitanism seems to be capable of escaping from the shrinking of the global present (the time of cosmopolitan *capitalism*) in order to look equally at the past, by shedding light on the roots of contemporary social inequalities, and at the future, by underlying the responsibilities to unborn generations.

In this context the political community is temporalized: the global sense of belonging together materializes through a nonreified time and space. At their heart the planet is profiled like a dynamic system of interconnected spaces and times that have a historically sedimented temporality and spatiality. This cosmos surely receives light from the global present that crosses it, but it is at the same time open to the future and aware of the past. It is constructed by a multiplicity of social and existential times and natural rhythms, indissolubly tangled together.

This temporal vision refers not only to ecological awareness. It is also concerned with a social and political dimension, with development models and their criticism, with sustainability and the principle of precaution. It is again linked to the idea of responsibility greater than that traditionally conceived by ethics (Adam 1998; Jonas 1985).

But the global movement not only calls our attention to the interlinking of cosmopolitan democracy and the future. It also emphasizes the relation between the present and the past. It points to the strategic question of memory: the teleological chains linking the past to the present but also the "places"-times attached to us by collective memories (Halbwachs 1950/1980), thus protecting them from empty and global space, which tends to swallow them up. Finally, it draws our regard to a present vivified and shaped by the numerous interconnected temporalities and by the play of their differences in global space.

The "temporalization of cosmopolitanism" (Cwerner 2000) carried by the movement allows not only the radicalization of criticism of global capitalism but also, as a result of enlarging temporal horizons and the reconquest of space as "friendly" dimension, the creation of the possibility to redesign the future as a potentially controllable dimension.

In the "acceleration society" the forms of resistance against eternal and ephemeral time produced by it become visible. They are forms of resistance that radically question the "organized irresponsibility" (Beck 2000, 227) that appears as the distinctive feature of present Western societies. To establish the connection between cause and effect, between before and after, allows us to critically reflect on the origins and dynamics of social processes and, at the same time, to rethink time and space.

One should bear in mind that the dramatic environmental, political, and economic risks run by our societies, will always remain, even if complex, the fruit of human choices. The "return of time" is also inevitably a return of responsibility to the center of the social stage.

Notes

1. *Neuzeit*, the German term meaning modernity or modern era, literally translates as "new time."

2. Decades ago Paul Virilio introduced the term *dromology* to conceptualize this process of progressive social and historical acceleration. See Virilio (1977).

3. See the images that illustrate this process in Harvey (1990:241–242).

4. From a historical perspective we can take into consideration two world wars, the Holocaust, totalitarian societies, ethnic cleansing, and genocide.

5. On the social movements of the era of globalization see, e.g., Della Porta, Kriesi, and Rucht 1999; Guidry, Kennedy, and Zald 2000; O'Brian, Goetz, Scholte, and Williams 2000; Burbach 2001. A crucial analysis for the understanding of the new social movements—an analysis that deals closely with, among other subjects, the different experience of time and space that they carry—is offered by Melucci (1996). An irreplaceable point of reference for a cultural analysis of contemporary social movements remains Touraine (1993).

References

Adam, B. 1998. *Timescapes of modernity: The environment and invisible hazards.* London: Routledge.

Archibugi, D. 2003. Cosmopolitical democracy. In *Debating cosmopolitics*, ed. D. Archibugi, 1–15. London: Verso.

Archibugi, D., and D. Held, eds. 1995. *Cosmopolitan democracy: An agenda for a new world order.* Cambridge, MA: Polity.

Archibugi, D., D. Held, and M. Köhler. 1998. *Re-imagining political community.* Cambridge, MA: Polity.

Balbo, L. 1991. Burnout. In *Tempi di vita* [Times of life] Milan: Feltrinelli.

Bartky, I. R. 1989. The adoption of standard time. *Technology and Culture* 30:25–56.

Bauman, Z. 2001. *The individualized society.* Cambridge, MA: Polity.

Beck, U. 1999. *World risk society.* Cambridge, MA: Polity.

———. 2000. Risk society revisited: Theory, politics, and research programmes. In *The risk society and beyond: Critical issues for social theory,* ed. B. Adam, U. Beck, and J. Van Loon, 211–229. London: Sage.

———. 2006. *Cosmopolitan vision.* Cambridge, MA: Polity.

Berman, M. 1983. *All that is solid melts into air: The experience of modernity.* New York: Simon and Schuster.

Blumenberg, H. 1986. *Lebenszeit und Weltzeit.* Frankfurt am Main: Suhrkamp.

Bourdieu, P. 1998. La précarité est aujourd'hui partout. In *Contrefeux: Propos pour servir à la résistance contre l'invasion néo-liberale,* 91–113. Paris: Liber-Raisons d'Agir.

Burbach, R. 2001. *Globalization and postmodern politics: From Zapatistas to high-tech robber barons.* London: Pluto.

Castells, M. 2000. *The rise of the network society.* Vol. 1 of *The information age: Economy, society, and culture.* Oxford: Blackwell.

Castoriadis, C. 1987. *The imaginary institution of society.* Cambridge, MA: MIT Press.

Catalano, G. 1999. *Space is the place: La velocità tecnologica nell'organizzazione spazio-tempo* [Space is the place: Technological speed in space-time organization]. Cosenza: Brenner.

Cwerner, S. B. 2000. The chronopolitan ideal: Time, belonging, and globalization, *Time & Society* 9 (2–3): 331–345.

Della Porta, D., H. Kriesi, D. Rucht, eds. 1999. *Social movements in a globalizing world.* London: Macmillan.

Diani, M. 2001. Social movements networks: Virtual and real. In *Culture and politics in the information age,* ed. F. Webster, 117–138. London: Routledge.

Giaccardi, C., and M. Magatti. 2003. *Itinerari dell'io globale* [Routes of the global self]. Roma-Bari: Laterza.

Gleick, J. 1999. *Faster: The acceleration of just about everything.* New York: Pantheon.

Guidry, J. A., M. D. Kennedy, M. N. Zald, eds. 2000. *Globalization and social movements: Culture, power, and the transnational public sphere.* Ann Arbor: University of Michigan Press.

Halbwachs, M. 1950 / 1980. *The collective memory.* San çcisco: Harper and Row.

Harvey, D. 1990. *The condition of postmodernity: An inquiry into the origins of cultural change.* Oxford: Blackwell.

Heller, A. 1999. *A theory of modernity.* Oxford: Blackwell.

Jedlowski, P., and C. Leccardi. 2003. *Sociologia della vita quotidiana* [Sociology of everyday life]. Bologna: Il Mulino.

Jonas, H. 1985. *The imperative of responsibility.* Chicago: University of Chicago Press.

Kern, S. 1983. *The culture of time and space, 1880–1918.* Cambridge, MA: Harvard University Press.

Koselleck, R. 1986. *Futuro passato. Per una semantica dei tempi storici.* Genova: Marietti. Original edition, *Vergangene Zukunft: Zur Semantik geschichtlicher Zeiten.* Frankfurt am Main: Suhrkamp, 1979; English translation, *Future past: On the semantics of historical time.* New York: Columbia University Press, 2004.

Leccardi, C. 2003. Resisting the "acceleration society." *Constellations* 10 (1): 34–41.

Lübbe, H. 1998. Gegenwartsschrumpfung. In *Die Beschleunigungsfalle oder der Triumph der Schildkröte*, ed. K. Backhaus and H. Bonus, 263–293. Stuttgart: Schäffer/Pöschel.

Martuccelli, D. 2001. *Dominations ordinaires: Exploration de la condition moderne*. Paris: Balland.

Marx, K. 1857–1858/1953. *Grundrisse der Kritik der politischen Ökonomie*, Berlin: Dietz.

Melucci, A. 1996. *Challenging codes: Collective action in the information age*. Cambridge, UK: Cambridge University Press.

———. 2000. *Culture in gioco: Differenze per convivere* [Cultures at stake: Differences for living together]. Milan: Il Saggiatore.

Nowotny, H. 1994. *Time: The modern and postmodern experience*. Cambridge, MA: Polity.

O'Brian, R., A. M. Goetz, J. A. Scholte, M. Williams. 2000. *Contesting global governance: Multilateral economic institutions and global social movements*. Cambridge, UK: Cambridge University Press.

Paolucci, G. 1986. *Il disagio del tempo: La metafora della scarsità di tempo nella vita quotidiana* [The hardships of time: The metaphor of time shortage in everyday life]. Rome: Ianua.

Pomian, K. 1981. La crisi dell'avvenire [The crisis of the future]. In *Le frontiere del tempo* [Time boundaries], ed. R. Romano, 97–113. Milan: Il Saggiatore.

Poster, M. 1997. Cyberdemocracy: Internet and the public sphere. In *Internet culture*, ed. D. Porter, 201–218. London: Routledge.

Rosa, H. 2003. Social acceleration: Ethical and political consequences of a desynchronized high-speed society. *Constellations* 10 (1): 3–33.

Stein, J. 2001. Reflections on time, time-space compression, and technology in the nineteenth century. In *Timespace: Geographies of temporality*, ed. J. May and N. Thrift, 106–119. London: Routledge.

Touraine, A. 1993. *La voix et le régard: Sociologie des mouvements sociaux*. Paris: Seuil.

Virilio, P. 1977. *Vitesse et politique*. Paris: Galilée.

———. 2000. *Polar inertia*. London: Sage.

Webster, F. ed. 2001. *Culture and politics in the information age*. London: Routledge.

2 Network Time

Robert Hassan

W E RACE THROUGH these opening years of a new millennium powered by a new engine: the computer. If I may be allowed to periodize, maybe somewhat excessively, I suggest that what steam power did for the nineteenth century and what the combustion engine did for the twentieth, the microchip is doing for the twenty-first—transforming it utterly. The car and the truck and the jet engine still dominate the communications infrastructures of our physical world, but with the networked computer we have transcended physical space and created a new and parallel world of virtuality. It is my contention that this virtual world, this cyberspace, is fast becoming the preeminent or preponderant space that is displacing the physical realm in terms of how we derive our information about the world and, as a consequence, how we make sense of it.

In this chapter I want to explore the temporal aspects of this change, to try to tease out and understand the nature of time in the networks of the information society. To do this, we need also to understand the other forms of time reckoning, such as that of the clock, which have dominated our relationship with time since at least the industrial revolution and the beginnings of Western capitalist modernity. The abstract and socially constructed time of the clock will also be related back to earlier forms of time reckoning, to nontechnological and nonabstract forms of time. These are the "embedded times" (Adam 2004) that exist in our bodies and in the natural world that surrounds us. We can see these as diverse times of emergence, of rhythms and

cycles and tempos that do not synchronize with the mechanical and unerr-
ing system of time based on numbers—a system that is the direct result of
the seventeenth-century Newtonian revolution in physics, which saw time as
both measurable and absolute. Embedded times were the governing times of
premodern cultures and societies. They were times that humans recognized
and understood more clearly than we do today, times in which humans were
able to exert a measure of *temporal control.*

Controlling Time

Time is social. From the earliest periods of human development as cultural beings, people and societies *created* time by giving duration, growth, decay, and
change intrinsic meaning (Nowotny 1989). The living body, nature, and culture
came together in ancient societies across the world to form a diversity of relationships with time. This social production of time, the imputing of significance
to the embedded times of the biological and natural world, constituted the deep
level of temporal relations that generations have passed down through the ages
to our own time. In social life this intermingling or clustering of temporal relations constitutes what Barbara Adam calls "timescapes." These form the basis
of our temporal being but are tacitly understood and are not consciously part of
everyday life. Everything has its own time, the time of duration, of cyclicality or
linearity, of growth and aging, of birth and death, but we move through these
and create connections between them with hardly a thought.

For Adam, however, "[t]he notion of 'scape' is important . . . as it indicates that time is inseparable from space, and second, that *context matters*"
(Adam 2004, 143; my italics). Context is where timescapes converge to create
this implicit temporal meaning. Many cultural practices have thus evolved
as contexts, as ways to understand and control time by grafting onto embedded times the rules or customs that imbue them with importance. We see,
for example, how a body time and lunar time converge in culturally significant ways in the ancient Chinese practice of *zuo yuezi.* This is the custom
where after pregnancy women go into a thirty-day period of confinement
that coincides with a lunar cycle. As part of a long list of dos and don'ts, the
mother is to avoid cold foods and drinks, winds or water or contact with
any other cold substance. There are variations of this practice in many other
cultures. Of course, to the modern sensibility there are no rational reasons
for such conduct. The primordial motivation, I argue through a foreground-

ing of the temporal perspective, was to create a cultural significance for the embedded temporality of pregnancy, to *order* it and bring it more directly under human understanding and therefore control.

Another example is the rhythms of the seasons. For millennia these have been incorporated into nearly all cultural systems. Their cyclical temporality was given significance and, hence, scope for ordering. The reasonable expectation of predictable seasonal change allowed cultivators to plan when to sow and to harvest crops. This gave them a form of *domain* over the past and the future through cultural memory and forecasting. In agrarian communities feast days evolved to celebrate these times and functioned as ways to symbolically connect with them and their meanings. For agricultural societies the rhythms of nature became synchronized with the rhythms of culture. Of course, for much of human history this synchrony could be so tight as to tie whole societies to the vagaries of nature. The individual human lifetime could thus be prolonged through continued bountiful harvests or cut short through unexpected drought or catastrophic flood.

These microcontexts of temporal-cultural production, however, were invariably played out against what Robert Banks called the "temporal backdrop of a cosmic drama" that organized religion brought to the social creation of time (Banks 1985, 107). The symbolic representation that is characteristic of all significant religious systems of thought meant that diverse cultures were, for example, able to project a "timelessness" that transcended their earthly finitude. Within Buddhism, Christianity, and Islam the past and the future stretch out, far beyond the life of the individual in the world. Religion thus creates a realm of timelessness. It developed the notion of "eternity," as in the Christian conception, where the "life everlasting" that is promised in the Apostle's Creed serves as an ultimate form of control. And through it the intuitively suspected void that comes after inevitable death is psychologically overcome. Such temporal strategies were able to lay the basis for a powerful form of understanding and control that provided premodern societies with a measure of order, structure, and, most important, seeming permanence through the temporal sureties of religion.

Clock Time

This relative control over temporal creation and experience that had emerged through symbolic layers of culture underwent a transformation (and a loss

of control) through the introduction of the clock. By viewing time and duration in the context of numbers, modern cultures and societies developed a
much-diminished relationship with the diversity of temporalities immanent
in culture, in the body, and in nature. These times were *rationalized* through
the rule of the clock, a mechanical abstraction that places time outside the
immanency of human creation and experience. The automatic measurement
of time functioned in such ways as to hollow out temporal diversity into an
empty, linear form that was antithetical to the ways in which humans had
related to time for thousands of years (Gurevich 1976). Modernity, industrialism, and capitalism incorporated the time of the clock as the universal system
of time. Rationalized time was of course good for the projects of modernity,
where "progress" and the future could be planned; and it was very good indeed
for a system of capitalist production where precision and punctuality were
essential for predictable (and profitable) commodity production. As Adam
writes: "The clock . . . changed the meaning of time. The machine time sup-
planted (but never quite eradicated) the experiential understanding of time
as change—as growth and ageing, seasonal variation, the difference between
past and future—and shifted the experience and meaning of time towards invariability, quantity and precise motion expressed by number. [Time] became
independent from time and space, self-sufficient, empty of meaning and thus
apparently neutral" (Adam 2004, 114).

Clock time was a slow-burning *revolution* in how we related to time (Thrift
1996). It took nearly four centuries for this transformation to become complete—symbolically with the introduction of Standard Time and the division
of the world into "time zones" at the 1884 International Meridian Conference
in London. From that point on what constituted time was both signified and
made real for increasing numbers of humanity through a technobureaucratic
construction. From that point on people in modern societies were schooled
from infancy that the numbers around a clock face measured the reality of
absolute time, and therefore the *experience* of time had to be measured by
it. And from that point on the control or relative autonomy we had over the
social production of time began rapidly to diminish.

Space *and* Time

Since the beginning of the revolution in information and communication
technologies (ICTs) around the late 1970s, the development of ontologies of

cyberspace has been a busy and productive intellectual industry. Much valuable and insightful work has been done and continues to be done on how individuals, industries, applications, and processes combine to produce a growing virtual dimension to our lives (e.g., Bauman 1998; Harvey 1989). Much of the literature, however, tends to dwell on the spatial aspect, in either an implicit or explicit way. This focus is perhaps unavoidable. Since at least the industrial revolution people have acquired the habit of thinking and naming, almost as a conditioned reflex, in spatial terms. Spatialized frames of reference shaped, literally, how we oriented ourselves in the world. Ideas such as the local neighborhood, the linguistic and ethnic community, the philosophy of the nation-state, and the ideologies of nationalism were rooted in a concept of space that became a basic unit of social life (Anderson 1982).

This is a practice we have carried into our contemporary time of "globalization," an integral part of which is the World Wide Web, which contributes to the further "shrinking" of the planet and the creation of a "global marketplace." In these postmodern and postnational times we now adapt fairly easily to ideas of contracting space and *action at a distance* through ICTs. People are now exposed to these concepts at an early age and are quickly inured to them—so much so that it is commonplace now to think of the digital network as a *shared* space. A user with a cell phone, or a wireless laptop computer, or Bluetooth-enabled PDA can connect with a friend or colleague who is similarly equipped from almost any two points on the face of the earth. In so doing they share a common space, a virtual space that both accept as being a "real" space, a "real virtuality" that has real-world effects.

But what of time? Missing from much of this intellectual endeavor and exhilarating technological development has been a corresponding theory or understanding of time. We have cyberspace so why not cybertime? If one pauses to think about it, this gap in what would be a more holistic understanding is rather strange given that space and time are indivisible elements—indeed one makes no sense without the other. We measure space through time, such as the time it takes to fly from Paris to Rome; and time "annihilates" space, in that the faster we travel, the more we "shrink" space. The problem is doubly strange because we are in fact so familiar with time.

A key to unlocking the problem lies, I think, in the fact that the clock has "displaced," as Adam puts it, our deeper relationships with the embedded times of our physiology and nature. The clock ticks "outside" the body and nature. It slices and measures and makes universal and uniform all forms of duration. Being born into this form of time measurement, as all of us were, endowed us with a distorted sense of what time is. Embedded times are in-eradicable, to be sure, but the logic of the clock has severed our connections with them or has diminished them to the point that we feel them only indis-tinctly. We shall return to this "feeling" for time presently. Let us continue, however, with a short vignette on how the clock meters our days and then move to the implications of this for a "feeling" for time and our social and cultural ability to have some kind of autonomy or sovereignty over it. We will then reevaluate the time of the clock and the time of experience in the context of "network time."

Timepieces are ubiquitous. Clocks tick or they electronically flicker every-where, reminding us of the time of the day. I write these words at a desk in a university office. In my immediate view there are four reminders of what "time it is": a clock on the wall, a watch on my wrist, a town-hall clock I can see from my window, and a little digital clock at the bottom right-hand cor-ner of my PC. These machines *drive* the rhythms of the day, rhythms with which we are all familiar. So practiced are we at synchronizing our lives to this tempo that we can roughly guess the time without needing to glance at a clock. Looking at them now, my contiguous timepieces tell me that it is now (more or less) 11:27 a.m. So motivated are we by temporal regular-ity that we have developed the ability to predict many events in the near fu-ture. For example, I know that in around half an hour from now there will be more human traffic outside my half-open office door. Lunchtime inexorably approaches, and people start to move from other offices. They will go out into the street to buy lunch or take lunch to the park. I know of three people who today, Tuesday, have classes to take at 1:00 p.m. Accordingly, in another ninety minutes or so, I feel confident that I will see them stride past with their laptops, assorted papers, and other teaching paraphernalia. In the af-ternoon the rhythm of time continues. Conversations will periodically break the silence in the hallway outside. Their sounds rise and fall in a Doppler effect (the aurality of time and space) as they pass my door, marking a fairly regular tempo into the day, as people move to and from meetings. Their talk, in general, is faster and conducted in more urgent tones if they are running late, then slower and noisier as they emerge from their meeting rooms. When my clocks agree (more or less) that it is 5:00 p.m., an increase in human traffic can be predicted that will once again be audible in space as people begin to leave their offices. Almost simultaneously, and over the next couple of hours, a larger spatial-temporal rhythm comes to life across the city where I live and, indeed, across all cities. This is when cars and trains and motorcycles and bicycles and pedestrians and joggers and shoppers are all stirred by what the hands on the clock tell us: that it is time to go home.

It is clear that we move unthinkingly with the rhythm of clock time, so deeply do we experience it. It is clear also that to a significant degree it controls us and synchronizes us to its mathematical rhythms. Less clear is how to *consciously* think about other forms of time and express our thoughts about the experience of these. This predicament may explain in part our lack of insight into the temporality of the network. This is indeed a problem. Clock time, as an abstract form of time, has been the time of modernity and of capitalist industrialism. It is a form of time reckoning that has inserted itself into our subconsciousness to the extent that most of us consider (when we do consider) that this is what time is. We can extrapolate from this to argue that because of the difficulty of "knowing" or "understanding" the embedded times of our bodies and of nature, we have let the mechanical clock "keep" time for us. In order to explore how we can recover or discover the embedded times that have been displaced from our social life by the clock—and now, seemingly, by the "real time" of near-instantaneity that is generated in the digital networks of the information age—we need to begin with a fuller articulation of the problem of feeling and understanding time.

In an essay called "Time Felt, Time Understood" J. T. Fraser analyzes the conundrum concerning our seeming inability to properly express what time is. It is a failure, he reminds us, that philosophers have recognized for at least fourteen centuries, since the time of Saint Augustine. He puts it this way: "The experience of time's passage is intimately familiar. Present, future, and past and the flow of time appear to be simple, obvious aspects of the natural world. Yet trying to explain to someone, who does not already know what is meant by the passage of time is not simply difficult, but seemingly impossible" (Fraser 2003, 17). Fraser is a respected interdisciplinary thinker on time, but in this work he goes on to make the argument that the trouble humans have in communicating effectively with each other about the nature of time, and our relationship with it, has a singular locus—in the evolutionary development of the brain. The part of the brain that deals with our experience of temporality, according to Fraser, is the most ancient realm of the brainstem and the midbrain, which together are referred to as the "reptilian brain" (ibid., 18). This reptilian brain is responsible for the working of the reflex system and lower levels of cognition. Surrounding the reptilian brain is the hippocampus and the limbic structures that control drives and motives. The outermost "and uniquely human structure," as Fraser puts it, is the cortex, which controls speech, and the associative areas of the brain. These layers interact and have evolved together in that they "share the same skull," but "each level retained its peculiar way of assessing reality and hence formulating—gathering and processing—knowledge. The older parts of the brain may be said to command knowledge felt, the newer parts knowledge understood" (ibid., 8).

In other words we "feel" the passage of time in the ancient structure of the brain, but we are unable to express this accurately because the "deeper regions of the brain" are "unavailable for cognitive examination" (Fraser 2003, 21). Putting it rather more crisply, Fraser writes: "Time understood subsumes time felt" (ibid., 22). Human creativity has found a partial way around this, according to Fraser, and that is through art. His article quotes poetry, such as that of Dylan Thomas, whose final lines of "Fern Hill" Fraser thinks go some way to addressing this temporal "asymmetry": "Time held me green and dying/Though I sang in my chains in the sea."

Theodor Adorno argued along similar lines when he insisted that music (or a certain kind of music) has the ability to "express the inexpressible" (Adorno 1973, 114). Adorno was a profound thinker who inspired a couple of generations to study and develop his "critical theory." But he was also accused of elitism when it came to popular culture and to music especially. Fraser is no elitist (and neither was Adorno), but in emphasizing rarefied forms of culture as the "solution" to "feeling" time, he speaks only to a limited stratum of society, those educated enough to read, "appreciate," and write poetry. The solution is therefore no solution at all, as it leaves the experiencing of time as a purely subjective process, unable to be adequately shared by individuals (except through an approximate understanding of a poem).

Moreover, Fraser cites no hard scientific evidence from medicine or neurology in his essay. Nor could he. This is because, first, there seems to be no current research in this precise area, and, second, the "problem" is a *social* science one. Through the clustering of timescapes, the coming together of people, processes, institutions, technologies, and the environment that surrounds us, social time is created. These are (or can be) times felt, but they are also times that are constructed by human agency, durations, emergences, rhythms, and so on that constitute the numberless individual and collectively created timescapes that fill our lives. Key to expressing these, to both feel *and* understand these, is a *control* over their production and the creation of their context. This does not mean a full autonomy, of course, but rather the ability to be part of the process of coming together with other ribbons of time—creating time-scapes—in ways that are not oppressive or alienating.

Imagine reading a book (in this case it will have to be Proust), and think of immersing oneself within it, to consciously connect with its narratives and its imageries. We can soon reach the point of losing track of clock time, where seconds and minutes and hours dissolve into nothing. Creating this contextually unique time is a form of temporal control. This could be seen as an individualized context, but it is something we can have (only too infrequently) when in social situations. In communication with others we can also get to the point where the clock does not matter, so deeply have we shared the flow and rhythms of the constructed time. Released from the domination of the clock, time dissolves and becomes the context. Listening, speaking, eating, writing, thinking, watching, breathing, concentrating, and daydreaming all generate their own temporal qualities. And these are qualities that can be "freed" for us to "feel" their combining and forming, unfolding and unforming in a living timescape.

The "problem" of being able to express this feeling for time, as Fraser sees it, is a problem that can only be overcome, however partially, through art. The problem, moreover, is enunciated in terms of a lack—a gap that stems from the hierarchical structure of our brain but that may be filled or eased somewhat through poetry or, in an extension of Fraser's rationale, through music or dance or painting. There is indeed a sense in which artistic forms express something inexpressible, but it is a deeply subjective interpretation—and neither is it necessarily about time. The gap or lack that is our inability to express the feeling of time is, as the logic of this essay would strongly suggest, the tyranny of the clock, which has for two hundred years and more separated humans forcibly from feeling and understanding the socially constructed nature of time. And so in a very real sense the problem is a *political* one because it involves a loss of control, which is a loss of freedom over what is increasingly being recognized as a basic right (Schor 1991).

We *are* time. As Ann Game writes, "To be *in* the body is to be in time" (Game 1991, 95). To order and shackle this time to the "outside" time of the clock is to alienate us. The experience of the time of the clock is therefore to experience an unfreedom. To regain control over time in the individual and collective sense is to win freedom back. To have more autonomy over how one relates to temporality, to be able to control "one's time" more, to have it organized in society more democratically, and to have the right to refuse to be swept up in the acceleration of society and the time-squeeze that is taking its growing toll on cultures and societies across the globalized and interconnected world is thus a central political challenge for the twenty-first century.

Ironically, it is with the dawning of the computer age—the source of temporal acceleration—that our serfdom, vis-à-vis the relationship to the clock, is beginning to change. Networked cultures and societies are now confronted with the historical opportunity to not only "control" time once more through our own contextual self-creation of it but also to rediscover and connect with the deeper embedded temporalities that exist within ourselves and in the natural world. In other words through the temporal worlds constructed by information technologies we stand on the brink of a new *engagement* with time. Before discussing these political questions more fully, we need to look more closely at what constitutes network time.

The Times of the Network

The global digital network is more than an infinite number of connections that enable people to communicate. It is more than a vector for binary information to flow through; it is more than a way for businesses to compress space and time in the constant search for "efficiencies" and speed; and it is more than an assemblage of technologies connected into a working whole. The network is alive. Literally. It lives and breathes and thinks and acts and reacts. It works furiously, at a breakneck pace, or cruises at a more manageable speed, stopping to check, to rest, to reflect, to leap forward or step back. It is alive because the network is you; it is us. It is everyone who operates a connectable device or uses a connected service or process.

In his 2003 book intriguingly titled *Living Networks* business consultant Ross Dawson maintains that worldwide electronic networks constitute a "*global brain* in which ideas procreate freely and [within which] we collaborate to filter an ever-expanding universe of information" (Dawson 2003, 3). *Living Networks* is a book written for business people and for would-be NASDAQ investors, so, somewhat predictably, much of the rest of the book continues in this fanciful and uncritical fashion. In this it is characteristic of its genre, what Thomas Frank calls the burgeoning "school of guru-interpretation" (Frank 2000, 242). The idea of the network as a "global brain," even as analogy, does not work because it suggests a centrality, a unity and an overall co-herence, that simply does not exist. Nevertheless, the notion that the network represents in some new way the living, technologized expression of hundreds of millions of people is useful and workable as a framework of analysis—as a way of viewing "the body as information processor" and the network as the global extension of that body (Tofts 1997, 94).

Networks do have, to use one of Dawson's more acceptable terms, a "pres-ence" (Dawson 2003, 115). This presence is virtual: a virtuality that is no less real for its being decentered and disembodied. What this virtual presence of more than one billion people constitutes is a larger virtuality, a virtual en-vironment or virtual *ecology*. Again, the virtual ecology of the network is a "real virtuality" because it involves real individuals who constitute part of it and works in tandem with digital systems on the reality of the concrete world to change and shape it. The virtual ecology is created, maintained, and sus-tained as a consequence of the users' capacity to be "always on" and through the system's logic, which is oriented toward "ubiquitous computing," which, in turn, creates the appropriate environmental conditions for what another business consultant, Jon Lebkowsky, neatly terms the "persistent connection" (Lebkowsky 2004).

The network ecology is evolving out of the nascent forms that cybernetic interaction on a large scale is now making possible. The idea (and the reality) of the cyborg (the fusion of humans with technological aids) has been with us for some time now (Haraway 1991; Licklider 1960; Negroponte 1995; Weiner 1948). Through theorists such as these, both science and social theory have made much headway in understanding the possibilities and implications of what a deepened, more entangled, and completely intractable relationship we humans have with technology. We are still, however, far from the science-fiction stage where "bits and atoms" combine (to use Nicholas Negroponte's phrase) into a proto-Terminator cyborg-being that is living flesh covering powerful computing and hardened steel.

Today we are in the preliminary stages of the evolving network society and are taking only the initial steps of what will doubtless be a long journey. Nevertheless, so intimate have we already become with mobile phones, per-sonal computers, PDAs, and so forth that it is already possible to view these as our cyborg extensions into the network, technologies that unite us with it and it with us. And it is here that the links are made that constitute the construction of an information ecology. The ecological framework is created and held in place by webs of communication that are becoming increasingly dense, normalizing the "persistent connection" that creates a "presence" or, more accurately, a "telepresence" that forms the growing digital environment. No longer are the components of the network reducible to their constituent parts—computer, server, user, software, time and space. They instead combine to form a living, amorphous system. They become the social and technological means of innumerable contexts-through-connection, the creation of digital times and spaces that individuals, groups, corporations, institutions, processes, and applications blend into lived realities. Contexts may combine and separate in the space of nanoseconds—or last for hours or days or weeks. Contexts traverse geographic space, dissolving it into the virtuality that is the network society (Manovich 2001, 25–26). Importantly, this digital environment or ecology is as real as the built environment that comprises the cities and towns and as actual as the natural ecology that provides the basic building blocks (the contexts) for life on the earth. It exists because intense matrixes of connectivity create the framework for concrete actions that have real effects on people and on the interpenetrative social, political, economic, and technological systems they construct.

Using the internet as his basis for analysis, John S. Quarterman (2002) hypothesizes that "[t]he Internet is an ecosystem. It is composed of many interacting parts, ISPs, datacenters, enterprises, end-users, each of them drawing sustenance from the others and from raw materials. Each of them needs to make informed decisions. This is an ecology. And this ecology whose life forms are corporations and people is also a market." Of course the Internet is one aspect of the network ecology. Our digital environment grows daily, hourly, as people connect through new devices and applications that enter the marketplace every week, suffusing the persistent connection deeper into everyday networked life. Some theorists call the time of the network "real time"; indeed, the term has become synonymous in the popular imagination with the speed of computer networks. *Real time* is, however, a misnomer. The term lends itself to the construction of a general consciousness that tends to obscure the actual temporality of the network. A much more interesting and potential-laden term is *network time*. This theoretical venture is tentative, as it should be, but the preconditions for its fully fledged emergence are already in place. As Jacques Attali (1982) argued: "a new perception of time . . . is always preceded by the invention of the instruments required for its measurement and followed by the appearance of a new master of social organization. . . .

Conversely, the theory for each new time structure would seem to be never totally formulated until the end of the given structure's domination" (cited in Klein 2004, 252).

With this in mind it is possible to see that, acting through a human/machine-generated ecology of interconnectivity, our long-standing relationship with the time of the clock is not only being "deconstructed" but is undergoing profound transformation. Hundreds of millions of individuals now inhabit—day in and day out, in their business and leisure, and in their public and private lives—a digital space where the time of the clock has less and less relevance. Crucial matters now are speed, connectivity, and flexibility. The times of the network are generated along a spectrum of compressed clock time, a "chronoscopic time" (Hassan 2003; Purser 2000). To be sure, the times that are generated in the new economy of speed tend to be fast, to be accelerated, but not on the plane of real time. So before describing the defining temporality of the network age, the question still needs to be asked: what is real time?

Computer programmers and systems designers coined the term to describe operating systems that could respond at high speed to the input of data. The computer technicians' online dictionary of Internet terms defines real time as something "occurring immediately," and on a surface level, at least, this is how most people would conceive of real time. This generalized definition, however, stemming as it does from a technical perspective, sheds little light on the social, cultural, and temporal implications that "occurring immediately" may signify. Michael Heim, in his *The Metaphysics of Virtual Reality*, gives a more intriguing definition. He writes that real time is "[s]imultaneity in the occurrence and the registering of an event, sometimes called synchronous processing" (1993, 157). This represents a significant shift from the technical definition. *Immediately* connotes a brief temporal lag (be it measured in minutes, seconds, or even nanoseconds). Heim's *simultaneity*, however, suggests "happening at the same time," a cancelling-out of temporal duration, delay, or latency between events. *Simultaneity* implies, then, a nontime, the shattering, or voiding, or "death" of time.

A problem here is that social theorists, and the media more generally, have taken the technician's term for indicating something that happens in digitally compressed clock time (fast, but still multidurational, multipatterned, etc.) and implicitly or explicitly use it to mean *no time*. For example, Castells, in his 1996 book *The Rise of the Network Society* argues that globalization and the information age are heralding the era of domination by real time, or what he calls "timeless time." Real time for Castells is also a kind of nontime, which means that as the network society becomes more encompassing of culture and society, "linear, measurable, predictable time is being shattered . . . in a movement of extraordinary historical significance" (Castells 1996, 433). In his speculative social theory, Paul Virilio is even more explicit in his book *Open Sky* when he writes that "the teletechnologies of real-time . . . are killing 'present' time by isolating it from its here and now, in favour of a commutative elsewhere that no longer has anything to do with our 'concrete presence' in the world" (Virilio 1997, 10).

If one thinks about the nature of time, however, it can be recognized that the concepts of "timeless time" or of the "killing" of time make no sense at all. Ontologically it is an impossibility. We are temporal beings living in a temporal environment—whether inside or outside the network. Temporal durations, patternings, rhythms suffuse everything—from the rapid heartbeat of a baby in the womb to the years it takes the oyster to grow its pearl from a grain of sand. Like trying to imagine "time before time began"—i.e., before the Big Bang, fifteen billion years ago—we evolved anthropologically and culturally ill-equipped to think in such terms.

The absurdity of simultaneous real time may be appreciated more readily if we think about our own involvement with the network society. For example, the combination of the Internet, with its technical capacities, and our own human capabilities ensures that this is an inherently *asynchronous* space. Nothing occurs instantaneously, or in real time. There exists instead an open-ended continuum within the network, measured (if we need to measure it) from picoseconds upward. For example, we can flash an email across the world in seconds or minutes and then wait for an unknowable period for a reply. This could come in seconds, minutes, hours, days, or never. Networks can fail; they can slow down or speed up; we could be using state-of-the-art technology or an old 486 PC with a dial-up modem. The multiform temporal dimensions that we are able to create, at least in potential, in the Internet have led Lee and Liebenau to insist that "we can regard the experience of using the Internet as one of pseudo-instantaneous access" (2000, 51).

Accordingly, real time and its social-theory meanings of "instantaneity" or "no time" need to be brought into proper technological and ontological perspective. Real time may be viewed, therefore, as the final goal of machine / human interaction, the very end of the temporal continuum that would stretch from "no time" to the speed of light. To be able to achieve true real-time response would mean the ultimate surrender of human agency to digital technology, where latencies have been driven out and where lags no longer occur. This would constitute the militarist dream of the achievement of absolute power through absolute speed (Virilio 1986) and the capitalist Nirvana where production and circulation function "at the speed of thought" (Gates 1995). Both dreams are destined, however, to be unrealizable because imperfect humans constantly get in the way of perfect systems.

Network Time as Connected Asynchronicity

The key to understanding the essence of network time is to appreciate the economic and ideological motivation that created (unintentionally it must be said) the information ecology—the drive toward systemwide flexibility. The system of Fordism, as David Harvey (1989) has shown, was predicated on synchronization, predictability, and planning. Flexible accumulation emerged as Fordism's antithesis in the 1970s. The computerization of this process contributed to the asynchronous ecology of information.

Connected asynchronicity is a central feature of the network society and network time—connected asynchronicity and the acceptance of the idea that people have the capability to create their own times and spaces (Adam 1998; Lefebvre 1990). Network time fundamentally changes our relationship with the clock—it doesn't negate or cancel it. Instead, the numberless asynchronous spaces of the network society, created and inhabited by people and ICTs in interaction, *undermine* and *displace* the time of the clock. What we experience, albeit in very nascent form, is the recapture of the forms of temporality that were themselves displaced by the clock. What digital networks make possible is the conscious creation of temporal contexts and the freeing of the embedded times in humans, in nature, and in society that form the timescapes that intersect our lives but that we have been unable to fully experience, appreciate, or understand because of the deadening implacability of clock time.

Asynchronicity connotes a temporal fragmentation, a smashing of the uniform and universal linearity of the clock into a billion different time contexts within the network. In a similar vein Olivier Klein maintains that because of the effects of high speed and computer technology a network-generated "fragmented time" is emerging alongside the "industrial time" of the clock. Indeed, argues Klein, this "new time structure, not totally formulated but already distinct," may signal a "return to the 'task oriented' work that Edward Thompson (1967) attributed to pre-industrial societies" (Klein 2004, 252–255). Thompson's research indicated that within preindustrial societies, before domination by the clock occurred, "task-oriented" time—i.e., the time it took someone to sow a particular-sized field or shoe a horse—was dictated by the task itself and the interaction between human, technological, and local circumstances. To time the work as "one hour," "sixteen hours," or whatever would have seemed an illogical way to look at the job. The straightforward "task orientation," Thompson concluded, was, to the preindustrial worker, "more humanly comprehensible than timed labour" (Thompson 1993, 358).

Thompson's task-oriented time, Klein's fragmented time, and our network time have important similarities in that they denote a time that is created and shaped by a context that emerges through the intersection of humans, socioeconomic forces, and technology. The latter two theorizations indicate the creation of a new space for new experiences with times that are able to go beyond the purely instrumental "task" that network designers initially set for them.

Within these digital spaces of asynchronicity we have the potential to create and experience (and therefore control) our own context-dependent times, where the clock will have marginal or no effect. In an online chat room, for example, it may be midnight where you are and midafternoon for one of your interlocutors, breakfast time for another. The interaction, however, takes place in network time. This may be fast if the network is running fast, faster if you have a whiz-bang computer and broadband fiber-optic access—or slow if network conditions are busy and you are using a copper-wire telephone connection and 28,000-bps modem. The important point is that this *context-created temporal experience is disconnected from the local clock times of the users*. The clock no longer governs, as it once did in the preinformation age. Much more fragmented and temporally contextual times are now able to vie with industrial time for sovereignty for the duration of our stay in the chat room, in our surfing of the Internet, in our conversations on a mobile phone, in our ICQ-ing at a wi-fi hotspot, or our texting à la mode, in reply to a fourteen-year-old niece in Toronto who asked what the weather is like where you are.

What we do when we enter the network, then, is to change the "normal" governing dynamics of modernist space and time. By doing that, we change the way the mind and body are potentially able to experience time and space. We have no sense organs for perceiving time, but our total awareness is able to become attuned to a greater temporal inventiveness. Such an effort at the level of our imagination is needed if we are to deal satisfactorily with a whole range of time-focused environments. Language captures some of the diversity of time experience that we may be able to create and explore. Such temporal diversity includes the potentials of latency and immanence, of pace and intensity, of contingency and context dependence, of time-distantiation and intergenerational impacts, of rhythmicity and time-scales of change, of timing and tempo, of transience and transcendence, of irreversibility and indeterminacy, and of the complex interrelation between the influence of the past, the present, and the projection into an open future (Adam 2004).

Gaston Bachelard noted this ability to change our nature and hence our awareness of space and time through the experience of environmental change. Bachelard had in mind our relationship with space, but the logic also applies to temporal dynamics that tightly interpenetrate the spatial. Bachelard (1966, 15) writes that "[b]y changing space, by leaving the space of one's usual sensibilities, one enters into a communication with a space that is psychically innovating. For we do not change place, we change our nature."

The Digital (and the Temporal) Is Political

Neoliberalism and the economic globalization it has rendered as reality through the revolution in information and communication technologies is a profoundly *political* project. It is a politics, however, that denies its own existence. The *ideology* of neoliberalism asserts that the transformation of economy culture and society that has occurred since the 1970s is not a political project at all but simply a getting back to basics, to where the unencumbered market functions neutrally (and nonpolitically) in the generation of wealth and the creation of opportunity for all. Indeed, much of the work of the institutions of politics—of governments and parliaments, of congresses, and of the daily work of numberless elected politicians—is now actively directed toward letting "market forces" do their "politically disinterested" work. As a result, the past quarter-century has seen wave upon wave of privatization sweep the planet. Public assets have been sold, or given away, or stolen, and private shareholder capitalism now dominates. Economic nationalism, the ability (and once the perceived duty) to develop national well-being through government-business alliances, is now seen as a hopelessly old-fashioned concept. Both parties now see the economy as essentially borderless and believe that the role of government is to cut the red tape that binds the free movement of capital and commodities and to let prosperity and individualism bloom. Or so the rhetoric goes.

That it has not worked out entirely as planned is now commonly asserted through a growing body of empirical economic and social data (e.g., UNDP 2005). Inequality and the attendant lack of opportunity are now the specters that haunt the world. The dynamics and momentum of neoliberal globalization have driven its logic and its effects into every register of economy, culture, and society (Hardt and Negri 2000). Accordingly, the personal has become the political through the agency of the digital. This has resulted in, as Zygmunt Bauman has observed, putting it rather mildly, an "absence of justice":

> On a planet criss-crossed by "information highways" human misery of distant places and remote ways of life is displayed by electronic images as vividly, harrowingly and humiliatingly as the distress of the humans close to home is during the daily strolls through the town streets. And on a planet open to free circulation of capital and commodities, whatever happens in one place has a bearing on how all other people live. (Bauman 2005, 4)

The networked society is thus at the same time an integrated and global *political society*—but one where the locus of political power has shifted decisively from relatively stable institutional forums to the rather more volatile settings of corporate boardrooms and the computer screens of funds managers in New York or London or Tokyo. The absence of justice is compounded by a global political vacuum at the institutional level—an immense lack of political will about taking on the near-sacrosanct role of the free market and its palpably destructive consequences. So in many disturbing ways neoliberal globalization, driven by market ideology and powered by planet-girding information technologies, is a system on autopilot, a system propelled by the abstract notions of competition, where each looks to his or her own and where, as Anthony Giddens has described it, "there is no-one in charge" (1999).

Political injustice and network time are part of this same logic in that they have emerged from the same globalizing processes and are driven by the same technologies. No matter which name we give to its dynamics—the information society, the networked economy, or simply "globalization"—the effect is a world of social and economic flux, a world that is up for grabs. This represents a historic opportunity, but precisely what is at stake needs to be understood. Today we exist within a double structure of time: that of the clock and that of the network. We move in and out of each realm multiple times each day. The clock governs us from the "outside," displacing experienced or embedded times, and network time is a temporality created by ICT users, across a flexible spectrum that is dependent, as we have seen, on levels of technological sophistication and the nature (the context) of the communication. The clock will still be part of our lives for the foreseeable future, but the future will be dominated increasingly by network time. The current phase of neoliberal globalization therefore represents a time of change and of potentiality. The opportunities for political transformation are already being exploited in the network society, as we will see shortly. To develop a momentum, however, the politics of temporality, of ownership and autonomy over the creation and experience of time, needs to be raised more consciously to the top of the agenda. This is because the future of neoliberal globalization and the network society is able to develop in two possible directions, and the extent to which theorists and activists see temporality as a central issue could decide which direction is taken. Let us look at the choices that confront networked civil society in the twenty-first century.

The first choice is no choice at all. It is to do nothing and leave globalization on autopilot. This is, in fact, what is largely happening today. Under the rule of the market most people allow economic and technological change to subsume them. People feel atomized and powerless, so they try to adapt to changing circumstances and synchronize with (not control) the speed of the network. The reality of network time and network communication for most people is to be impelled by business, by profit, and the need to look always for ways to be more "efficient" and "productive." Speed is fetishized and short-term outcomes valorized. This is the unidirectional path of continued social, economic, and cultural acceleration, where the blizzard of signs and symbols, of imperatives and demands, all concentrate into a singular instrumental plane, into what Ron Purser has called a "constant present" (2000). Users are compelled by the momentum of the now. Control in this context is almost impossible: take your time and you lose the sale, suffer a drop in efficiency, or miss the "valuable" connection. Deviate from the instrumental script (not doing what you are paid to do), and you run the risk of being marginalized and driven from "the game"—which is increasingly just holding on to your job and keeping the boss happy. Within this networked ecology individuals, communities, and societies are headed toward a kind of digital serfdom. As Paul Virilio (1995) sees it, "the twin phenomena of immediacy and instantaneity" represent the "inaugural value" that ushers in a "new epoch" that will be a "dictatorship of speed." And as Kevin Kelly (1998) predicts, in such a society, a society on autopilot, a society without transformative human agency—"the computer wins."

Alternatives to this baleful scenario exist, however, and alternatives flourish within the neoliberal preponderance. The exercise of a democratic choice is currently building a grassroots politics that is developing across cyberspace and across the physical world. The consequences of neoliberal speed and commodification outlined above are being consciously rejected by millions of people across the world today. The most important development here is that it is being done from within the network society itself, using the tools of speed and instrumentalism that run counter to the ways they were intended. Using the panoply of connectivity that ICTs provide, activists, theorists, and the many who are simply fascinated by what computers can do are creating alternative times and spaces where alternative visions can be projected and alternative politics developed. Global networks have developed and continue to develop, where ideas are formed and discussed and political action is translated into agency in the physical realm.

It is a form of politics that can be characterized, in the words of Herbert Marcuse (1991, 63), as the "Great Refusal." Marcuse is theorizing along the lines of Fraser and Adorno about the transformative possibilities of art when he proposes, "Whether ritualized or not, art contains the rationality of negation. In its advanced positions, it is the Great Refusal—the protest against that which is. The modes in which man and things are made to appear, to sing and sound and speak, are modes of refuting, breaking, and recreating their factual existence."

It is this "rationality of negation" of the "factual existence" of the neoliberalized network society, the denial of it as the only possible reality, that constitutes the common thread in the immense diversity of what has been called the "global civil society" or, more formally, the World Social Forum (Anheier, Kaldor, and Glasius 2004 / 2005). From within these categories of negation new virtual and physical worlds are emerging. We see their "advanced positions," to use Marcuse's phrase, in the "open-source" movement that grew during the 1980s as a response to the domination by corporations such as Microsoft, whose ruthlessly guarded proprietary software has left users with few options. The movement catalyzed a global stratum of those who write computer code or who are activists concerned about questions of free speech in cyberspace. In the introduction to his 1999 book *Code and Other Laws of Cyberspace* Lawrence Lessig, one of the founders of the open-source movement, argues for control, but control of a specific kind: "Liberty in cyberspace will not come from the absence of the state. Liberty there, as anywhere, will come from a state of a certain kind. We build a world where freedom can flourish not by removing from society any self-conscious control; we build a world where freedom can flourish by setting it in a place where a particular kind of self-conscious control survives" (1999, 190).

Blogging (a kind of online personal publication) is much less skill-intensive than code writing, and maybe for that reason it has exploded in the 2000s. Blogs are said to grow at the rate of one every second (Technorati 2005). They can (and do) reflect almost every whim that individuals have. But they are also increasingly political, and it is here that they have their greatest potential. To enter and engage with a political blog—and there are tens of thousands of them—is a profoundly temporal network experience. What most of them do is to reprint or provide links to news articles in the mainstream media. Instead of that news item disappearing into the archives of the datasphere very soon after it has been published, bloggers *hold it in time* and in virtual space to discuss, analyze, or promote it. Facts are questioned, motivations speculated upon, and consequences considered in a way that was not possible in the days when newspapers or television dominated. This is a form of temporal control. Blogs and their readers and writers constitute a temporal context where the time of the clock, the time of business, or locality and zone do not matter. Ideas and discussions dwell in cyberspace until people have thought them through, had enough of them, or moved on to the next one—or back to a previous one.

Moreover the logic of control and autonomy from what Jean-François Lyotard saw as *knowledge as a commodity* through computerization (1979, 5) is being developed in the vast epistemological experiment that is Wikipedia, the online encyclopedia where anyone can write up an entry on any subject. This may seem like a recipe for disaster, but the millions who visit the site are able to question "facts" and dispute entries. Most entries are hyperlinked to checkable sources, and those that are not are always susceptible to validation by one's own efforts. People can add to entries by giving insights and perspectives, including evidence from valid sources that may have been forgotten or ignored, or by simply commenting on an entry in the discussion pages. Egregious, racist, or other offensive entries or comments are edited out by others. Overall, Wikipedia evolves and develops as a changing and effervescent source of knowledge and constitutes a genuine alternative to the logic of commodification, instrumentalism, and the relegation of knowledge to the dusty archives of physical library shelves. Again, like the example of the blog, visiting and contributing to Wikipedia is a temporal event. Through blogging, personal and collective forms of control over ideas, knowledge, and the means with which to orient oneself in the world becomes possible through the experience of being part of its production and dissemination.

Using open source, creating or contributing to a political blog, or creating an entry or discussing an entry on Wikipedia, are all technopolitical acts. They are a form of what Douglas Kellner (2001) has termed a "technopolitics." Through the powerful communicative means that ICTs make possible, the creation and distribution of alternative political ideas are generated. Networks create a political ecology in which activists can develop a new form of agency. On this Kellner (2001, 2) writes, "Deploying computer-mediated technology for technopolitics . . . opens new terrains of political struggle for voices and groups excluded from the mainstream media and thus increases potential for resistance and intervention by oppositional groups."

Use of the word *terrains* reveals again the habit of thinking principally in terms of space, but Kellner's logic applies just as much to the temporal. And as the logic of this chapter would suggest, the temporal has to become central to political struggle in the coming years. Time and temporality must be recognized as a realm where control and autonomy can be self-generated by individuals and groups in a world where previously these had to be taken from those in power. Activists need to create for themselves the time to think, to reflect, to organize, and to act. The examples given above are evidence of a rhizomatic activity that amounts to a political and creative *reestablishment of social control over time, space, and speed*. In a diversity of circumstances and at multiple levels of awareness people *are* coming to realize that the computer, mobile communications, and the networks that bring these erstwhile business tools to life have uses that can be resistant and subversive. Political actors who have been marginalized from the institutional dynamics of democratic processes, or who have found them to be ineffectual, have discovered through their own technical application, spaces and times of alterity that are able to be developed to work against the dominating pressures of neoliberalized networks.

The coming to consciousness of the importance of autonomy and control over one's experience of time in the network society is a political imperative that needs to be implicated in the ways in which we now practice politics.

Millions are making what in effect is a technopolitics by themselves, but the actual potential of what they are making happen everyday needs to become explicit. This consciousness raising is itself a political task, and it requires the constant work of theorists and activists who recognize what the temporality of the network is capable of producing.

Earlier in this chapter I cited the final lines of Dylan Thomas's "Fern Hill," which J. T. Fraser quoted by way of an illustration of the power of art. For Fraser art represented a partial overcoming of the inability of our reptilian brain to fully appreciate the experience of time. In the light of the arguments set out here, one can use a stanza from the same poem to describe more fully, I think, the power of democratic politics to bring about a rediscovery and reestablishment of our experience of time, not only in the network society but in every other realm of life:

> In the sun that is young once only,
> Time let me play and be
> Golden in the mercy of his means

References

Adam, Barbara. 1998. *Timescapes of modernity: The environment and invisible hazards.* London: Routledge.

———. 2004. *Time.* Cambridge, MA: Polity.

Adorno, Theodor. 1973. *Negative dialectics.* New York: Seabury Press.

Anderson, Benedict. 1982. *Imagined communities: Reflections on the origins and spread of nationalism.* London: Verso.

Anheier, Helmut, Mary Kaldor, and Marlies Glasius, eds. 2004/2005. *Global civil society.* London: Sage.

Bachelard, Gaston. 1996. *The poetics of space.* Boston: Beacon.

Banks, Robert. 1985. *The tyranny of time.* Homebush, NSW: Lancer Books.

Bauman, Zygmunt. 1998. *Globalization: The human consequences.* Cambridge, MA: Polity.

———. 2005. The demons of an open society. www.lse.ac.uk/collections/LSEPublic LecturesAndEvents/pdf/20051020-Bauman1.pdf (accessed Jan. 25, 2007).

Castells, Manuel. 1996. *The rise of the network society.* Vol. 1 of *The Information age: Economy, society, and culture.* Oxford: Blackwell.

Dawson, Ross. 2003. *Living networks.* London: FTPrentice Hall.

Frank, Thomas. 2000. *One market under God.* London: Secker and Warburg.

Fraser, J. T. 2003. Time felt, time understood. *KronoScope* 3 (1): 15–26.

Game, Ann. 1991. *Undoing the social.* Milton Keynes: Open University Press.

Gates, Bill. 1995. *The road ahead*. New York: Viking.

Giddens, A. 1999. *Runaway world: How globalization is reshaping our lives*. London: Profile Books.

Gurevich, A. J. 1976. Time as a problem of cultural history. In *Cultures and time*, ed. L. Gardet, A. J. Gurevich, A. Kagame, C. Larre, G. E. R. Lloyd, A. Neher, R. Panikkar, G. Pattaro, P. Ricoeur, 71–83. Paris: UNESCO Press.

Haraway, Donna. 1991. A cyborg manifesto: Science, technology, and socialist-feminism in the late twentieth century. In *Simians, cyborgs, and women: The reinvention of nature*, 149–181. New York: Routledge.

Hardt, Michael, and Antonio Negri. 2000. *Empire*. Cambridge, MA: Harvard University Press.

Harvey, David. 1989. *The condition of postmodernity*. Oxford: Blackwell.

Hassan, Robert. 2003. *The chronoscopic society: Globalization, time, and knowledge in the network economy*. New York: Lang.

Heim, Michael. 1993. *The metaphysics of virtual reality*. New York: Oxford University Press.

Kellner, Douglas. 2001. Globalization, technopolitics, and revolution. www.gseis.ucla.edu/faculty/kellner/essays/globalizationtechnopoliticsrevolution.pdf (accessed Jan. 25, 2007).

Kelly, Kevin. 1998. The computational metaphor. *Whole Earth* (winter): www.wholeearth.com/ArticleBin/201.html (accessed Jan. 25, 2007).

Klein, Olivier. 2004. Social perception of time, distance, and high-speed transportation. *Time & Society* 13 (2/3): 245–263.

Lebkowsky, Jon. 2004. The future of affinity: Living networks with social software. Paper presented to the CenTex Chapter of the World Future Society, Austin, TX, Nov. 19, 2004. http://weblogsky.com/2004/11/the_future_of_affinity_living.html (accessed Jan. 25, 2007).

Lee, Heejin, and Jonathan Liebenau. 2000. Time and the Internet. *Time & Society* 9 (1): 43–53.

Lefebvre, Henri. 1990. *The production of space*. Oxford: Blackwell.

Lessig, Lawrence. 1999. *Code and other laws of cyberspace*. New York: Basic Books.

Licklider, J. C. R. 1960. Man computer symbiosis. http://memex.org/licklider.pdf (accessed Jan. 25, 2007).

Lyotard, Jean-François. 1979. *The postmodern condition: A report on knowledge*. Manchester: Manchester University Press.

Manovich, Lev. 2001. What is new media? In *The language of new media*, 1–26. Cambridge, MA: MIT Press.

Marcuse, Herbert. 1991. *One-dimensional man*. Boston: Beacon.

Negroponte, Nicholas. 1995. *Being digital*. Rydalmere, NSW: Hodder and Staughton.

Nowotny, Helga. 1989. *Eigenzeit: Entstehung und Strukturierung eines Zeitgefühls*. Frankfurt am Main: Suhrkamp Verlag.

Purser, Ron. 2000. The coming crisis in real time environments: A dromological analysis. http://online.sfsu.edu/rpurser/revised/pages/DROMOLOGY.htm (accessed Jan. 25, 2007).

Quarterman, J. S. 2002. Monoculture considered harmful. *First Monday*, no. 2 (Feb.): http://firstmonday.org/issues/issue7_2/quarterman/index.html (accessed Jan. 25, 2007).

Schor, Juliet B. 1991. *The overworked American*. New York: Basic Books.

Technorati. 2005. http://technorati.com/.

Thompson, E. P. 1993. Time, work-discipline, and industrial capitalism. In *Customs in common: Studies in traditional popular culture*, 352–403. Orig. pub. in *Past and Present* 38 (1967): 56–97.

Thrift, Nigel. 1996. *Spatial formations*. London: Sage.

Tofts, Darren. 1997. *Memory trade: A prehistory of cyberculture*. Sydney: 21C Press.

UNDP. 2005. *Report on the World Situation 2005: The Inequality Predicament*. New York: United Nations.

Virilio, Paul. 1986. *Speed and politics*. New York: Semiotext(e).

———. 1995. Speed and information: Cyberspace alarm! *CTheory* (Aug. 27): www.ctheory.net/text_file.asp?pick=72 (accessed Jan. 25, 2007).

———. 1997. *Open sky*. Trans. Julie Rose. London: Verso.

Wiener, Norbert. 1948. *Cybernetics: Control and communication in the animal and the machine*. Cambridge, MA: Technology Press.

3 Speed $= \dfrac{\text{Distance}}{\text{Time}}$

Chronotopographies of Action

Mike Crang

I WANT TO BEGIN WITH some of the grand claims and narratives of changing temporality heralded via information technology. I also want, however, to write into these the way changes in time are bound up with changes in space and to propose that spatialities and temporalities are mutually constitutive. I begin with stories of compression and dispersal— that is activities intensifying in time and allegedly dispersing in space. In this tale I foreground discussions of acceleration and speed in a real-time society. From this I suggest how flexibility of location and timing of activities can be seen through information and communication technologies (ICTs). Finally, I highlight several specific aspects of flexibility in both time and space but also start to figure how the two dimensions act together.

The imbrications of space and time in a networked world are clear at many levels. For instance, the insertion of ICTs into service provision via telephone "call centers" enables locational flexibility in provider location and regional, then national and increasingly global, distantiation via their relocation to countries such as India. ICTs not only allow a global reach but also use space to overcome time. The perhaps over-cited example of continuous global financial trading has to be seen, therefore, in the context of the use of ICTs to first overcome the difficulties of distantiated interactions and then to actually capitalize on this. We thus develop from using ICTs to coordinate widely scattered activities, bringing information together into a central office in the financial district, to using offices in different time zones to enable "around-the-clock" working. At the extreme this has been seen as the "supersession of space and the annihilation of time" (Castells 1996, 470). Castells provided a lengthy and influential account of the resulting spatial and temporal transformation. His most influential idea, that we are witnessing a society organized around informational capitalism, which itself gives rise to a global space of flows, highlights a new spatiality driven by the ability of ICTs to reconfigure the relationships of people and places. I wish to pick up from his work the dimensions of such a transition. The most usual and obvious sense here is that the friction of distance is reduced, that is distance presents less of a barrier to movement in space. While there has typically been the assumption of a broadly linear relationship of spatial and temporal distance (i.e., the further away in space, the more time to get there), this starts to break down. This relationship had never been absolutely linear nor socially even—so aeroplanes shrank intercontinental distances for a "kinetic elite," while reduced public transit services slowed others. One way of visualizing this development is via "space-time" maps, where we might draw a choropleth line to indicate how far an individual might travel in a given time in different directions. Such space-time contours suggest New York is just twice as long a journey from London as the west-country city of Exeter—where London and New York are just six hours apart by plane, whereas London and Exeter are three hours by train; or, indeed, from where I sit on Tyneside, Amsterdam, London, and Paris are all about an hour's flight, while Glasgow is more than two hours by train. Of course, this way of phrasing things emphasizes the speed of networks by leaving aside the times of getting to, going through, and coming from airports and the experienced time of waiting—though increasingly this too is becoming a site of social division and differentiated velocities, with premium services of high-speed links, and faster check-ins for first-class passengers, and even accelerated border controls for some fliers. Consequently the space-time contours will look different for the frequent flier fast-tracked through the airport (Newcastle to London via city airport one and two-thirds hours), the budget flier routed through airports miles from his or her destination town (Newcastle to Stansted and into London two and two-thirds hours), the train traveler (three and one-third hours) through to the cheaper coach (five hours) and budget bus (seven hours) traveler.

For all the uneven and variable patterns, time is related to distance covered. ICTs, however, shake up this time-space proximity map, allowing the possibility of near instantaneous communication irrespective of distance. In that sense it may be quicker to phone someone in New York than to walk up to the next floor of the office, and an email takes much the same time as either. This sort of trend points in two directions—first, that 60 percent of email and phone traffic never leaves the building but also that the City of London has more data flows connecting it to Manhattan than it does to, say, East London suburbs, and Manhattan is as linked to London as it is to, say, the Bronx. All this creates "a relation of intercity proximity operating without shared territory: Proximity is deterritorialized" (Sassen 2000, 226). Within cities notions of "centrality" thus have to be refigured, especially where cities are oriented more strongly to global networks than to regional or local hinterlands (Sassen 2001). This division is bound into what Castells (1989) called the "dual city," sharply divided between prosperous "knowledge workers" and those incapable of finding a place in the "new economy" (other than, ironically, in servicing the needs for baby-sitting, house cleaning, and similar work as servants of the knowledge workers who require assistance to find time to pursue their frenetically busy lives). Castells sees a space of flows produced through global nodes and hubs, often themselves sealed off from localities in what he calls real virtual spaces (such as corporate offices, hotels, and airports) that act as cocoons for the elite. The "dual city" is simultaneously "globally connected and locally disconnected" (Castells 1996, 404), where some are relegated to the dark spaces between the networks. This networked society produces not just fluidity, however, but new fixities, as hubs are themselves constructed and entail massive infrastructural investments, producing new concentrations of skilled labor, centers of power, and so forth (Sassen 2000). So these complex space-time topographies refigure the production of centrality and marginality, fluidity and fixity.

Castells suggests this means reconceptualizing current geographies as dominated by this "space of flows." This characterization has some problems, however, since "'global' and 'local' social processes have been framed in binary opposition, as mutually exclusive and inherently antagonistic explanations for urban development which pit local cultures against globalizing economic transformations" (Smith 2001, 2), which tends to imply that flows are always dynamically global while stubborn resistance is the best that places can muster. But the theory does enable us not only to examine the density and scale of flows in a given time and space but to see them as creating new temporalities and spatialities. That is, they are reshaping our temporal and spatial coordinates and sensibilities. This includes a necessary temporal corollary to a space of flows—since Castells sees space as a "crystallized time" (1996, 411). He suggests a sequence of hegemonic forms of temporality, with industrial capitalism producing and produced by clock time and now informational capitalism entailing a time in which linearity is replaced by instantaneity and discontinuity: "Timeless time . . . the dominant temporality in our society, occurs when the characteristics of a given context, namely, the informational paradigm and the network society, induce systemic perturbation in the sequential order of phenomena performed in that context. . . . The space of flows . . . dissolves time by disordering the sequence of events and making them simultaneous, thus installing society in an eternal ephemerality" (Castells 1996, 464, 467).

Related analyses sketch a movement from premodern unified temporal order, to modern order of quantified and commodified time, and on to a postmodern era of simultaneity and an "extended present" (Roberts 1998). Such epochal accounts tend to focus, however, on only one aspect of temporality, whereas as Adam (2003, 59) notes, we could pick out five often diverging trends, the five "Cs": the creation of time to human design (C_1), the commodification of time (C_2), the compression of time (C_3), the control of time (C_4), and the colonization of time (C_5). Even if these categories align to form a timeless time, and that is not inevitable or universally true, within each category there are uneven and contested elements. So, although we create new temporalities and rhythms, it is true as any long-haul flight would remind you, that "embodied time is lived and experienced alongside, despite of, and in conflict with the culturally constituted social relations of time" (Adam 61; see also Vannini 2002, 2121). This means that "[c]ause and effect, linearity, spatiality, invariability, stability, clarity and precision are not being replaced but have alongside and superimposed contrasting temporal principles such as instantaneity, simultaneity, networked connections, ephemerality, volatility, uncertainty as well as temporal multiplicity and complexity" (Adam 2003, 74).

The effect is also one of competing temporalities—with global times, national times, and local times all now interacting in one place (Sassen 1999, 2000). Of course this is not entirely novel. We can look back to the informational world of telegraphy to find similar clashing temporalities. From extensive transport networks came the need for standardizing time—where Brunel's Great Western station in Bristol duly fitted its clock with two minute hands, eight minutes apart, one for local and one for national time. But media also brought conflicting temporalities into contact, as when telegrams flashed news around the British Empire. So before her Diamond Jubilee procession, the Queen-Empress Victoria went to the telegraph room in Buckingham Palace, pushed a button, and sent a signal to the Central Telegraph Office in St. Martin's le Grand, and the message "Thank my beloved people. May God bless them" was on its way around the globe. Within two minutes it had passed Tehran, and as her carriage, surrounded by cavalry, bobbed down the Mall, her thanks and blessings had reached the Cape, West Africa, and the Caribbean (Morris 1968, 21, 27). More jarring was the flow of news, where packet steamers took weeks to bring clippings of the London press to places like Sydney, bearing stories of plans and impending events that were published in local papers that had to reconcile them with real time but abbreviated telegraphic headlines that reported the outcomes—leaving battle plans being speculated upon in one story brought by boat but final outcomes in the headlines supplied by telegraph. The butting into one another of activities and consequences is not new, then, but the scale and tempo has indubitably increased—as has the valorization of speed.

Real Time and the Accelerated Society

The notion of temporal acceleration finds its apogee in the work of Paul Virilio, for whom space is being transformed or, indeed, being obliterated by the speed of modern society. He argues that "constructed geographical space has been replaced by chronological topographies, where immaterial electronic broadcast emissions decompose and eradicate a sense of place" (Boyer 1996, 19). ICTs do not simply allow the spatial stretching out of activities so that the same level of activity is dispersed; they also increase the level of interaction so that

> decentralization would take on an altogether different sense from that of autonomy accorded to regions, [and] it would signal the end of the unity of place of the old political theatre of the city, and its imminent replacement by a unity of time, a chronopolitics of intensivity and interactivity, "technicity" succeeding the continuity [long durée] of the City, architecture of information systems definitively replacing the system of architecture and of contemporary urbanism. (Virilio 1998a, 61)

Virilio suggests that modern society valorizes speed and acceleration, and this is now the engine of division in life chances as spatial location might once have been. Some are plugged in to a global time, of distantiated real-time interaction, and others are cut off into a local time, where events are, if anything, slowed down. For example, while the connected are able to pay their bills online and access international communications and media, others find physical facilities closed and more poorly serviced, which actually makes daily activities slower. Virilio sees society split by speed, where "one part lives in an electrical world of relative speed—transportation—, the second with absolute speed of transmission of information in real time" (Virilio 1998b, 185).

Virilio suggests the replacement of bureaucrats, the powerbrokers of the age of reason, with dromocrats in the age of speed, whose space-time contours chart a "dromosphere" (Virilio 2000a, 44; 2003, 42). These map power on the scale of "plus d'espace en moins de temps" [more space in less time] (Lantz 2000, 398), where the capacity to "compress and accelerate temporal processes is a prime index of wealth and power" (Roberts 1998, 117). If we use the long-term trends identified by Adam (2003), we might track this process through the evolution of the commodification, compression, control, and colonization of time. She suggests Virilio delineates three epochs of time compression—nineteenth-century transport, twentieth-century transmission, and twenty-first-century transplantation—each with its own distinct means of enhancing independence of the social relations of time from space and the body. So the nineteenth and twentieth centuries are marked by accelerating detachments from places:

> With the invention of trains, cars and aeroplanes, at the turn of the last century, the relation of time and space has been altered. The speed at which bodies can move across space has been massively increased, the time it takes dramatically shortened. Since their inception, all improvements in these modes of transport have been primarily in time compression. However, these increases in speed, as Virilio insists, brought with them a range of contradictions and paradoxes. Thus, for example, while cars, planes and trains have become progressively faster, the time spent in transit has not been compressed at an equal rate. (Adam 2003, 67)

Indeed, for all the talk of speed, recent studies suggest that current overland travel in central London is no faster than the ox cart attained in Roman Londinium. ICTs have received much attention as a means for bypassing this congestion. Indeed, the linkage of ICTs to speed to urban cohesion has a long pedigree in social commentary. We can go back to Casson's (1910) "The Invention of the Telephone" to find the argument that

> [i]t is one of the few social laws of which we are fairly sure, that a nation organizes in proportion to its velocity. We know that a four-mile-an-hour nation must remain an inert mass of peasants and villagers; or, if after centuries of slow toil, it should pile up a great city, the city will sooner or later fall to pieces of its own weight.... Mere bulk, unorganized becomes its own destroyer. But when ... Morse's telegraphy clicked its signals from Washington to Baltimore, and Bell's telephone flashed its vibrations of speech between Boston and Salem, a new era began. In came the era of speed and the finely organized nations. In came cities of unprecedented bulk, but held together so closely by a web-work of steel rails and copper wires that they became more alert and cooperative than a tiny hamlet.

Here communication is seen as connecting to a scale of shared temporality, binding places together, expanding the possible scale of community (Innis 2004). Similarly, mass mobilization of the populace was heralded by Le Corbusier as offering a chance to unify the city (Stallabrass 1999). For Virilio, however, the current epoch means communication will lead to disintegration rather than integration. According to Virilio it will entail nothing less than a "crisis in the notion of physical dimension," where the "tyranny of distances" between geographically scattered people gives way to the "tyranny of real time" and the "city of the past slowly becomes a paradoxical agglomeration in which relations of immediate proximity give way to interrelationships over distance" (quoted in Graham 1998, 170); hence we move from an urbanization of real space to an urbanization of real time (Virilio 1997a, 7). This leads to a rupture where we are "no longer part of chronological time; we have to conceptualize it instead as chronoscopic time. Real space, he suggests, is making room for decontextualized 'real-time' processes and intensity takes over from extensity" (Adam 2003, 68).

The different and embedded temporal regimes, the "polychronies of various heres and theres are linked in the isochrony of immediate teleactivity, telepresence or teletopia" (Luke 1998, 171). Accordingly, Virilio implicates "[t]elecommunications in dissolving the 'here' and the 'now,' serv[ing] both to break down distance, physical distance, and to create psychological 'distance'" (Leach 1999, 77). This occurs because the "instantaneity of ubiquity results in the atopia of a singular interface. After the spatial and temporal distances, speed distance obliterates the notion of physical dimension. Speed suddenly becomes a primal dimension that defies all temporal and physical measurements" (Virilio 1997b, 385). Virilio offers the strong sense of how tele-communications allows the general confusion and intermingling of places, an effect previously reserved for theatrical or exhibitionary spaces: "The cathode-ray window brings to each viewer the light of another day and the presence of the antipodal place. If space is that which keeps everything from occupying the same place, this abrupt confinement brings everything precisely to that 'place,' that location that has no location. The exhaustion of the physical, or natural relief and of temporal distances telescopes all localization and all position" (quoted in Leach 1999, 75).

Instead, then, of mobilizing people for movement through the city, the people are stationary, and places are mobilized (Vannini 2002; Virilio 2000a, 63–64). Time is no longer experienced as an acceleration of events but as a cutting adrift. "Chronological and historical time, time that passes, is replaced by a time that exposes itself instantaneously" (Virilio 1997b, 363), and the "passing time of chronology and history is replaced by time which is exposed to the absolute speed of light" (Virilio 2000a, 38), where we lose a sense of passage and trajectory in favor of shorter and shorter exposure times revealing events. Since Leibniz, space has been seen as the order of coexistence and time as the order of succession, but what Virilio is arguing is that there is now coexistence in time and that the distinction no longer holds. Virilio suggests this undermines democracy—which depends on expectation and memory—and stable categories of belonging and exclusion (Chesneaux 2000; Mandarini 1998). Paralleling Castells, he produces the concept of the "time accident," which occurs as a result of the temporal compression of data and the risks of the synchronization of knowledge, meaning that we have now passed from the visible velocity of substance to the invisible velocity of the accident (Virilio 2000b, 2003, 26). In this sense Virilio sees progress as creating the seeds of its accidents, producing the possibilities of larger and more dramatic technical failures, and failures that have to be predicted as possible yet cannot be rationally planned for become a form of time pollution (Virilio 1997a).

Virilio grasps the urgency and significance of the time-space shifts enabled through ICTs, and Castells offers a sense of fundamental transformation, but both seem locked into binarized outcomes that do not really speak to the complexities of space-times formed in current life. First, in all these accounts we need to ask how the everyday and bodily gets coded as the authentic yet also the slow. We should be suspicious of the habitual coding of the everyday as small scale and local and not equate "the human with the near and local, the slow and the small" (Thrift 2004, 54). So İ want to ground my account in the everyday, not as some "ultimate non-negotiable reality" (Felski 2000, 15) but rather as an arena of entanglement and complexity. Let us "call up the intricate web of itineraries weaving the thread of time into our daily lives," not necessarily through close social ties but the spaces of daily mobility and communication to offer a chronotopia combining analyses of pace (rhythm analysis) with analysis of places (Paquot 1999, 68). Stories of acceleration and squeezing more activities into the day are part of the imaginary of a digital life. The flipside is that they need to be fitted in by double-shifting women and enable long hours by overachieving men in informational sectors (Perrons 2003). We also find a shift from valorizing "leisure" to valuing busyness (Gershuny 2005). ICTs become another time-saving technology to cram more into the hectic day—a day that they may cause to seem more hectic.

Acceleration, Flexibility, Time, and Densification

We need to develop a conceptual approach that addresses the effects of information and communication technologies, and I want to start by outlining a range of temporal implications. To do this, I want to lay out six initial temporal impacts associated with the new media. First, ICTs speed services, though this can be a sociospatially selective benefit. Here new media offer quicker access, for instance by obviating travel time, bypassing physical queues, or offering preferential access, by enabling swift provision of information. ICTs accordingly alter the duration and pace of events. Such outcomes, let me say, contra Virilio, are contingent for different people in different places—phone banking may beat traveling to the bank and queuing, or being placed in a phone queue preference system may not be any advantage at all. Equally, online banking may be faster than both, or getting access to a PC, starting it, getting a connection, and processing may be just as slow. Nor is this to say that all networked access is equal or spatially invariant.

For the user there are issues of bandwidth and data-transfer speed over the network—with different parts of the city now having, and being marketed as offering, superior access—be that wi-fi or broadband cabling of different types. The differential speeds do not end there, though, since supplier software now may be used to sort through customers in an online or telephone queue to grant preferential access—so that premier rate and highly valued customers may be recognized and receive customized attention—or indeed be routed to their personal account adviser—other valued customers might be given the next priority, and those whose custom is deemed incidental or problematic may wait until any slot is free (Graham 2005). When the automated telephone message announces, "Your custom is valued; please hold until an agent is free to deal with your call," it may well mean your custom has been precisely valued and you will wait accordingly. Moreover, we must think about the "externalities" of this speed. With many users accessing services electronically on the basis that it is faster, there may be a slowing down for those without such access. An organization may reroute effort into online provision and reduce physical facilities to balance the online expansion. Such facilities will typically be the ones in poorer, less-profitable areas. As a result, for all those gaining faster access, others may be actively slowed. Networking thus goes along with, reflects, and enables the unbundling of provision into more differentiated access (Graham and Marvin 2002).

Second, there is the "timing" of activities, in terms of when they need to or can occur in the day. ICTs enable the time shifting of activities to formerly unavailable time slots. The flexibilization of times enabled by ICTs breaks down work/leisure time constraints, partly by breaking down spatial boundaries—as people access work at home, conduct business calls on trains, and indeed shop from the office, with recent market research suggesting peak purchasing, especially of holidays, around early to midafternoon on Mondays (Coremetrics 2005). Rather than focusing on the "death of distance," one might equally address the "death of diurnal time" (Presser 2003, 5). ICTs are evidently, one of the factors enabling and compelling up to 40 percent of U.S. households to work nonstandard hours. Presser, however, omits the way space is used to enable this colonization of time. So to return to the introduction to this chapter, and the globalization of work via informational networks, we need to think of the impact of people in different time zones and work patterns, meaning work keeps arriving from elsewhere around the clock—at the extreme resulting in work patterns that are decoupled from local times and reoriented to clients in different time zones (Laguerre 2004, 230). The global financial market is one example but a diurnal chronograph of Internet access gives a sense of temporal ebbs and flows in the networks (see Figure 3.1). Here the circadian geography of different temporal and spatial peaks of usage of different media produces a complex pattern of global connectivity. The corporate dream is to use this geography so that work can be done continuously around the globe, each worker sending off material to be processed by another while the sender is absent, to be awaiting him or her, completed, upon his or her return. The worker's nightmare is the incessant flow of demands unrelated to his or her own time rhythms.

Laguerre (2004, 224) highlights the contrast of a civic calendrical time with a flexible, globalized cybertime. The civil week is

> organized along several axes that give it its stability, channel its deployment and spatialize its content: these are the differentiations of space (the workplace versus the home), the divisions of time (work time versus rest time), the temporal harmonization of collective activities (people doing the same types of work at the same time), the linearity of chronological order (the work week versus the weekend), the temporality of physical presence (face-to-face interaction in the

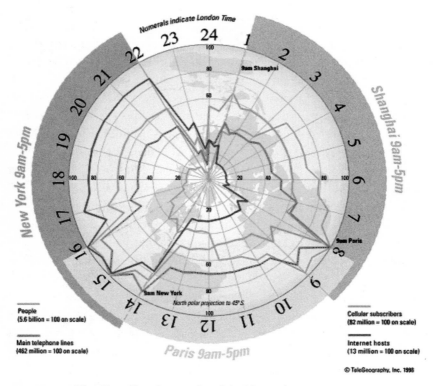

FIGURE 3.1 The Circadian Geography of the Network.
Copyright © Gregory C. Staple 1998.

carrying out of activities), and the policing of time through the surveillance of the diverse boundaries of the civil day and civil week (blue laws, firm schedules and the temporal regimentation of society).

All of which contrast with a putative cyberweek, which is

> organized along a different set of axes: hybridity (real time is mixed with virtual time as people move back and forth from one type to another in the process of completing a specific task), multiplicity (one has different temporalities to choose from), ubiquity, "going everywhere" by using the Internet as "the network of all networks" (one is able to accomplish a task in a continuous time period despite the vagaries of different time zones), flexibility (the work can be done at any place, and interconnectivity can occur at any time), recombination (several tasks can be accomplished at the same time), compression (one can squeeze a week's time into a few days), expansion (a task that can be done in a week may now be spread beyond the boundaries of the civil week), telepresence (one can replace or substitute virtual presence for physical presence), and telespatiality (one can indicate the role of human agency in the transnationalizing and globalizing of cyberspace).

The result is a blurring of boundaries between work and leisure, on diurnal and weekly scales. Even leaving aside full-time teleworking, we have wider trends for information workers to do more work from home (Perrons 2003), which can produce significant difficulties in maintaining old spatial and temporal boundaries that regulated workloads (Tietze and Musson 2002). Laguerre stresses flexibility as improving quality of life because of "the freedom to pick and choose where and at what time" to work "because it is so easy to switch on the computer on Sunday morning and get back to work" (Laguerre 2004, 230). This observation rather downplays the notion (which he also mentions) that the time when you could be available for work expands and that the arrival of email from other time zones implodes local rhythms. It is only easy to answer your email on a Sunday if you have no other family responsibilities then, though knowledge workers may use flexible hours to pick up children from school but then log back on after the children have gone to bed (Perrons 2003). Whether you can pick and choose when and where to work depends on your employment type. Networked work may be flexible, or it may be intrusive, or indeed both. The effect may be a tension, as seen by Nowotny between pressure for a "managerial" self-maximization through time efficiency and biological and social identifications grounded in "slowness" and other rhythms (Roberts 1998, 118). This results in desynchronizations and resynchronization of global and local times into an "omnipolitan" time—one linked to a virtual world urban agglomeration and pace rather than embedded in a locatable single city, with recombinant technicized rhythms playing over territoriality and telemetricality to produce a new "terraformation" (Luke 1998, 167–168).

What this suggests is two ways of assessing the changing temporal regime—relational or additive (Ellegård 1999). Relational time refers to when in the day or week we would like to, have to, or are able to perform tasks; additive approaches focus on the total time committed to activities. A large discussion has followed additive analyses of temporal substitutionism—which looks at the finite amount of time and assesses the extent to which "online" activities substitute for "real-world" ones. In terms of ICTs, users have tended to express concern over how much time the new media use up—and whether this is better or worse use of that time than former activities. Media accounts portray alienated net users or as Mitchell pithily put it: "they picture us all huddled at home in our underwear typing email messages to one another" (Mitchell 1999, 9). This, however, portrays ICT use as an end in itself (which it may be, in, say, game playing). Instead, I want to emphasize ICTs not as ends but as means, as tools that often enable other activities. This requires that we see online time not solely as an end point in a zero-sum situation, where time online is not available for other activities, but also as a facilitator of offline activities ([re]organizing where to meet, when to meet, etc.) and possibly as a means to reduce the time spent on "chores" such as household provisioning, finances, and so forth (see Gershuny 2003). Time-use data suggest that "each extra minute on the Internet is associated with about one-third of a minute reduction in personal care time, one fifth of a minute less visiting, half a minute less watching television . . . [and], nearly one-fifth of a minute of extra time devoted to going out—eating or drinking in a public place, going to the theater or cinema"; and longitudinal measurement of changes in time use by people adopting net technologies actually suggests an even stronger positive relationship with socializing and specifically with going out to public places (Gershuny 2003, 158, 164). ICTs here make time.

There is the possibility that ICTs, while promising to save time, like so much domestic technology, actually just reallocate time within a household, changing who does what rather than how long it takes, or even expanding time on a task by, say, increasing frequencies of activities (for a debate see Bittman et al. 2004; Gershuny 2004). The frequency of events may or may not alter the total time taken on a task—for instance the ease of amending documents may lead to more frequent if less extensive redrafting, or easier access to financial information via online banking may encourage more active micromanaging of accounts, or, to take the opposite effect, grocery shopping might be done less frequently via larger orders if we are no longer faced with having to load, carry, and offload the products. Returning to Laguerre's cybertime, it points out the significance of "when" tasks occur as in itself vital even without changing the overall time taken. Online grocery shopping or phone banking may be no quicker at all, but if it can be done in the evening, it may fit around other more valued or constrained tasks—such as work hours, child care, and so forth. This chapter suggests that this maneuverability of complex interrelationships of tasks is a more important consideration than the speed with which tasks are accomplished.

We might distinguish a third set of temporal impacts on relations between activities such as time lags between action and event. Castells and Virilio talk of real time here as the compression of this time lag. This has been argued to undermine time for reflection in a "deliberative democracy" so that, contrary to claims of "e-government" and "cyberdemocracy," the effect of rapid decisions is to exclude meaningful public participation via debate—replacing it with forecasts and polls (Chesneaux 2000). Real-time management software does not have a discrete sequence of plans, implementation, event, assessment, replan but rather an automation of responses embedded in the software (Graham 1997). At the grand level financial markets have automated trading systems, whose collective real-time, preprogrammed responses to price falls in 1987 crashed the markets. At the prosaic level urban traffic-management systems continually monitor flows of traffic and reprioritize junction lights and so forth. The effect, then, is that the "event is fused immediately with event reactions. Digitalization destroys duration, or that somatic space for human volition and analysis that falls between the act perceived and the act interpreted" (Luke 1998, 165). This enabling of real-time responses also enables a shift from planned actions and consequences measured on an external calendar to continual recalibration and reaction to events. On a person-to-person level this can be seen where people may not plan so far in advance but rely on mobile phones and so forth to enable them to get together with people more flexibly, the so-called approximeeting; ICTs here may not only change our use of time but also our sense and measures of it, away from abstract external time ("I'll be there at 9 a.m.") to one embedded in activities or a relational time between individuals and tasks ("I am just arriving at the station, how far away are you?") (Green 2002, 283; Laguerre 2004, 238; Ling 2004, 70)—and indeed from absolute space to relative space ("How far are you from me? The bar?"), answers to which may be denominated in time as much as distance. Time-space data is readily and frequently used to organize mobilities, not against some abstract frame of reference but producing shared time-space relevancies and shared coordinates (Laurier 2001). These trends form part of the way the collective ordering of time is ceding to the individual where shared preordained meal times, and timings, are replaced by a series of flexibly negotiated and mediated encounters (MVRDV 1998, 60).

In terms of tempo in a networked society, both email and phones have their own expectations of timings. The phone anticipates a synchronous medium—it rings, and it is socially expected that you will pick it up, so it punctures the recipient's time. Even if the recipient screens the call or ICTs such as voicemail allow them to respond later, any interaction in the end relies on both parties conversing simultaneously—meaning they share time though not space. Email is increasingly being compressed from having an asynchronous, postal temporality (send and wait, receive and open when suitable, reflect, compose and send) to one where send and reply ("zap it back") parallels the tempo of the phone—a transition bridged by text messaging. So the impact we can pick out of the temporalities of ICTs is changes in the sequencing of events, where one event needs to happen before another. Real-time compression means more and more is simultaneous. Things are done alongside each other and concurrently where ICTs enable and maybe promote multitasking and a polychronic approach to time—that is performing several tasks simultaneously rather than sequentially (Adams 1998, 100; Lee 1999; Lee and Whitley 2002). This densification may be by allowing the interleaving of activities—we set one process running and start another while we wait for the first to complete, enabling us to coprocess. The feeling of the denseness of activity is crucial to felt dimensions of acceleration and speed and feelings of stress, as well as empowerment (Southerton 2003; Southerton, Shove, and Warde 2001). Accordingly, if we look not at data on just time use but multiple uses of time, we find denser patterns of multitasking for women (Sullivan 1997, 229–231). ICTs may alter not only the duration of processes but also the experiential intensity and fragmentation of periods of time.

The final effect I want to highlight is the need for the synchronization of events. That is, who needs to be copresent in either space or time or both? This effect reveals some paradoxes: media can result in people in the same location communicating over time (leaving a message, etc.), they can result in people in distant locations communicating simultaneously (by telephone or chat), or people at different places and different times may communicate (using voicemail, email, text messages, etc.). The degree of separation is variable, but the impact affects different people and activities unevenly. It is this sense of synchronization and choreography that means ICTs are intertwined in daily life in complex ways. There is a dialectical relationship of the orchestrational and liberating capacity of ICTs. They hold "the promise to help people cope with the compression and fragmentation of time. But in so doing they lock their users into certain practices and habits, at the same time requiring an extensive if routinely invisible supporting infrastructure" with the "unintended consequence of tying people into an ever denser network of inter-dependent, perhaps even dependent, relationships with the very things designed to free them from just such obligations" (Shove and Southerton 2000, 315). Moreover, the organizational webs become more flexible and complex to manage when

> by speeding things up, or offering increased flexibility, contemporary technologies, systems and infrastructures of mobility permit the fragmentation of episodes into smaller and smaller "units" thereby increasing the challenge of co-ordinating what become separate events. In addition, and in order to cope, individuals adopt responsive strategies that enhance their ability to follow space-time trajectories of their own choosing. But when everyone else is doing the same, the problem of co-ordination increases further. (Shove 2002, 5)

The resultant time crunch and need to coordinate ever-more-extended and complex networks of tasks tend to result in an increasing sense of stress for users (Southerton 2003). As more people become more flexible and tasks are intensified, and with more people communicating from dispersed, maybe mobile, locations, the "decentralization of communication creates new webs of potential interaction between atomized individuals, which on the one hand increases the communication activities carried out, while at the same time fragmenting that communication into more numerous communications of shorter duration" (Green 2002, 284).

Coordinating Action in Space Time

We have seen that focusing on the timing of activities reveals a variety of effects, but these make little sense unless one sees them anchored in daily life, which occurs not only in time but in space. The classic approach to such issues is time geography. Broadly speaking, time geography is concerned with the location of activities in both time and space and the constraints this imposes on human action. For our purposes we can take one of its main developments as the application of the formula for speed (distance covered divided by time taken) not as a diagnostic of society but as an operating function. Hence it has been concerned to map out how far people can move in a given time—to map so-called activity spaces (Vilhelmson 1999). These are, as it were, chrono-topographic envelopes of time-space. If, for example, someone has an hour's free time, you can work out the maximum distance he or she can travel and return. Generally, the further this person travels, the longer it takes, and the less time he or she can spend at the destination before turning around—what is formed is a prism (see Figure 3.2).

Given different capacities (a bicycle, a car, and the relative position on a road or bus network), such idealized shapes are likely to be extended and distorted in various shapes (for examples see Dijst 1999). So, as I mentioned earlier, three hours' activity space from London might include Newcastle,

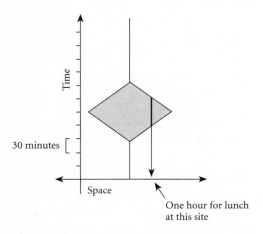

FIGURE 3.2 One Person Selects a Lunch Location.
SOURCE: Mark 1997, 315.

Edinburgh, Amsterdam, or Barcelona, while a similar activity space starting from Aberystwyth might reach only Bristol or Liverpool. Consequently social inequalities map into chronotopographic reach. Different people have different powers of speed and mobility deriving from the means at their disposal and their location. Within the notion of activity space we can disaggregate the "potential" activity space—that is all the places physically feasible to reach—and the "awareness space"—that is the places a person believes are feasible. The actual activity space used is shaped by the awareness space and is usually only a subset of the potential—though for late-running, over-optimists their believed possibilities may exceed the practical ones.

Networked systems and locative media are currently being designed to maximize the fit of potential and awareness spaces. First we may think of those attempting to provide maximal and optimal information on travel. Increasingly, bus networks display real-time information, and vehicles may have satellite navigation and traffic transponders—warning of road maintenance or congestion and allowing people to route around it. So devices are using locational cues to interact with place-related information in real time. Take the locative media used in "Amble Time," which takes these very time-geographic ideas and uses real-time data to answer questions such as "Is there time to stroll to the park? Can I stop off at the museum?" It takes a conventional tourist map and adds time by using a GPS system through a Personal Data Assistant. So given your average walking speed, it creates a chronotopographic envelope that indicates everywhere you could walk in a given time. Given current location and final destination and when you need to get there, it can show places you could visit along the way and still arrive on time. As your position changes and time ticks by, the envelope slowly shrinks and morphs until eventually it highlights the shortest path to your destination (www.carolstrohecker.info / ProjectPages / ambletime.html).

Most activities are not about solitary individuals though. In arranging a meeting, for example, we are attempting to coordinate two or more patterns of activity space, to create an overlap of shared time-space where all parties can be copresent (see Figure 3.3). Such interactions are constrained by the speed and pattern of mobility of each party and the temporal and spatial location of activities that form fixed "bases" in their schedules. And here the effects of "approximeetings" and other networked technologies are dramatically transforming how these possibilities are explored and enacted. But they are transforming them through the kinetic inequalities highlighted by

Virilio. Therefore, we can look empirically at the way time use is constrained by gendered patterns of activities, such as child care (Bianchi et al. 2000; Sullivan 2000). It is not only the case that women spend more time on care work and domestic responsibilities; these are fixed at points in the day and involve an often increasing number of locations in a less-temporally standardized, more individualized society with flexible work time (Jarvis 2005). Even if "the place and time of work are singular and fixed, the spaces and times of care are complex and fluid—the notion of 'home' obscures the diversity of places and times that are implicated in childcare," be they friends' houses, school crèches, doctors' surgery, or any of numerous other possibilities that are often not readily appreciated by those not involved (McKie, Gregory, and Bowlby 2002, 912). It is perhaps not surprising that if we move from additive studies of time to relational ones, looking at the when and where of activities, we find constrictions of women's activity spaces and potential opportunities (Kwan 1999, 2000a).

The relational perspective also suggests focusing on which times are fixed or flexible and which places are fixed or flexible (Vilhelmson 1999, 181). Table 3.1 shows the pattern of combinations of things that are locationally and temporally flexible to those that are specified, and to which can be added the category of whether activities are optional or obligatory. What is notable in empirical studies is that "although spatial fixity of bases is important, the

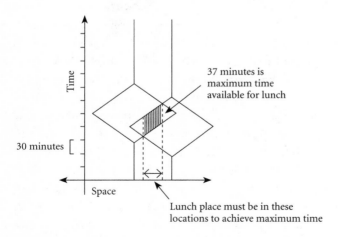

FIGURE 3.3 Two People Plan a Lunch Meeting.
SOURCE: Mark 1997, 316.

TABLE 3.1 Typology of Fixed and Flexible Space-Time

		Place of activity	
		Fixed	*Flexible*
Time of activity	Fixed	Activity required Specific place	Activity required Optional place
	Flexible	Activity optional Specific place	Activity optional Optional Place

SOURCE: Vilhelmson 1999, 181.

temporal constraints . . . operate in a far more rigid manner" (Dijst 1999, 196). Moreover, ICTs impact these patterns, first, as "constraint relaxation" (Kwan 2002), enabling us to, say, work from home or shop online, making more activities locationally more flexible or at least relocating them, and possibly making the time of activities more flexible. We might thus complicate Table 3.1 by looking at which activities are rendered more flexible and which are not, so, for instance, being able to tell child-care providers on your mobile phone that you will be late does not make you get there quicker, nor can you parent remotely (Jarvis 2005). Indeed, if we look at fragmented, multitasking, flexi- bilized networkers, who should be part of a footloose kinetic elite, we can, in fact, find them more dependent on locally embedded, immobile support networks to sustain their complexly organized flexible households through child care or services in kind (Jarvis 1999).

Evidently ICTs do shift constraints. For some activities we move not only the temporal fixities but also the spatial ones. ICTs change the terms of pres- ence in time and space by altering our extensibility—that is our ability "to overcome the friction of distance through transportation or communica- tion . . . [and] the scope of sensory access and knowledge acquisition and dispersion" (Adams 1995, 267). ICTs augment our physical activity space. If we can act at a distance, then standard measures of what is accessible to us through physical activity space are not fully adequate (Kwan 2000b). The literature is replete with examples of wider geographical reach, and this chapter started from the clear and massive evidence and effects of this. We should be careful, however, of the implications. First, even if one gains loca- tional flexibility, that is not the same as locational indifference. So contrary to predictions, and endless commercial advertising, networked or wireless access rarely means working from the top of the mountain. In fact, in most high-tech industries we see massive agglomerations in key urban quarters because copresence with colleagues, suppliers, and clients to interact, brainstorm, and work through issues is, if anything, more vital than before (Pratt 2002). Mediated access may create some flexibility, but it can also create other spatiotemporal fixities, so in terms of the outline of temporalities discussed earlier in the chapter there may be contrasting and offsetting effects, depending on which dimension of time is studied. Let us take the example of online grocery shopping. Certainly, travel time, and maybe the time in choosing goods, is reduced. It may be that shopping online at home can be done alongside other activities, densifying time, and it definitely allows time shifting of shopping—where many shoppers place orders late at night or during short breaks in the workday. Online shopping should also obviate travel constraints in accessing large, usually out-of-town, stores. Empirical work, however, suggests that distance from the shop is not the key factor in deciding on use, and while the flexibility of when one places the order helps some consumers, others find the frequency or tempo disabling (Crang, Crosbie, and Graham forthcoming). Thus those with frenetic and volatile lifestyles (perhaps the archetype of online shoppers) find that planning orders in advance requires a stability of consumption patterns and a future fixed time to receive the order, both of which can be problematic.

New media, though, do more than just liberate or extend our capacities from fixed bases. Research suggests that the locational flexibility offered by mobile phones and mobile computing enables some people to turn previously "dead time" and offline space—for instance waiting for the bus—into "useful" periods, enabling especially informational workers to pack in more activities and intensify their existing networks (Jain 2002). In terms of work patterns flexibility rapidly becomes an issue of intrusion—where adverts that boast you can work from the beach beg the question of whether you can ever then go to the beach without having to work? It moves to a logic of "always-everywhere availability" (Green 2002). If we look at a range of occupations, many have now been remodeled to accommodate the mobilization of work and the reshaping of space-times: roadside diners become the sites of informal and formal business meetings, a vehicle's front-passenger seat is referred to as a "desk" by traveling workers, and the road itself becomes a site of work. Here "fast subjects" are actually trying to reconcile the delays, obstructions, and "wasted time" of travel with demands for continual work and availability

(Laurier 2004). In these moments we can see the interplay of ICTs enabling new uses of time-spaces and time-spaces shaping the use of ICTs in a recursive pattern. As more ICTs offer the chance to do more, in more places, so people are expected to move further "away" yet to still be "available." While it is tempting to focus on the ability of media to move out of the office and home, we also need to recall the effect on fixed spaces. In the case of highly informationalized groups the technologies used to coordinate their lives become, in effect, the portable infrastructure of their family lives, while the domestic realm itself is mediated and made fully electronic (Morley 2003, 449–450). Recent work among busy, middle-class, "dual-career" families in California showed them living tightly scheduled lives, with parents continually balancing conflicting demands of work and family:

> In this situation, the issue of which parent is to pick up which child from which place at which time is negotiated daily by the participants, on the move, by mobile phone and email. When they get home, the children may reel off their activities for the next day while the parents dutifully enter them into their palm pilots, checking for problems with the scheduling of their other appointments as they go and promising their children to page them confirmation of their "pick-up" point/time by mid-afternoon of the next day. This is a world in which virtual parenting now has to carry some part of the burden of child care and where being in electronic contact with a child (welcoming them home with a text message, hoping that they've "had a good day") is what "good parenting" is now about. (Morley 2003, 447)

Although these may be extreme cases, the effect illustrated is a shifting yet intensely complex pattern of copresence in either space or time or both. Media form part of a dense tissue of time-space technologies, which stress the relational links of different speeds, rhythms, and time frames.

Conclusions

I have argued that what we are seeing is the importance of relational times and spaces and their co-implication. The effect of network time and space is to emphasize the specific and relative qualities of each. Relational approaches stress that the significance, experience, and indeed usefulness of time-spaces depend on how they are connected to other times, places, and activities (Crang 2001, 2005). I have been suggesting in this chapter that not only is this an analytic or epistemological claim, but also it is becoming ontologically more important in the time-spaces of mediated interaction.

Throughout the chapter, though, I have endeavored to show how outcomes are complex and differentiated. Although we may easily suggest Virilio's theory of speed is itself overquick to suggest one set of outcomes, it does highlight the differential effects of speed and mobility. To take a perhaps overused quotation, it is well to remember that

> different social groups and different individuals are placed in very distinct ways in relation to the flows and interconnections. This point concerns not merely the issue of who moves and who doesn't. . . . [I]t is also about power relation to the flows and the movement. Different social groups have distinct relationships to this anyway-differentiated mobility: some are more in charge of it than others; some initiate flows and movement, others don't; some are more on the receiving end of it than others; some are effectively imprisoned by it. . . . This is, in other words, a highly complex social differentiation. There is the dimension of the degree of movement and communication, but also dimensions of control and initiation. (Massey 1993, 61–62)

There are multiple speeds implied in network time-spaces. Rather than thinking simply of an endless onward rush, we might look at them as a turbulent torrent. There are back eddies, ripples, fast parts, slow pools, and so forth, and flows may be braided and overlain (Grosz 1999). Some people may be slowed, others accelerated. Some times may be densified or fragmented and others extended or attenuated in long waits. My point is not to counterpose frenetic speed to some rounded authentic, everyday time of the past but rather to suggest our daily rounds are always made up of, and shot through with, different temporalities that have long been subject to a variety of temporal and spatial modulations.

We need to see technologies as feeding into these time-spaces in recursive and interactive patterns. ICTs offer the promise and ability to do more, to reach further or cram more into the time-space of our lives. The effects of many people using these technologies, however, can render those time-spaces massively complex. They begin to require advanced technologies to coordinate them. There is a quick slippage from new technological ability to taken-for-granted necessity. This comes about through the adaptation of our space-time rhythms, assumptions, and expectations. Some people may start out using ICTs to control their time-space and extend their ability to act.

Others may have much less choice but find that new time-space realms re-compose their working and social worlds without their control. Still more of us probably experience mixtures of both, using new technologies to enable us to juggle and cope with changes over which we have little control. Recursively, we may all find that what we adopted as liberatory technology comes back to haunt us by dominating our activity, becoming embedded in our everyday taken-for-granted assumptions of time-space. In the end ICTs are altering not just the content but the shape of time-space, with both time and space now being relative dimensions, not absolute containers of action.

References

Adam, B. 2003. Reflexive modernization temporalized. *Theory Culture and Society* 20 (2): 59–78.

Adams, P. 1995. A reconsideration of personal boundaries in space-time. *Annals of the Association of American Geographers* 85 (2): 267–285.

———. 1998. Network topologies and virtual place. *Annals of the Association of American Geographers* 88 (1): 88–106.

Bianchi, S. M., M. A. Milkie, L. C. Sayer, and J. P. Robinson. 2000. Is anyone doing the housework? Trends in the gender division of household labor. *Social Forces* 79 (1): 191–228.

Bittman, M., J. M. Rice, and J. Wajcman. 2004. Appliances and their impact: The ownership of domestic technology and time spent on household work. *British Journal of Sociology* 55 (3): 401–423.

Boyer, M. C. 1996. *Cybercities: Visual perception in the age of electronic communication.* New York: Princeton Architectural Press.

Casson, H. 1910. *The history of the telephone.* Chicago: A. C. McClurg. (Available online from Project Gutenberg: http://etext.virginia.edu/toc/modeng/public/CasTele. html [accessed Jan. 24, 2007]).

Castells, M. 1989. *The informational city.* Oxford: Blackwell.

———. 1996. *The rise of the network society: Networks and identity.* Oxford: Blackwell.

Chesneaux, J. 2000. Speed and democracy: An uneasy dialogue. *Social Science Information* 39 (3): 407–420.

Coremetrics. 2005. Are shoppers buying on company time? Nov. 14: www.coremetrics. com/news/media/2005/pr05_11_14_company_time.html (accessed Dec. 8, 2006).

Crang, M. 2001. Rhythms of the city: Temporalised space and motion. In *TimeSpace,* ed. J. May and N. Thrift, 187–207. London: Routledge.

———. 2005. Time: Space. In *Spaces of geographical thought: Deconstructing human geography's binaries,* ed. P. Cloke and R. Johnston, 199–217. London: Sage.

Crang, M., T. Crosbie, and S. Graham. Forthcoming. Technology, timespace, and the remediation of neighbourhood life. *Environment and Planning A.*

Dijst, M. 1999. Two-earner families and their action spaces: A case study of two Dutch communities. *GeoJournal* 48:195–206.

Ellegård, K. 1999. A time-geographical approach to the study of everyday life of individuals: A challenge of complexity. *GeoJournal* 48:167–175.

Felski, R. 2000. The invention of everyday life. *New Formations* 39 (winter): 13–32.

Gershuny, J. 2003. Web use and net nerds: A neofunctionalist analysis of the impact of information technology in the home. *Social Forces* 82 (1): 141–168.

———. 2004. Domestic equipment does not increase domestic work: A response to Bittman, Rice, and Wajcman. *British Journal of Sociology* 55 (3): 425–431.

———. 2005. Busyness as the badge of honor for the new superordinate working class. *Social Research* 72 (2): 287–314.

Graham, S. 1997. Cities in the real-time age: The paradigm challenge of telecommunications to the conception and planning of urban space. *Environment and Planning A* 29 (1): 105–127.

———. 1998. The end of geography or the explosion of place? Conceptualizing space, place, and information technology. *Progress in Human Geography* 22 (2): 165–185.

———. 2005. Software-sorted geographies. *Progress in Human Geography* 29 (5): 1–19.

Graham, S., and S. Marvin. 2002. *Splintering urbanism: Networked infrastructures, technological mobilities, and the urban condition.* London: Routledge.

Green, N. 2002. On the move: Technology, mobility, and the mediation of social time and space. *Information Society* 18:281–292.

Grosz, E. 1999. Thinking the new: Of futures yet unthought. In *Becomings: Explorations in time, memory, and futures,* ed. E. Grosz, 15–28. Ithaca, NY: Cornell University Press.

Innis, H. 2004. *Changing concepts of time.* Oxford: Rowman and Littlefield.

Jain, S. 2002. Urban errands: The means of mobility. *Journal of Consumer Culture* 2 (3): 419–438.

Jarvis, H. 1999. The tangled webs we weave: Household strategies to co-ordinate home and work. *Work, Employment, and Society* 13 (2): 225–247.

———. 2005. Moving to London time: Household co-ordination and the infrastructure of everyday life. *Time & Society* 14 (1): 133–154.

Kwan, M. P. 1999. Gender and individual access to urban opportunities: A study using space-time measures. *Professional Geographer* 51 (2): 210–227.

———. 2000a. Gender differences in space-time constraints. *Area* 32 (2): 145–156.

———. 2000b. Human extensibility and individual accessibility in cyberspace: A multi-scale representation using GIS. In *Information, place, and cyberspace: Issues in accessibility,* ed. D. G. Janelle and D. C. Hodge, 241–256. Berlin: Springer-Verlag.

———. 2002. Time, information technologies, and the geographies of everyday life. *Urban Geography* 23 (5): 471–482.

Laguerre, M. 2004. Virtual time: The processuality of the cyberweek. *Information, Communication, and Society* 7 (2): 223–247.

Lantz, P. 2000. Sens, puissance, vitesse. *Social Science Information* 39 (3): 395–405.

Laurier, E. 2001. Why people say where they are during mobile phone calls. *Environ-*

ment and Planning D: Society and Space 19 (4): 485–504.

———. 2004. Doing office work on the motorway. *Theory, Culture, and Society* 21 (4/5): 261–277.

Leach, N. 1999. Virilio and architecture. *Theory, Culture, and Society* 16 (5/6): 71–94.

Lee, H. 1999. Time and information technology: Monochronicity, polychronicity, and temporal symmetry. *European Journal of Information Systems* 8:16–26.

Lee, H., and E. A. Whitley. 2002. Time and information technology: Temporal impacts on individuals, organizations, and society. *Information Society* 18:235–240.

Ling, R. 2004. *The mobile connection: The cell phone's impact on society.* Oxford: Elsevier.

Luke, T. 1998. Moving at the speed of life? A cultural kinematics of telematic times and corporate values. In *Time and value,* ed. S. Lash, A. Quick, and R. Roberts, 162–181. Oxford: Blackwell.

Mandarini, M. 1998. From epidermal history to speed politics. In *Virtual futures: Cyberotics, technology, and post-human pragmatism,* ed. J. Broadhurst Dixon and E. Cassidy, 88–99. London: Routledge.

Mark, D. M. 1997. Cognitive perspectives on spatial and spatio-temporal reasoning. In *Geographic information research bridging the Atlantic,* ed. M. Craglia and H. Couclelis, 308–319. London: Taylor and Francis.

Massey, D. 1993. Power-geometry and a progressive sense of place. In *Mapping the futures: Local cultures, global change,* ed. J. Bird, B. Curtis, T. Putnam, G. Robertson, and L. Tickner, 59–69. London: Routledge.

McKie, L., S. Gregory, and S. Bowlby. 2002. Shadow times: The temporal and spatial frameworks and experiences of caring and working. *Sociology* 36 (4): 897–924.

Mitchell, W. 1999. *E-topia: Urban life, Jim, but not as we know it.* Cambridge, MA: MIT Press.

Morley, D. 2003. What's home got to do with it? Contradictory dynamics in the domestication of technology and the dislocation of domesticity. *Cultural Studies* 6 (4): 435–458.

Morris, J. 1968. *Pax Britannica: The climax of an empire.* London: Faber and Faber.

MVRDV. 1998. *Farmax: Excursions on density.* Rotterdam: 010 Publishers.

Paquot, T. 1999. The post-city challenge. In *The urban moment: Cosmopolitan essays on the late-20th-century city,* ed. R. Beauregard and S. Body-Gendrot, 79–95. London: Sage.

Perrons, D. 2003. The new economy and the work-life balance: Conceptual explorations and a case study of new media. *Gender, Work, and Organization* 10 (1): 65–93.

Pratt, A. 2002. Hot jobs in cool places. The material cultures of new media product spaces: The Case of south of the market San Francisco. *Information, Communication, and Society* 5 (1): 27–50.

Presser, H. 2003. *Working in a 24/7 economy: Challenges for American families.* New York: Russell Sage.

Roberts, R. 1998. Time virtuality and the goddess. In *Time and Value,* ed. S. Lash, A. Quick, and R. Roberts, 112–129. Oxford, Blackwell.

Sassen, S. 1999. Juxtaposed temporalities: Producing a new zone. In *Anytime*, ed. C. Davidson, 114–121. Cambridge, MA: MIT Press.

———. 2000. Spatialities and temporalities of the global: Elements for a theorization. *Public Culture* 12 (1): 215–232.

———. 2001. Impacts of information communication technologies on urban economies and politics. *International Journal of Urban and Regional Research* 25 (2): 411–418.

Shove, E. 2002. Rushing around: Coordination, mobility, and inequality. Lancaster, UK: Department of Sociology, Lancaster University. www.lancs.ac.uk/fss/sociology/papers/shove-rushing-around.pdf (accessed Jan. 24, 2007).

Shove, E., and D. Southerton. 2000. Defrosting the freezer: From novelty to convenience. *Journal of Material Culture* 5 (3): 301–319.

Smith, M. P. 2001. *Transnational urbanism: Locating globalization.* Oxford: Blackwell.

Southerton, D. 2003. Squeezing time: Allocating practices, coordinating networks, and scheduling society. *Time & Society* 12 (1): 5–25.

Southerton, D., E. Shove, and A. Warde. 2001. *"Harried and hurried": Time shortage and the co-ordination of everyday life.* Warwick: CRIC.

Stallabrass, J. 1999. The ideal city and the virtual hive: Modernism and emergent order in computer culture. In *Technocities*, ed. J. Downey and J. McGuigan, 108–120. London: Sage.

Sullivan, O. 1997. Time waits for no (wo)man: An investigation of the gendered experience of domestic time. *Sociology* 31 (2): 221–239.

———. 2000. The division of domestic labour: Twenty years of change? *Sociology* 34 (3): 437–456.

Thrift, N. 2004. Driving in the city. *Theory, Culture, and Society* 21 (4/5): 41–59.

Tietze, S., and G. Musson. 2002. When "work" meets "home": Temporal flexibility as lived experience. *Time & Society* 11 (2/3): 315–334.

Vannini, P. 2002. Waiting dynamics: Bergson, Virilio, Deleuze, and the experience of global times. *Journal of Mundane Behavior* 3 (2): www.mundanebehavior.org/issues/v3n2/vannini.htm (accessed Jan. 25, 2007).

Vilhelmson, B. 1999. Daily mobility and the use of time for different activities: The case of Sweden. *GeoJournal* 48:177–185.

Virilio, P. 1997a. *Open sky.* London: Verso.

———. 1997b. The overexposed city. In *Rethinking architecture: A reader in cultural theory*, ed. N. Leach, 380–390. London: Routledge.

———. 1998a. Critical space. In *The Virilio reader*, ed. J. Der Derian, 53–65. Malden, MA: Blackwell.

———. 1998b. Architecture in the age of its virtual disappearance. In *The virtual dimension: Architecture, representation, and crash culture*, ed. J. Beckmann, 178–187. New York: Princeton Architectural Press.

———. 2000a. *Polar inertia.* London: Sage.

———. 2000b. *A landscape of events.* Cambridge, MA: MIT Press.

———. 2003. *Unknown quantity.* London: Thames and Hudson.

4 Protocols and the Irreducible Traces of Embodiment

The Viterbi Algorithm and the Mosaic of Machine Time

Adrian Mackenzie

MACHINE TIME, it has often been argued in critical thought, is inhuman or nonlived time. Machine time is a relatively abstract, taken-for-granted term that refers to the speed at which mechanisms and devices carry out operations. Usually, responsibility for the deleterious and positive effects of technological speed is attributed to the high rate at which movements are carried out. For much critical theory this ever-increasing rate (expressed prosaically, say, in CPU speeds used to advertise computers or in Moore's Law) reduces temporal complexities, memory, and subjective experience to attenuated abstractions, to nonlived spaces and times, to intervals and orderings that are inimical to human lifeworld structures. Adverse reactions to machine time are particularly strong in the domain of media and images (Virilio on autonomization of perception is a good example [Virilio 1997]). This chapter argues that it would be useful and perhaps important to reconsider machine time in less-abstract terms. This involves finding middle ground between the temporality of technologies as material orderings of movement and the temporal flows of subjective experience. Through a case study of a specific telecommunications algorithm, it suggests seeing machine time as a mosaic of relations and orderings of actions brought into proximity.

One symptom of the aggregate or mosaic nature of machine time can be found in the very proliferation of different timings attached to contemporary computing and information technologies. They include seek time, run time, read time, access time, available time, real time, polynomial time, time division, time slicing, time sharing, time complexity, write time, processor time, hold time, execution time, compilation time, and cycle time. While some of these timings are related (for example, read and write time), many are unrelated or antagonistic to each other (for example, real time and polynomial time). The relations between different timings are heterogeneous. While compilation time and execution time of a fragment of software may be closely associated for a programmer, the time complexity of a whole system comprising many different processes may be most relevant for people using networked computers. Machine time has many interstices, and they have implications for how we think about changes in perception, experience, movement, embodiment, sociality, and meaning associated with contemporary telecommunications and information networks. Attending to the constitution of contemporary machine time would both continue long-standing attempts (Derrida 1989; Husserl 1991) to find ways of reactivating the forgotten sense of the lifeworlds we inhabit and bring into dialogue some recent work in sociology, social studies of science and geography, new media, and cinema studies that has addressed these changes in terms of structures of feeling, networks of actors, spaces and times of calculation (Thrift 2004a), formal properties of media (moving images in particular) (Hansen 2004; Rodowick 2001), and new forms of sociality (Knorr-Cetina and Bruegger 2000).

Framings of Machine Time

The study of machine time is difficult. How do we frame the time of machine operations? This question underlies much sociological and philosophical thought from the late nineteenth century onward, when electric media and the physical and life sciences together started to challenge the verities of perception and action in new ways. Two related responses appear in recent accounts. For media theorists such as Friedrich Kittler machine time falls below the threshold of consciousness and thereby withdraws into the background of average everyday life: "What remains a problem is only recognizing these layers [of software], which like modern media technologies in general, have been explicitly contrived to evade perception" (Kittler 1997). This withdrawal is very much a structural feature of systems of control, information, and communication, and it permits, among other things, their annexation of everyday communication as forms of property. In a broadly similar vein media theorists such as Manovich (1996, 2001), Rodowick (2001), Lunenfeld (2000), and

Cubitt (1998) understand digital media in terms of the formal properties and attributes that rupture habits of communication, perception, and representation. In relation to time such changes can only radically undermine the foundations of subjective experience in time consciousness.

For recent theorists such as Mark B. N. Hansen the task is not to affirm the way in which information processing evades perception but to understand the challenge it poses to our understanding of embodiment, communication, and time more generally: "Viewed in this way, the digital era and the phenomenon of digitization itself can be understood as demarcating a shift in the correlation of two terms: media and body. Simply put, as media lose their material specificity, the body takes on a more prominent function as a selective processor of information" (Hansen 2004, 22). In Hansen's terms machine time does not simply evade perception. It is a radical restructuring of perception as selection from fluxes of information (or images in his analysis). In particular, machine time can, in some sense, be said to enlarge the frame of the now itself. In Hansen's case, a relatively complex neurophenomenological account of the constitution of time consciousness ensues.

Across this range of responses a relatively abstract characterization of machine time remains intact. Even in his deeply interesting combination of neurophenomenology with concepts of embodiment and affect, Hansen's account of machine time remains relatively asocial. All complexity, dynamism, and potential is again located in "the body," which takes on "a more prominent function." Machine time, as a contingent effect generated by large numbers of machines connected together in materially and socially heterogeneous networks and infrastructures, remains unanalyzed. The problem, therefore, is to find ways of articulating the uneven, mixed timings that emerge within real networks of interoperating systems and to understand these timings as living-nonliving syntheses, not as confrontations between the living subject and dead, deadly machines. Machine time in networked, distributed information technologies is a truly complex assemblage, with many different interfaces, points of intersection and slippage, competing dynamics and intensifications.

In a somewhat different context, Elspeth Probyn asks "how we can cross over from the solitary space-time of individual categories in order to renew a critical emphasis on the proximity of sites. . . . Living in the space-time of a world rendered local, means that we have the capacity to be intimately confronted with the implications of our actions" (Probyn 2001, 184). The key issue in this passage concerns the shift from "solitary space-time" to "proximity to sites," proximity to others, and this curious, slightly awkward idea of intimately confronting the implications of our own actions. This shift is doubly relevant for an analysis of machine time. For on the one hand, contemporary communication networks are largely put in the service of forms of proximity (in time and space). Here are located all the effects of real-time media and telethesia so widely discussed in critical theory in recent decades. On the other hand, proximity refers to the clustering together of different times and spaces in composites that "implicate" actions with each other. On this latter point sociological studies of the time and space of global financial trading systems indicate how temporally complex the implication of actions can become.

Algorithm as Articulation

As a preliminary crossing out of the solitary category of machine time we could think of some of the different conventional, artificial, inorganic, living, social, and semiotic materials that come together today in computing devices such as mobile phones and wireless networking equipment. In such equipment machine time emerges from specific articulations of materials in relations on widely varying scales—semiconductor fabrication; network protocols; licensing agreements; quotidian rhythms of work; branding; marketing; travel and consumption (see, e.g., Donald Mackenzie's [1996] account of the relation between the design of nuclear test simulation and the working day of high-energy physicists); the implementation of standards; protocols; the marketing of network bandwidth to individuals, institutions, and corporations; the effect of diurnal rotation of the earth on the electromagnetic spectrum, and so on. Everywhere in this mélange articulations of different material constitute contemporary machine time. It only takes one particular algorithm to show this composite texture.

Algorithms are often seen as the abstract heart of software and digital technologies. Given that software has gradually taken shape as a new kind of substance, halfway between matter and mind, and has propagated throughout the matrices of everyday life, analysis of algorithms has a certain importance. In some accounts, for instance Steven Wolfram's cosmology, algorithms serve as ontological foundations of the universe. In many other accounts of technology, information, or network society, algorithms are seen as all the same. From the perspective of humanities and social sciences, algorithms, like mathematics and geometry, belong to a worldview that quantifies, orders, and sequences events and movement. As I will argue, however, to treat algorithms as a general expression of mental effort, or, perhaps even more abstractly, as a process of abstraction, is to lose track of proximities and relationalities that algorithms articulate. Regardless of how central algorithms are to mythologies of computation, information, economy, life, or universe, they are rarely discussed in themselves and rarely attended to as objects of analysis.

When they are examined, for instance by patent attorneys, algorithms are treated as the mechanical expression of mental effort. For instance, the several hundred patents currently associated with an algorithm discussed at length below—the Viterbi decoder algorithm—are all judged as embodying singular applications of human individual or collective intelligence. The creation of value, particularly intellectual value, is the foundation of intellectual or "vectoral" forms of property. Algorithms are a key object of ownership. Current disputes over software patents hinge on the mode of existence of algorithms. In these disputes the issue concerns the creation of algorithms and how that creation can be made over into a form of property. Of particular interest is how the creation of an algorithm occurs as a mental act. What distinguishes algorithms from other forms of invention? The connection to be made here concerns algorithms as embodiments of mental effort or thinking. Considering how algorithms come into being and evolve, it is hard to deny some contribution from mental effort. The thought embodied in an algorithm does not simply represent a preexisting object, nor does it create a new thing. The philosopher John Dewey suggested that thinking occupies a temporally intermediate reconstructive position that brings out some order in a discordant situation. It is hard to argue with the idea that algorithms embody highly refined, often formalized repetitions, but these repetitions themselves accomplish a movement that reduces discord. Algorithms handle repetition in interestingly variable ways. Furthermore, the repetition of algorithms themselves, the ways in which they are imitated and altered as they circulate, is in no way mechanical or abstract. Algorithmic functions shift and refract as they repeat movements. They move toward the fringes of bare mechanical repetition, where hidden states, indistinct feelings, and sensations cluster around the "bright nucleus" of intellect and action that mechanism represented for Bergson (1911).

Viterbi Algorithm: Evolution, Telecommunications, and Language Processing

The Viterbi algorithm runs across telecommunications, new media, and a contemporary incarnation of a biopolitical knowledge project, bioinformatics. The algorithm dating from 1967 is widely used in telecommunications networks to create and discover position and sequence in flows of signals. It has become a fundamental element in wireless, satellite, and space communications. Andrew Viterbi, a now retired telecommunications engineer, designed the algorithm and started a company that designs and fabricates semiconductors based around the algorithm. In telecommunications applications these chips enable satellite, cellular phone, and wireless networks to communicate despite high levels of electromagnetic noise. In bioinformatics the Viterbi algorithm is currently used to find weak similarities and evolutionary kinship between protein or amino acid sequences within families of functionally related biomolecules.

The Viterbi algorithm deals with situations where the generation of sequential system states cannot be directly observed. This could be because they are lost in evolutionary history (bioinformatics) or because a signal transmitted in the crowded electromagnetic environment of a city (or interplanetary space) is noisy or variable. According to the account given in Wikipedia, the Viterbi algorithm was originally conceived

> as an *error-correction* scheme for noisy digital communication links, finding universal application in decoding the *convolutional codes* used in *CDMA* and *GSM* digital cellular, dial-up modems, satellite, deep-space communications, and *802.11* wireless LANs. It is now also commonly used in *speech recognition*, *keyword spotting*, *computational linguistics*, and *bioinformatics*. For example, in speech-to-text (speech recognition), the acoustic signal is treated as the observed sequence of events, and a string of text is considered to be the "hidden cause" of the acoustic signal. The Viterbi algorithm finds the most likely string of text given the acoustic signal.

In general, the algorithm finds the most likely series of hidden events that could have given rise to the observed events. The fact that the algorithm merits an article in Wikipedia attests to its significance as an embodiment of thought and an organization of movement.

The basis of Viterbi's application to speech processing, bioinformatics, and telecommunications, or to language, life, and media, to use more abstract terms, hinges on the idea of finding the most probable hidden states that would account for the currently observed behavior in a system. The movement accomplished by the algorithm is reconstructive in Dewey's sense. It realigns a problematic situation. For instance, in an 802.11b wireless network, a GSM cellular telephone network, a satellite, or the Cassini Saturn probe, data to be transmitted is coded using a particular approach called *convolutional coding*. In convolutional coding the computational processing capacity of the transmitter and receiver is used to compensate for noise and errors produced in the transmission channel. Intensified movements in transmitter and receiver compensate for disturbances or errors arising from what cannot be made fully part of the system, the medium of propagation of signals. Convolutional codes get their name from the way in which they base what they transmit at the current point in time on what has been transmitted earlier. They begin to build summaries of what has preceded the current moment into each moment. The "convolution" consists in this turning inward of encoding to include information about what was transmitted before. Each packet, datagram, or frame represents not just information but a relation to other information. A convolutional code "enlarges the frame of the now itself" (Hansen 2004, 252) in a specific way and in relation to particular forces.

Interpreting Algorithms:
Imperative, Brute Force, and Abstraction

Does not this enlarged now still remain mechanical, however? How can an algorithm be understood as anything other than mechanical? The prevalent interpretation of algorithms sees them as programs, as sets of instructions to be carried out in sequence in order to accomplish some task. Presenting an algorithm as a recipe means treating it as imperative. This means that the algorithms lend themselves to being seen as commands that are carried out mechanically. Other interpretations or formalizations of algorithms that appear much less mechanical are well known although less commonly used. It would be interesting to analyze the social dynamics of formulations of algorithms. For instance, "functional programming" is based on the recursive evaluation of expressions, something that appears far less mechanical yet is also less widely used. (On this score see Graham 2004 for an entrepreneurial description of how an early e-commerce business used functional programming to out-accelerate competitors in the dot-com boom.)

Computer science textbooks usually classify algorithms in a relatively small number of categories based on how the algorithm works. Divide and conquer, search and enumeration, probabilistic, heuristic, and dynamic programming are five main categories. Most books on algorithms are actually catalogs of algorithms combined with explanation and examples. The Viterbi algorithm belongs to the class of dynamic programming algorithms. There are two frames that unify algorithms as a field of operational practice. The first is a limit notion of "brute force," where the "programmer relies on the computer's processing power instead of using his or her own intelligence to simplify the problem" (Raymond 1996, 91). Brute force, at least from the perspective of programmers, lacks grace or abstraction, but it may be the best technique when a smart solution would cost a lot of programming time. In his recent work on "qualculation" Thrift (2004b) argues that the availability of large amounts of computer processing capacity distributed in the built background of everyday life is supporting new apprehensions of space and time based on movement. From an algorithmic perspective the sheer availability of processing power means little. The question is how to order and select possible operations to create a consistently concatenated set of movements. In this selection the key question is a relevant abstraction that responds to the needs of a situation.

A second overarching abstract perspective on algorithms as forms of movement is offered by computational or algorithmic complexity theory. This body of mathematical theory specifies the computational time and space in which the algorithm runs, and it summarizes using a specific notation, the big-o notation (see National Institute of Standards and Technology 2005). Knowing the complexity of an algorithm can help decide whether it is feasible to run it given the speed and memory of the system. Choosing or creating a different algorithm can drastically alter the temporality of computation. For instance, the flow of sensation and movement associated with contemporary action real-time games relies intimately on algorithmic orderings found in graphics calculations. Brute force approaches to animation do not work. The proofs and formalisms of algorithmic complexity theory express the time and space of any particular class of algorithms, and part of the working knowledge of programmers is some awareness of how different algorithms affect the time and space of computation.

Fold in Time: Stochastic Processes and Convolution

In terms of algorithmic complexity theory and computer science as operational knowledges of machine time, we can treat an algorithm as a framing of time and space, as the creation of a duration. For instance, in convolutional coding a practical folding of time occurs. It takes us away from algorithms understood as linear sequences of steps to be carried out mechanically, to algorithms conceived as establishing relations between things that are disjointed, by concatenating events in paths. Convolutional codes are executed by software and more often by VLSI (Very Large Scale Integrated) chips fabricated for use in cell phones, wireless networks, and other communication equipment. But the implementation of the algorithm in silicon does not necessarily imply that the algorithm is purely mechanical or that it is governed by repetition. Rather implementation changes the texture of the mechanism in certain ways. The power of the imperative style resides in its promise of exact repetition. This is what makes it mechanical—the specification of what is to be repeated. As Henri Bergson (1911, 46) argued, however, "Repetition is only possible in the abstract: what is repeated is some aspect that our senses, and especially our intellect, have singled out from reality, just because our action, upon which all the effort of our intellect is directed, can move only among repetitions." Convolutional codes pose an obstacle to any reading of algorithms as repetition because they assume that events are not fully determined and therefore not definitively repeated. This begins to undermine a mechanistic understanding of algorithms as repetition. Different vectors of repetition interpenetrate. The Viterbi algorithm works with convolutional codes that themselves grapple with stochastic processes. These are processes in which the next state of the system is not fully determined by the previous state. A game of Snakes and Ladders is a stochastic process because each move is partially determined by a dice roll. It is the stochastic character of the Viterbi algorithm that both affects the qualitative outcome of repetition and alters the terrain on which machine time moves.

Probabilistic processes have been of great interest ever since population became a thinkable entity—something that could be counted and controlled—in the nineteenth century. Probability and randomness have a number of different conceptual layers in the Viterbi algorithm. First, the algorithm regards all signals, sequences, or systems in probabilistic terms. In particular, it treats them as a Hidden Markov Model. A Markov model is a way of understanding stochastic processes. It models situations by assuming that the next state or event in the system is dependent only on the present state, not past states, and by assuming that the most probable next state can be known. For instance, a game of Snakes and Ladders can be modeled as a Markov process because the next move depends entirely on the present state of the board and a roll of the dice. (More formally, the conditional probability distribution of next moves in Snakes and Ladders depends on a current state and roll of the dice.)

Every algorithm, apart from so-called brute-force algorithms, contains a twist or kink that affects the flow of the computational process. The Hidden Markov Model is one twist or kink at the heart of the Viterbi algorithm. It treats the received signal as a set of states that correspond to a Markov model that cannot be observed directly. Via the Hidden Markov Model, the Viterbi algorithm turns the communication situation inside out. The combination of a known and finite set of system states and probability is turned inside out by the algorithm because it treats the Markov model as hidden. The object of making a Hidden Markov Model is to deduce the most probable sequence of internal states that could have given rise to the observed sequence of signals.

We can begin to see how this twist might be useful in communication systems. Something blocks access to what is actually happening in the situation. In telecommunications, including satellite, cellular, and wireless network communications, many different kinds of interference and noise affect the transmission of digital signals. The task is to work out the most probable sequence of signals that could have given rise to the observed signals. Again, counter to the images of mechanical determinism sometimes associated with digital technologies or information systems, the algorithm engages with and provides an elaborate figure of an unpredictable and intrinsically dynamic environment. It moves to the fringes of mechanical action, where similarity or repetition begins to blur.

The Sociality of an Algorithm

Where does this convoluted displacement of repetition come from? What has happened to machine time to contort it into such unfamiliar, uncertain patterns of operation and movement? A simple explanation of the core of an algorithm, again drawn from Wikipedia, provides one clue:

> Assume you have a friend who lives far away and who you call daily to talk about what each of you did that day. Your friend has only three things he's interested in: walking in the park, shopping, and cleaning his apartment. The choice of

what to do is determined exclusively by the weather on a given day. You have no definite information about the weather where your friend lives, but you know general trends. Based on what he tells you he did each day, you try to guess what the weather must have been like.

You believe that the weather operates as a discrete *Markov chain*. There are two states, "Rainy" and "Sunny," but you cannot observe them directly, that is, they are hidden from you. On each day, there is a certain chance that your friend will perform one of the following activities, depending on the weather: "walk," "shop," or "clean." Since your friend tells you about his activities, those are the observations. The entire system is that of a hidden Markov model (HMM).

You know the general weather trends in the area and you know what your friend likes to do on average. . . .

You talk to your friend three days in a row and discover that on the first day he went for a walk, on the second day he went shopping, and on the third day he cleaned his apartment. You have two questions: What is the overall probability of this sequence of observations? *(Wikipedia 2005)*

The explanation is simple and, symptomatically, refers to an everyday situation. It renders the core of the algorithm as a social situation. It renders the Viterbi algorithm thinkable as a set of questions about the weather. The problem of reconstructing how the weather turned out somewhere else hardly seems important, but it exemplifies the movement that Dewey ascribes to thinking. It does, however, embrace a complication. A social interaction (calling a friend to find out what he or she has been doing) furnishes the basis for implementing a form of controlled movement (deducing the weather) that is not itself intrinsic to that interaction. This aspect of the Viterbi algorithm, I suggest, introjects a communicative relation from everyday life. An introjection of sociality into the organization of repetition begins to break down any simple opposition between machine and human time.

Dynamic Programming and the Logistics of Intensive Movement

In classifications of algorithms the Viterbi algorithm is broadly regarded as a "dynamic programming" algorithm. This second major formal aspect of the Viterbi algorithm stems from operations research, a field originating in World War II logistics. Computer science textbooks usually contain at least one chapter on dynamic programming. Dynamic programming addresses the problem of finding optimal routes or paths through networks or grids. A typical metaphor is the problem of how a tourist walking Manhattan could visit the most attractions with the least walking. Given the gridlike street layout, there are many different paths that could be taken to include MoMA, the Empire State Building, Times Square, and Wall St. (Another version of the problem, a slightly older metaphor, is the traveling-salesman problem. How can a traveling salesman visit all the towns in the region doing the least driving?)

Many different situations can be translated into the model of the Manhattan tourist itinerary, even nonspatial ones. When a bioinformatics textbook claims "development of new sequence comparison algorithms often amounts to building an appropriate 'Manhattan'" (Jones and Pevzner 2004, 160), it emphasizes the intimate connection between space (data structures) and itineraries or paths (algorithms). The movement of tourists visiting attractions dotted on the grid of Manhattan's streets provides a useful spatial model or "data structure" for other forms of movement. So, too, the Viterbi algorithm maps sequences of events, the possible outputs of the Markov model, onto a grid. Dynamic programming is then used to find the optimal path through the grid, which in turn translates into the most probable sequence of states in the model that could have yielded that output. Logistical problems concerning networks, ranging from flight scheduling to text searching, make use of dynamic programming approaches. Dynamic programming models all problems in terms of traversals of directed acyclic graphs (DAGs) or networks in which movement can never go in circuits. By transforming problems such as sequence comparison into a graph / network data structure, and carefully planning the order in which computations are carried out, dynamic programming algorithms drastically reduce the time needed to find the optimal itinerary.

The dynamic programming technique has been imitated and varied in applications across bioinformatics, logistics, and telecommunications because it lays down an especially effective concatenation of steps between source and destination. No technologically determined acceleration in hardware or processor speed is at stake in this movement. Rather, by virtue of a reversal that lies at the heart of dynamic programming algorithms, the Viterbi algorithm traverses the distance between input and output counterintuitively. That is, it carries out calculations in a different order from that dictated by a practical sense of the world as something to be acted on effectively. These calculations undergo topological transformations and reordering in time. The transformations in computational time wrought by dynamic programming proceed via a process of intensification of movement that needs to be explained rather than simply attributed to algorithms or to abstraction per se. The hack at the center of "the creative production of abstraction" in the Viterbi algorithm is not based on a better representation of something, for instance, of the prototypical situation modeled in software. Nor is it based on a solution that puts an end to movement.

In finding the shortest path through a network, the problem is to minimize repeat visits to nodes. In this sense the algorithm seeks to reduce repetition, not to multiply it. Dynamic programming is a tactic to avoid doing calculations that have already been performed or returning to points in the network that have already been visited. Every repeated calculation equates to the tourist backtracking over the same ground. To minimize repetition, dynamic programming abstracts from the particular to the general. Rather than trying to solve the specific problem of how to get from one point to another most directly (for example, the minimum number of blocks to walk to visit all the popular sights), dynamic programming algorithms build a table or array containing the best scores for all possible movements (for instance, between all known tourist destinations in Manhattan). A new, conventional order, that of the table or matrix, replaces the topology of the network or the topography of the city. Movements in the ordered space can be carried out without repetition because the table represents the cost of different movements. Expressed in the most elementary form, by solving the general problem of movements between every point, dynamic programming makes finding the best movement between two chosen points much more efficient. Somewhat paradoxically, by tackling all problems to start with, it accelerates solving a particular one. The creative "hack" is to reverse the intuitive approach that would start with the particular and then generalize from it. Dynamic programming imagines all movements in order to choose one.

Mental Objects, Repetition, and Concatenated Worlds

Where have we moved in relation to algorithms as ideal distillations of machine time? Solitary machine time is replaced by proximities between sights and by an implication of different kinds of action with each other. Three general features emerge from the Viterbi algorithm. First, an algorithm differs from "brute force" or bare mechanical repetition by virtue of some abstraction that hacks, twists, or folds the space and time of computation. For instance, the Viterbi algorithm accepts "hidden states" as a given, not as something to be excluded. The abstract ideal of bare repetition does not capture the pragmatic reality of algorithms. To treat algorithms as pure repetition would be to overlook the inventive variation embodied in every algorithm. The Viterbi algorithm accepts a certain nonideality as a given. An algorithm often turns uncertainty into a feature that allows repetition to gain traction in situations where conditions are far from ideal, where evolutionary history or abundant communication generates constant variations and differences. In this sense it moves to the fringes of repetition.

Second, the treatment of repetition found in the algorithm is variable. It is not pure repetition but a mixture of different repetitions that intensify movement rather than simply automate it. For instance, the Viterbi algorithm assumes that observed events occur in a sequence. It also assumes that every observed event corresponds to one hidden event. Having made idealized assumptions about the existence of events in sequence, the algorithm starts rearranging that sequence in order to move through it differently and to associate things in the sequence with one another. For instance, as mentioned above, dynamic programming algorithms make all possible moves in advance and then combine them in synthetic forms to quickly find the best move. Although repetition is ordered in algorithms, it is modulated and varied in ways that augment difference rather than simply reducing it to the same.

Third, through algorithms, variation in repetition becomes associative and concatenates different relations. Algorithms seem to distill pure repetition. They seem to be one of the most complete forms of repetition. After all, the very notion of an algorithm is of an ordered sequence of operations that can be carried out by anyone or by anything. How, then, can we say that an algorithm enlarges the "frame of the now"? As much social theory argued over the last century (at least beginning with Nietzsche), pure or "bare" repetition is a normative ideal that serves to stabilize power relations and social forms. Repetition is at best a provisional accomplishment, not a given, amidst variation. Actually, repetition constantly varies and differs, as it is imitated. This variation itself may be imitated, and in an important sense this is what algorithms offer—something made to be imitated. (For instance, as I mentioned earlier, the Viterbi algorithm has been imitated and varied in several hundred patented versions.) The practical function of computer science courses, textbooks on algorithms, software libraries, and VLSI chips is to make treatments of repetition imitable. Algorithms socialize repetition by making it imitable. The force of an algorithm in establishing repetition is dependent on the linkages it establishes, the predicates or attributes it brings into relation and corporealizes as a force with specific intensity and quality.

These features allow us to begin to understand algorithms from the perspective of force and desire and to fit living invention and repetition together. William James (1996, 107) wrote: "Two parts, themselves disjoined, may nevertheless hang together by intermediaries with which they are severally connected, and the whole world may hang together similarly, inasmuch as some path of conjunctive translation by which to pass from one of its parts to another may always be discernible." Following James's logic of conjunction, we could say that algorithms function as associative objects. Algorithms make the world they work in hang together in certain ways and not others today. They give weight to relations, and they treat relations as real by holding things together and by making some conjoined path of translation discernible.

Conclusions: Machine Time as Practice of Relationality

Any technology confronts the realization that no foundation can fully secure its operations. This exploration of the Viterbi algorithm is motivated by the idea that technical infrastructures and operations are not simply mechanical foundations of forms of life and sociality. Their appearance as infrastructure or as machine time is relative to the irreducible traces of embodiment and sociality that they carry with them. These traces are legible at the cost of some willingness to regard technical arrangements as analyzable practices of relationality. Algorithms are "global phenomena" in a specific sense proposed recently by Aihwa Ong and Stephen Collier (2005, 11):

> Global phenomena are not unrelated to social and cultural problems. But they have a distinctive capacity for decontextualization and recontextualization, abstractability and movement, across diverse social and cultural situations and spheres of life. . . . At the same time, the conditions of possibility of this movement are complex. Global forms are limited or delimited by specific technical infrastructures, administrative apparatuses, or value regimes, not by the vagaries of a social or cultural field.

In their orderings of computation and communicational times and spaces, algorithms such as Viterbi demonstrate specific kinds of decontextualization.

The combination of convolutional codes and Viterbi decoding contributes to the possibility of billions of radio signals propagating at the same time in urban environments. The overall argument in this chapter, however, has concentrated on suggesting that this decontextualizing effect only succeeds in organizing machine time by folding different relations together.

Two significant temporal restructurings result from this folding together of relations. The incorporation of past states into each message begins to break down the punctual, discrete nature of repetition. A flow of information begins to look more like a phenomenological "now," composed of retentions and protentions. The treatment of itineraries by putting the general before the specific, by solving all problems in order to solve the particular, treats movement in space as a crowd phenomenon, not as a solitary movement.

The argument that machine time is relational and heterogeneous is both an empirical claim concerning the actual state of communications today and a more general claim about how technology can be thought today. The value of examining a particular algorithm is showing how complex the patchwork of orderings, materialities, and social orderings of communications can be. Unpacking a particular algorithm also begins to lend historical depth to machine time. The mixture of statistics, logistics, information theory, and signal-processing conventions present in the Viterbi algorithm points to several centuries of governmentality, sciences, commerce, organizational practice, and management. These diverse materials are sedimented not just in perception but in things. Because they increasingly rely on hidden states, algorithms construct microworlds from concatenations, collections, and paths that it brings into mosaic conjunction. These microworlds possess qualities that change our experience of force, movement, feeling, and duration.

References

Bergson, Henri Louis. 1911. *Creative evolution.* Trans. Arthur Mitchell. New York: Holt.

Cubitt, Sean. 1998. *Digital aesthetics.* London: Sage.

Derrida, Jacques. 1989. *Edmund Husserl's "Origin of geometry," an introduction.* Lincoln: University of Nebraska Press.

Graham, Paul. 2004. *Hackers and Painters: Big Ideas from the Computer Age.* Sebastapol, CA: O'Reilly.

Hansen, Mark B. N. 2004. *New philosophy for new media.* Cambridge, MA: MIT Press.

Husserl, Edmund. 1991. *On the phenomenology of the consciousness of internal time (1893–1917)*. Trans. John B. Brough. Dordrecht: Kluwer.

James, William. 1996. *Essays in radical empiricism*. Lincoln: University of Nebraska Press. Orig. pub. 1912.

Jones, Neil C., and Pavel Pevzner. 2004. An Introduction to Bioinformatics Algorithms, Computational Molecular Biology. Cambridge, MA: MIT Press.

Kittler, Friedrich. 1997. There is no software. In *Literature, media, information systems*, ed. John Johnston, 147–155. London: G & B Arts International.

Knorr-Cetina, Karin, and Urs Bruegger. 2000. The market as an object of attachment: Exploring postsocial relations in financial markets. *Canadian Journal of Sociology* 25 (2): 141–168.

Lunenfeld, Peter. 2000. *Snap to grid: A user's guide to digital arts, media, and cultures*. Cambridge, MA: MIT Press.

Mackenzie, Donald A. 1996. *Knowing machines: Essays on technical change*. Cambridge, MA: MIT Press.

Manovich, Lev. 1996. The labor of perception. In *Clicking in: Hot links to a digital culture*, ed. Lynn Hershman-Leeson, 183–193. Seattle: Bay Press.

———. 2001. *The language of new media*. Cambridge, MA: MIT Press.

National Institute of Standards and Technology. 2005. Big-O notation. www.nist.gov/dads/HTML/bigOnotation.html (accessed Jan. 24, 2007).

Ong, Aihwa, and Stephen J. Collier. 2005. *Global assemblages: Technology, politics, and ethics as anthropological problems*. Malden, MA: Blackwell.

Probyn, Elspeth. 2001. Anxious proximities. In *Timespace: Geographies of temporality*, ed. Jon May and Nigel Thrift, 171–184. London: Routledge.

Raymond, Eric. 1996. *The New Hacker's Dictionary*. Cambridge, MA: MIT Press.

Rodowick, David Norman. 2001. *Reading the figural, or, Philosophy after the new media*. Durham, NC: Duke University Press.

Thrift, Nigel. 2004a. Movement-space: The changing domain of thinking resulting from the development of new kinds of spatial awareness. *Economy and Society* 33 (4): 582–604.

———. 2004b. Remembering the technological unconscious by foregrounding knowledges of position. *Environment and Planning D: Society and Space* 22 (1): 175–191.

Virilio, Paul. 1997. *Open sky*. London: Verso.

Viterbi, Andrew J. 1967. Error bounds for convolutional codes and an asymptotically optimum decoding algorithm. *IEEE Transactions on Information Theory* 13 (2): 260–267.

Wikipedia. 2005. Viterbi algorithm. http://en.wikipedia.org/wiki/Viterbi_algorithm (accessed Jan. 25, 2007).

Wolfram, Stephen. 2002. *A new kind of science*. Champaign, IL: Wolfram Media.

2 DIGITAL TIME: TEMPORAL DIMENSIONS OF MEDIA AND CULTURE

5 Truth at Twelve Thousand Frames per Second

The Matrix *and Time-Image Cinema*

Darren Tofts

. . . this jump by which I place myself in the virtual.
—*Gilles Deleuze,* Bergsonism

T O ALL APPEARANCES it looks like any other movie bust. A dumpy cop, a pair of cuffs in one hand and a flashlight in the other, approaches a spread-eagled perp. The woman in the fetish gear turns swiftly and disarms the cop with a pinpoint succession of blows to the arm and face. Then it happens. She leaps into the air with an impossible elegance and assumes a stylish martial arts vogue, hanging frozen in space several feet above the cop, who also seems to have succumbed to this sudden pause in time. The only thing that moves in the three seconds this maneuver takes to unfold is our viewpoint of the scene, which rapidly sweeps around the tableau in a breathtaking 180-degree arc. The effect is awesome, sculptural, as the woman's body floats as a pure mathematical point in space, a pure instant of attention. The spell of this composite image of intense duration is broken as quickly as it is cast, however, as the woman proceeds to beat to other rhythms, disarming three more cops in rapid succession.

This scene occurs three minutes into the Wachowski Brothers' film *The Matrix* (1999). As an establishing shot it introduces pretty well everything that is important to the development of the film: the high-tech noir aesthetic, a subaltern appropriation of the ICT network, and the messianic pursuit of "the One." Its singular moment of action is so dramatic in its impact that we may blink in disbelief at what we think we have just seen, as the spectacular sequence resolves itself into diegesis and the plot ticks over. Let us return to that leap. This first instance of the film's most celebrated special effect, bullet-time photography, is memorable as much for its brevity as for its virtuosity. Although we encounter other instances of it during the course of the film (including the virtual dojo set piece with Morpheus and Neo), our opportunity to savor them is no less fleeting. In a film that refers to itself frequently we are, however, given a number of hints on how this pleasure might be achieved. During a "training program" on the seductive ways of the Matrix, Neo is instructed by Morpheus to do a double-take: "Look again." What he thought was a woman in a red dress has become his nemesis, Agent Smith, his gun point-blank in Neo's face. No leaps to bullet time here, just the command from Morpheus to "Freeze it." The training program succumbs to his bidding, and the throng of passers-by stops in midstride. This is Neo's second lesson on the hyperreal. In the earlier "loading program" Morpheus welcomes Neo to "the desert of the real" with the click of a button and the complacent flourish of a man who doesn't have to leave his chair to switch channels between the real world and its simulacrum.

Rewind, Review, Reality Check

As Neo learns the ways of the Matrix, we, too, learn the ways of *The Matrix*. In his elegant critical study of the film Joshua Clover argues that this confluence is precisely what the film is all about. Immersion is the common metaphysical currency that unites both the characters within the fiction and the spectators who watch them struggle with its manipulation of the real. *The Matrix* is a film informed by, preoccupied with, and directed toward a regime of digital media and their ubiquitous place in our lives. For Clover bullet-time photography is an index of the film's overt obsession with immersive effects, their overwhelming and enveloping audiovisual appeal. This is especially reflective of the film's appropriation of the aesthetics and gaming strategies of video games and their emphasis on interaction within a high-res mise-en-scène. *The Matrix*, in other words, cries out to be played, as well as watched and listened to. Its set pieces invite us, like Morpheus, to "leap at will from scenario to scenario. And it's within our grasp to accelerate, slow or stop the action" (Clover 2004, 51).

In this the film's signature bullet-time photography is designed explicitly with DVD in mind, especially in relation to that medium's superior ability to pause an image into crystalline stillness. With DVD we can control time, much like the cyberfemme Trinity does in her opening jump into the transcendence of bullet time. Trinity's leap is a springboard for an installation in being, as she is plunged into a time out of time. We can review the image's effects and slow them down even further, sustaining her momentary control of time in the fabric of "the construct" or simply play it over and over again for the pleasure of what Clover calls its "visual ecstasy" (2004, 66). Spatialization in the time-based medium of film has never been pushed so far in such a way. It gestures to the history of film converging with gaming and interactive video to form a kind of virtual or immersive cinema.

Look Again

The Matrix blurs the fictional situation of its characters with the actual realities of its audience. Both have the ability to control and interact with immersive effects. But there are other confluences at work here. As an instance of immersive cinema, the film is the perfect illustration of Gilles Deleuze's concept of the "time-image," discussed in the second volume of his extensive study of the cinema. Trinity's leap is a synecdoche of the time-image as Deleuze describes it, and *The Matrix* is an example of what Deleuze, at the end of *Cinema 2*, anticipates as a cinema to come, as the form continues its "investigations" into the emerging context of the electronic image and the replacement of nature with information (Deleuze 1989, 265). If, as for Clover, the film is a correlative of late-twentieth-century digital culture, it is also an allegory of what for Deleuze, writing in the mid-1980s, were the "as yet unknown aspects of the time-image" (1989, 266).

Look again. Are you reading *The Matrix* or reading Deleuze? The opening paragraphs of this essay are filtered with direct quotations from both Deleuze's cinema books and his earlier study of Henri Bergson (Deleuze 1966), much of which informs the conceptual basis of the latter. If we learn the ways of *The Matrix* in understanding the Matrix, we have much to learn about the time-image from *The Matrix* as well. Inversely, the more we read Deleuze in this context the more it sounds like he is describing *The Matrix*. The fluency with which Deleuze's prose blends in with the previous discussion of Trinity's leap is suggestive of something more profound than a creative rereading or misprision of his writing. Since so much of Deleuze's articulation of the time-image is based around the notion of the "interval," it is timely to pause for one.

Sculpting Time

The concept of bullet time is iconically illustrated in a sequence well into the film, when Neo dodges a stream of bullets fired at him by Agent Smith's henchmen. The visual conceit is that he has mastered the virtuality of the construct and can move with an infravisible speed, apparently frozen in time relative to the speed of a bullet. Bullets ripple past him as a stream of visible shockwaves, as if they are passing through a liquid membrane. This facility is merely a forecast of Neo's complete mastery of the Matrix later in the climactic showdown with Agent Smith in the subway. Here he stops bullets in midair, casually plucking one out for inspection. As in a Warner Bros. cartoon, the rest of the barrage fall impotently to the ground in a pantomime of inertia. The analogy with animation is significant here, in that the technique of bullet-time photography was designed to simulate the gravity-defying and visually spectacular gymnastics of Japanese anime. The mechanics of this immersive effect were based on traditional techniques of cel animation, whereby a sequence of still images is integrated into seamless movement by computer-generated "in betweens." Indeed, when Neo halts the flight of the bullets, he is like an animator slowly flicking the pages to check the flow of difference between individual drawings—an artist totally aware of and in command of the mechanics of his medium.

As it is used in the film, bullet time is effectively a form of capturing super slow motion; a ratio of around twelve thousand frames per second. It is a way of sculpting time, of capturing extraordinary moments of transcendence, when members of the resistance appropriate the very immersion they seek to overthrow and use it to their advantage. The so-called flow-mo quality of the swooping or panning around such time sculptures is actually reminiscent of the act of walking around and surveying a sculpture in an art gallery, a four-dimensional experience of a static object. The perspective we have of the characters frozen in midair registers our privileged perception of their privileged moments in the Matrix. Our perception, too, is of a time out of time, the time of the interval, of remote control and digital versatility.

John Gaeta, the visual effects supervisor on the film, describes this sculpting of time as "virtual cinematography." The term refers, in part, to the creation of immersive effects that enable people to perform impossible actions akin to animation. It also refers to a conception of cinema that is virtually, if not totally, inflected by digital technologies. Lev Manovich (2001) argues that the convergence of traditional filmmaking practices and digital technologies has profoundly changed the visual culture of the moving image. For Manov-ich the progression from the use of special effects in movies to special-effects movies made entirely of computer animation amounts to a redefinition of the very concept of cinema. Digital cinema is for Manovich a conceptual as much as technological category that takes into account the degree to which digital compositing and computer animation have transformed the traditional prac-tices of scripting, shooting live action, and editing. In this sense cinema has become "a particular case of animation that uses live-action footage as one of its many elements" (Manovich 2001, 302). Central to this broader transition within cinema as a hybrid form is a shift from temporal to spatial montage. Manovich argues that visual effects such as compositing, enhancement, and animation heighten the layering and complexity of the scene, deemphasizing the linkage or sequencing of scenes. "The logic of replacement, characteristic of cinema, gives way to the logic of addition and coexistence. Time becomes spatialized, distributed over the surface of the screen" (Manovich 2001, 325). Another way of putting this is that the advent of digital cinema represents a greater emphasis on the spectacle of the shot, the image. The translation of commercial cinema releases to DVD underlines Manovich's distinction, as films are organized as an inventory of separate events taken out of sequence. Watching a film on DVD as a continuous event of movement is merely one option. Interacting with it as a discontinuous database facilitates the person-alized navigation of discrete sequences and shots as experiences in their own right. Another way of putting this is that digital cinema is a cinema of the time-image rather than the movement-image.

Execute Jump Program

At the end of *Cinema 1* Deleuze outlines a "beyond of the movement-image." His articulation of the "new mental image" anticipates not only his second volume on the cinema but also the digital transformation of the cinema and its privileging of detail over whole in the medium of the Digital Versatile Disk. "The new image would therefore not be a bringing to completion of the cinema, but a mutation of it. . . . The mental image had not to be content with weaving a set of relations, but had to form a new substance" (Deleuze 1986, 215). For Deleuze the movement-image was the focal characteristic of classic cinema before the Second World War, and montage is central to it. Mon-tage is the reliable mechanism by which duration is elicited from the relations between individual shots within the closed system of the film as a whole. The movement-image refers not only, or simply, to the illusion of change and modulation over time. In this it solidified a historical tradition of reassurance within representation, when the artifice of movement cohered with and measured a rational order of things: an image, in other words, "corresponding to human perception" (Deleuze 1986, 82). The concept of the movement-image also signifies an economy of images that, in their relations to each other, expresses time as a dispersal or movement through images elsewhere: "The shot is movement considered from this dual point of view: the translation of the parts of a set which spreads out in space, the change of a whole which is transformed in duration" (Deleuze 1986, 20).

The time-image associated with modern, postwar cinema, on the other hand, reverses this subordination of time to movement: "The image had to free itself from sensory-motor links; it had to stop being action-image in order to become a pure optical, sound (and tactile) image" (Deleuze 1989, 23). Rather than being the measurement of action and movement, time is expressed in a pure state at the level of the image itself. As a consequence of this foregrounding of the image as event in itself over the image as vehicle of movement, a "cinema of seeing" emerged (ibid., 2), in which optical and sound situations contracted the image to greater presence instead of dilating it. These audiovisual situations precipitated a "new breed" of signs, what Deleuze called "opsigns" and "sonsigns." For Deleuze this cinema of seeing, of situations, was heightened by a different conception of time and continuity. Montage is challenged by what he calls a "false continuity" that no longer corresponds to human perception, or at least a rational form of perception grounded in the "laws" of association, continuity, resemblance, contrast and opposition (ibid., 276). Deleuze argues that the postwar period was a time of rupture and discontinuity, when "new forces" were at work in the image" (ibid., 271). The postwar period "greatly increased the situations which we no longer know how to react to, in spaces which we no longer know how to describe. These were 'any spaces whatever,' deserted but inhabited, disused warehouses, waste ground, cities in the course of demolition or reconstruction. And in these any-spaces-whatever a new race of characters was stirring, kind of mutant: they saw rather than acted, they were seers" (ibid., ix).

Sounding very much like the mise-en-scène of *The Matrix*, this description identifies the conceptual breeding ground for a different sensibility, a different way of viewing and representing the world. Deleuze recognized this sensibility in the dispersive, elliptical, and wavering quality of Italian neorealism, with its "deliberately weak connections and floating events" (Deleuze 1989, 1). Reality in this cinema was ambiguous, "aimed at," "to be deciphered" rather than reproduced: "this is why the sequence shot tended to replace the montage of representations" (ibid., 1). In French new wave cinema this sensibility could be traced in its jump cuts and disjunctive, irrational narrative structures, together with an emphasis on "optical and sound situations" that tend toward "a point of indiscernibility" (ibid., 9). For Deleuze these are the audiovisual signs of a new kind of image and, implicitly, the collapse in the rational movement-image of classical cinema: "[i]mages are no longer linked by rational cuts and continuity, but are relinked by means of false continuity and irrational cuts" (ibid., ix). They evince a breakdown in a certain kind of perceptual order and "belief in the external world" by disrupting the flow of extended and extendable sequence (ibid., 277). In both Italian neorealism and French new wave cinema, Deleuze identifies a distinguishable and conspicuous emphasis on description, on seeing rather than action. His reflections on the work of Jean-Luc Godard are suggestive of his overall thesis: "This descriptive objectivism is just as critical and even didactic, sustaining a series of films, from *Two or Three Things I Know about Her*, to *Slow Motion*, where reflection is not simply focused on the content of the image but on its form, its means and functions, its falsifications and creativities, on the relations within it between the sound dimension and the optical" (ibid., 10).

What is foregrounded with this emphasis on "descriptive objectivism" is a profound interstice or interval. The interval for Deleuze is an indeterminate pause, a dislocated transition that is neither here nor there. It is nonsequential, neither an end to one sequence nor the beginning of another. It is at such moments of nonlinkage, this loosening of the sensory-motor schema, that "'a little time in the pure state' . . . rises up to the surface of the screen" (Deleuze 1989, xi). This interval is what we glimpse when Trinity reaches the apex of her leap into virtuality. Or more accurately, the image forces us to "grasp" it, so dramatic is its punctuation of the action. Deleuze characterizes such moments in terms of extremity, of intolerable, unbearable or sublime conditions: "It is a matter of something too powerful, or too unjust, but sometimes also too beautiful . . . which henceforth outstrips our sensory-motor capacities" (ibid., 18). For Deleuze the interval is also marked by "almost imperceptible passages" that completely subordinate movement to time (ibid., 270). Drawing on Kant, he asserts that the time-image is "transcendental," that it is "out of joint" (ibid., 271). Trinity's leap is transcendent in the literal sense of the word, in that it is not feasible in the world of reality. As a leap in the virtuality of the Matrix it is the norm rather than an aberration. It is the cybercultural equivalent of Henri Bergson's metaphysical lump of sugar, the famous analogy with which he described his concept of duration in *Creative Evolution* (1907). In *Bergsonism* Deleuze observes that although the lump of sugar is spatial, it "also has a duration, a rhythm of duration, a way of being in time that is at least partially revealed in the process of its dissolving" (Deleuze 1991, 32). It is precisely this "rhythm of duration" that is captured with bullet-time photography.

The Crystal Method

Deleuze recounts Bergson's remark that he must "'wait until the sugar dissolves,'" noting that his impatience reveals his own duration, that it beats to a different rhythm from the dissolving sugar (Deleuze 1991, 32). For Bergson this reveals important differences in duration that are relative to each other. Clover's assessment of bullet time beats to another rhythm altogether. Clover asserts that the most dissatisfying quality of bullet time is, ironically, its speed, the fact that "it happens too quickly and slips away well before the sense of amazement" (Clover 2004, 50). Three seconds in the context of a fast-moving fight scene is indeed quick by any standards, but we need to remember that Trinity's position in space is a sculpture of imperceptible speed, not stillness. The reflexive iconography of Trinity being momentarily frozen at the apex of her leap gestures, yet again, to the invocation to "Freeze it." Clover is to Trinity what Bergson is to his dissolving sugar. The crucial difference, which is a difference in duration, is that whereas Clover wants to slow things down, Bergson wants to speed things up. Clover, unlike Bergson, is in a position to do something about it. As rhythms of duration, or images of being in time, however, both Trinity's leap and Bergson's sugar are articulations of the time-image as interval, as a break in movement. The arc of perception we trace around the image of Trinity is a descriptive act. It is a characteristic of the interval, a time-image that, like jump-cut editing, leaves an indelible and urgent impression on memory.

But there is movement. False movement. As with other instances of bullet time, Trinity's leap is the object of a mobile point of view within the film. The dramatic sweeping arc that describes her spectacle is not diegetically motivated, nor does it embody the point of view of any character within the film. It is an effect of the interval, an effect of different rhythms of duration. Its movement is as false as Trinity's stasis is illusory. What appears to be movement is, in fact, the perceptual reinforcement of how fast she is moving relative to anyone else at that particular point in time. It underlines the difference in rhythms of duration and in no way enables us to see how fast she is moving. But it also implies the very scrutiny that we have at our disposal with DVD, the facility to shift angles and points of view and to modify the speed with which we view the sequence, speeding it up, slowing it down, or freezing it altogether. Like Neo we are animators, capable of pausing images and plucking them out of sequence for our pleasure.

For Deleuze false movement implies false continuity, which he discusses throughout *Cinema 2*. In doing so he heightens the emphasis on the interval as a descriptive passage between images that carry the weight of contiguity: "even when there is a pure optical cut, and likewise when there is false continuity, the optical cut and the false continuity function as simple lacunae, that is, as voids which are still motor, which the linked images must cross" (Deleuze 1989, 213).

The animators of bullet-time photography, like all animators, are masters of false continuity. Persistence of vision is the ultimate trompe l'oeil technique of illusion, of the suggestion of continuity between static images. Warner Bros.' Matrix Web site describes the technique of bullet-time photography in terms that bring cel animation immediately to mind: "To execute the impossible, *The Matrix* VFX team painstakingly arranged 120 Nikon still cameras along a path mapped by a computer tracking system, fired the cameras in sequence around the unfolding action and scanned the images into the computer. After the computer interpolated between the scanned frames, the completed series of images was combined with a digital background" (Warner Bros.).

Movement and continuity in animation, false in a physical sense, is real in a virtual sense, if we can allow this oxymoron to stand for the time being. Perhaps a better way to describe the virtuality of animation is to emphasize the role played by our memory. Deleuze provides a telling example of this in relation to Luis Buñuel's and Salvador Dalí's *Un chien andalou*: "the image of the thinning cloud which bisects the moon is actualized, but by passing into that of the razor which bisects the eye, thus maintaining the role of virtual image in relation to the next one" (Deleuze 1989, 57). The suggestion of a virtual image (the cloud splicing the woman's eye) is an event of memory, a phenomenological event of persistence of vision. For Deleuze the key process at work here is the interplay between the actual and the virtual, which coexist as a time-image of the intolerable and unbearable. In *Bergsonism* Deleuze quotes from Bergson's *Creative Mind* (1941) to draw attention to the relations between memory and duration. The discussion is significant in that it uncannily anticipates Deleuze's own account of the opening sequence of *Un chien andalou*, but it also underlines the interplay or coexistence of the actual and the virtual in animation: "In fact we should express in two ways the manner in which duration is distinguished from a discontinuous series of instants repeated identically: On the one hand, 'the following moment always contains, over and above the preceding one, the memory the latter has left'; on the other hand, the two moments contract or condense into each other since one has not yet disappeared when another appears" (Deleuze 1989, 51).

This interplay or mutual coexistence of the actual and the virtual filters throughout the pages of *Cinema 2* like a long dissolve. Bergson's sugar cube has a lasting duration for Deleuze, and it especially reveals its presence about a third of the way through the text when, in a surprising move, he unexpectedly describes the time-image in terms of crystals. "The crystal-image may well have many distinct elements, but its irreducibility consists in the indivisible unity of an actual image and 'its' virtual image" (Deleuze 1989, 78). The crystal image is for Deleuze a perception of "the most fundamental operation of time" (ibid., 81), in which the past (virtual) and present (actual) states of an image coexist. This is most forcefully enacted in Trinity's leap in the virtuality of the Matrix. Our perception of the event as something unfolding in a present is simultaneously overwhelmed by its flight into the past as a memory of itself.

It is this quality of its happening at the moment of its passing that recalls Deleuze's remarks on the opening sequence of *Un chien andalou* as well as Clover's reflections of the image as being always already in rewind mode. The status of the "crystals of time" is appropriately evocative in this respect, since the actual and the virtual within the crystal image are reversible (Deleuze 1989, 69). This brings us back to a place we have been before, to look again at the confluence of the Matrix and *The Matrix*. For Deleuze the decisive characteristic of the crystal image is its "indiscernibility" (ibid., 69), its blurring of the actual and the virtual: "the optical image crystallizes with its own virtual image" (ibid., 69). The interplay between real and imaginary conditions is the key to the phenomenology of immersive effects, for both the rebels in the film and for those watching the film. The regime of immersive effects gives rise to a kind of "crystalline narration" that is reflexive and bound up with "pure optical and sound situations to which characters, who have become seers, cannot or will not react, so great is their need to 'see' properly what there is in the situation" (ibid., 128).

We could easily replace *situation* with *simulation* here and have a very tidy summary of *The Matrix*. In explaining the ambient everywhere of the Matrix to Neo, Morpheus describes it as a world that has "been pulled over your eyes to blind you from the truth." Neo has trouble adjusting optically as well as conceptually to this new reality and is reminded that he is using his eyes for the first time in his life. Neo's transcendent quest is not simply to accept the duplicity of false consciousness but to realize that to live in his actual present, 2199, is to inhabit the interval, to toggle between actual and virtual realities. For the film's audience in 1999 a similar challenge presented itself in relation to the ambivalent lure of immersive effects. The desire to succumb to virtuality was one of the great attractions of the film, to escape temporarily into an all-encompassing otherness of way-cool martial arts prowess and disembodied telepresence. Clover persuasively argues that in embracing the virtual we are in fact renewing our own contemporary technocultural conditions, of which we may not be fully cognizant. The time of *The Matrix* is the time of the Matrix. For Clover the film is about "digitech" (Clover 2004, 40), the late-twentieth-century obsession with digital technologies and the simulations they make possible, from the Internet and mobile audiovisual telephony to video games and interactivity. Although grounded in allegory, the film's conflation of the Matrix and *The Matrix* conforms to the mutual coexistence both Bergson and Deleuze describe in relation to the actual and the virtual. As Clover puts it, digitality "allows one to both image and to imagine an all-encompassing spectacle" (40).

In a curious play on the classical concept of mimesis, the film draws on the image of the mirror to crystallize this confluence of images and imaginings, avatars and bodies, characters and spectators. Having chosen the red pill and made his commitment to transcendence, Neo notices a strange distortion in his image in a mirror. Its surface quakes and coagulates like quicksilver, enticing him to touch it and immerse himself in its strange commingling of actuality and virtuality. He is already starting to see, to see that he is already "mesmerised by digital fabrication" (Clover 2004, 19). As are we. The strange relations between digital fabrication in the film and in our own world, of which *The Matrix* is merely one instance, are as commonplace as looking at oneself in the mirror. Deleuze, in yet another anachronistic instance, may well have been talking of *The Matrix* when he observed that "the mirror-image is virtual in relation to the actual character that the mirror catches, but it is actual in the mirror which now leaves the character with only a virtuality and pushes him back out-of-field. . . . When virtual images proliferate like this, all together they absorb the entire actuality of the character, at the same time as the character is no more than one virtuality among others" (Deleuze 1989, 70).

Cyberculture is another name for this absorption. We have become accustomed to living simultaneously IRL and URL, f2f and in cyberspace: even our transcriptions of the real are indelibly inflected by the virtual. It has become second nature to conceive of quotidian experience as an interplay between actual and virtual states of being. *The Matrix* is one of a number of cyberculture films that explore this blurring of metaphysical states of being. These films, such as *Total Recall, Dark City, Johnny Mnemonic, Strange Days*, are in their own way articulations of a new economy of distributed networks, convergent media, and immersive technologies. As signs of the times, they posit a world of extremes, intimations of a virtual gestalt for which there is no exit, a world in which we have already started to suspect that we are "inside something from which we might not be able to escape" (Clover 2004, 41).

The Matrix was made for an audience literate in the logics of immersive cinema and virtual cinematography. It offered a crystalline reflection on what it means to live routinely in a world of parallel and intersecting realities. In this *The Matrix* is an essay on method. The crystal method is a way of relating to the blurring of actual and virtual states in the domain of cyberculture. *The Matrix* is perhaps the most telling allegory we have yet encountered of what we are becoming in an age of digital versatility, when time-based media have morphed into crystalline description and the beat of a different duration.

For all the critical confusion surrounding Deleuze's description of the crystal image, the definition he provides in his glossary seems pretty straightforward: "the uniting of an actual and a virtual image to the point where they can no longer be distinguished" (Deleuze 1989, 335). The confounded would do well to read *The Matrix* in tandem with *Cinema 2*, flicking between pages like an animator.

References

Clover, Joshua. 2004. *The Matrix*. London: British Film Institute.

Deleuze, Gilles. 1966. *Le Bergsonisme*. Paris: PUF.

———. 1986. *Cinema 1: The movement-image*. Trans. Hugh Tomlinson and Barbara Habberjam. Minneapolis: University of Minnesota Press.

———. 1989. *Cinema 2: The time-image*. Trans. Hugh Tomlinson and Robert Galeta. London: Athlone.

———. 1991. *Bergsonism*. Trans. Hugh Tomlinson and Barbara Habberjam. New York: Zone Books.

Manovich, Lev. 2001. *The language of new media*. Cambridge, MA: MIT Press.

Warner Bros. Beyond bullet time: Creating virtual cinema. http://whatisthematrix. warnerbros.com/rl_cmp/rl_production_04.html (accessed Nov. 9, 2006).

6 The Fallen Present

Time in the Mix

Andrew Murphie

There is history because, from the origin onwards, the present is, so to speak, always delayed with regard to itself.
—*Vincent Descombes,* Modern French Philosophy

One day the day will come when the day will not come.
—*Paul Virilio,* Open Sky

THE GENESIS OF THIS CHAPTER was not a new media technology but a picture of a polar bear. It was found at the Web site of a Danish newspaper. The photographer catches this bear, huge and agile, midleap between patches of ice, forming a bridge over the black water. What was the picture meant to capture? Perhaps it was just the slightly perilous present moment in the life of this particular bear, caught in freeze frame, a present become history through the delay of photography. Perhaps the picture is a metaphor for the genuinely perilous future for all these bears and for the increasing fragility of the ice on which they depend for survival. For me, however, the picture of the bear also captures something else, more even than most photographs. This is the strange paradox of the present moment. It seems at once highly charged and almost inconsequential. Although the leap may be exciting, what matters in the case of the bear is landing on new ice. The leap has no meaning in and of itself. It is not a leap into the void (there is no sitting around in cafés suffering the ennui of the banal present for hungry bears!). Its meaning is found in the links to its immediate past and future, in the "extended" now or duration of the leap as an event. For the viewer of the photograph the paradox is inverted—the present is not nearly so highly charged, but we can read all kinds of consequences in it (metaphors about global warming and so on). We seem to have caught the present in its essence, and it is all leap. It is as if (and only by virtue of the technology of photography?) the leap contains within it the past and the future. If the present does contain past and future, however, what does that make the present?

Such well-known paradoxes will be considered in this chapter, from the perspective of the contemporary fate of the present within network cultures (the very network cultures, no doubt, that bring pictures of leaping polar bears to us in Australia via Danish-newspaper Web sites). A survey of ideas—drawn from cultural theory, cognitive philosophy, and neuroscience—will explore different understandings of the nature, conception, and potential of the present. This will allow for a further understanding of the complex politics of a network society.

I hope I will be forgiven for the necessarily scant nature of what is really a series of sketches and, worse, for a linking of these sketches that tends at times toward the shamelessly syncretic. I will begin by describing what I am calling the "fallen present." This is at once a state of sin into which the network society has fallen, as described by critics such as Paul Virilio; a failure of the present to live up to the metaphysics of immediacy central to much of modern culture and technics; yet also a relatively new territory peculiar to network cultures, one that perhaps fundamentally complicates our concept of what the present is (or is not). This complication will be sketched briefly via a consideration of the peculiar kinds of delay—and subsequent need for "latency tolerance"—found within the experience of networked technologies. I will then take a step back to describe a kind of contemporary obsessive-compulsion surrounding the present, a doomed but highly charged series of attempts to reconstruct presence that often seems to inform the use of network technologies. This compulsion will be characterized as a version of what Derrida (1996) has called "archive fever." I will then argue, however, for a kind of presence—presence as remix or open-ended synthesis. Here I will consider Deleuze's surprisingly little-remarked account of the electronic image. This will be juxtaposed with DJ Spooky's (Paul Miller's) use of the remix to potentialize the present without essentializing it. Here I will tease out Deleuze's notion of what I am calling a differential image and suggest in passing the idea of a rich but differential present as something often embraced by network cultures, in opposition to these cultures' tendencies toward obsessive-compulsion. This differential present is the present not as a guarantee of full and complete presence but rather as expression of the ongoing slippage of presence, its relational qualities that, like the never-ending permutations of the electronic or differential image, can never be resolved. This will lead me to consider (all too briefly) some useful ways of thinking out a differential, relational present. The ideas involved will include Henri Lefebvre's "rhythm-analysis," neurologist Detlef Linke's consideration of the role rhythms play in thinking processes, and Tim van Gelder and Francisco Varela's account of the differential temporality of thought. Central here will be what Varela (1999) calls, following William James, the "specious present." This is a complex present that often gives the impression of immediacy but is in fact a multifaceted assemblage of different durations at micro and macro levels. In the light of all these ideas I will finally consider what I am calling the "ontogenetic politics of cognition." This is the politics by which thinking processes are interfered with at the very level of their formation—in other words, in whatever it is that we might consider the "present moment" to be. This is therefore a politics that takes account of both macro- and microcognitive processes, and also what William E. Connolly (2002b) has called a "neuropolitics." It is a politics central to bringing together new technologies, new techniques, human thinking processes, and actions within network cultures.

The Fallen Present

If, as Vincent Descombes suggests, history requires a delay in which reflection can take place, then networked technologies seem to destroy history as they suck everything into an overburdened present. Brought to us real-time in what Baudrillard (1988) called the "ecstasy of communication," the networked present seems inescapable yet beyond our control. This is also Paul Virilio's well-known diagnosis. He writes of the "time of an endless perpetuation of the present" in which "contemporary man no longer arrives at, achieves, anything" beyond a tightly coordinated and rather mechanical "total performance syndrome" (1997, 143). New technologies carry a large part of the blame. Via "teleaction" networks take us away from the meaningful here and now to a "time-world of the real instant" within the network. For Virilio the present is reduced to an electronic present, a vacuous "all-powerful and all-seeing now" whose "pitiless nature is incommensurable with the nature of the age-old localization of the hic et nunc" (1997, 143)—the here and now.

History is challenged, not just as an idea but palpably. Past knowledges and practices lose value within the market, as different cultural histories meet up within the new networks and tear each other apart. At the same time, the future is in crisis. A series of social, environmental, and cognitive catastrophes (global warming famously brings all three together) creeps closer to the horizon of the present, but this is a horizon blurred by an electronic haze.

There is worse. There is, as Virilio and others have noted, a real challenge to the fundamental ontogenesis of human thought within which the present is constituted as experience. This challenge is made more powerful each day by the global technics of memory or "global mnemotechnics" (networked teletechnologies and media-memory devices, from digital recorders to databases) (Stiegler 2003a). For Bernard Stiegler this global mnemotechnics "directly challenges consciousness as such," but it is not only consciousness that is challenged. Memory, the synthesis at the basis of human thinking processes, the unconscious are all challenged by the new networks (and increasingly by technical interference with the brain itself, via drugs, procedures, and even simple cognitive training). What world results for Stiegler? For Stiegler the world becomes one of "hyper-industrialisation: namely, the submission of all retentional devices, including biological ones, to industrial exploitation." This is a world in which "conscious time and its bodily support" become dominated by "the new markets opened up by technoscientific developments" (Stiegler 2003a).

We can see that Stiegler warns that the consequences of too close an engagement with real-time networks are dire—not only for our sense of history but for our sense of everything, indeed for the very possibility of sense. In pursuing more of the present, we lose it completely. Somewhat unsurprisingly, this leads to a series of crises in "an ecology of the mind" (Stiegler 2003b, 166) that I have discussed elsewhere (see Murphie 2005).

Here I will take onboard the lessons of Virilio, Stiegler, and others concerning the threat of a perpetual, hypermediated present. Yet while embracing the criticism of the worship of a real-time present, I want also to propose an alternative, and richer, concept of nowness, one also found in network cultures. In fact, the fallen present of network cultures is perhaps more complex than it at first seems. First, the fallen present is indeed a present that is fallen or corrupted. This is no longer the present that once so freely gave us a sense of a local, habitable here and now. It is perhaps the mechanical, reductive present of Virilio's "total performance syndrome" (1997, 143). It is the state of sin into which the entire network society has fallen—contaminating everything and everyone. It brings "you"—as it transforms "you" into data and signal—remorselessly into the network via new technologies of mediation, biometry, and data surveillance. This is the present promoted by much of the commerce of network cultures and the present found in the promise of globalized, just-in-time production. We feel every day the constant fall into this present—a fall away from historical purpose or future hope (both substituted by short-term goals of improving immediate performance—the total performance syndrome).

Yet the fallen present is also a concept meant to describe the falling of the present away from itself. Here the fallen present describes the fact that the leap of the bear cannot really be frozen, except in an image. Put simply, despite the technological effort expended to keep us there, there is no simple present in the way we often think of it. We certainly cannot "live in the present" and it alone. So the fallen present also describes the fall of the reliance of culture on the concept of "knife-edge present" (Varela 1999, 268), of a present in which "things" can be located outside of change, in which events "happen" simply, in which perhaps "we" can find ourselves, and find ourselves "free agents" in time, at a constant "point of decision" about what to do next. This is also the false present in which we often think that thinking takes place. It is the present that perhaps forms the basis for what Derrida (1978, 279) famously called a "metaphysics of presence." It is an illusion, if a powerful one, and if networks seem to suck us into this present, they also sometimes open our eyes to it as an illusion.

For some thinkers this means that there are better cultural questions to be asked regarding time in the network than those about the perpetual present. These questions concern a series of mismatches, time lags, and disjunctions, or "reality fragmentations." This alternative approach to the "fallen present," involving the abandoning of the very concept of a simple present in favor of a present that includes these lags, mismatched durations, relational disjunction, and fragmentation, ironically allows an enriched notion of nowness. I will suggest that, as well as causing so many problems, recent technologies have, in fact, made it possible for the present—if only we will let it—to take up the burden of history in a much more complex set of delays and relays.

Latency Tolerance

For me one of the most haunting images of time in the network is found in Adrian Mackenzie's account of network gaming. Mackenzie describes playing with a gamer who not only seemed able to anticipate his opponent's every move but to work with "the delays introduced on the network we were both playing on" (2002, 166). Mackenzie points out that this is a phenomenon "which is well known in real-time applications" called "latency tolerance" (ibid.). This question of latency tolerance is also relevant to the human constitution of the experience of time, as we will see.

As Mackenzie points out, we might think of networked gaming as a classic example of a loss of the richness of time to the fixed parameters of the eternal, preprogrammed, networked present, as "nothing happens, except what was programmed" (Mackenzie 2002, 159). Yet there is a fundamental contradiction within network culture here. On the one hand, the promise (and the fear) is of getting caught up in the total performance syndrome of the program. This is enforced temporally in that by "promising instantaneity between an event and its reception, real time seems to eradicate delay" (ibid., 160). On the other hand, there is a subtler promise (and fear) that "there must be delays somewhere, otherwise capital would not deploy itself in real time as information or live spectacle" (and, otherwise, some gamers would not be better than others, precisely in their ability to constitute and act within network temporalities). In short, information has no value if everyone has it as soon as they want it. There is increasingly a financial reward for controlling the differential access to the time of information. As even basic information theory suggests, information is both produced and accessed differentially. Far from producing one simple present in which everything melts into one blinding light of unity, on the networks time often seems to "fall apart." Mackenzie notes that the game he discusses, Avara, sometimes placed a message onscreen—"Reality fragmentation detected" (ibid., 167).

This complex constitution of the present is not restricted to games. Many virtual reality artists have been concerned with such questions—for example, Char Davies and Ulrike Gabriel, both of whom have used the rhythm of the user's breath as an interface, have drawn attention to the constitution of a modulated duration between algorithmic and physiological times / rhythms. Others have pointed to the increased potentialization of the time of biological generation (the opening up of the "moment" of ontogenesis) using biotechnologies (see Cooper 2002). In both cases it becomes obvious that, as Elizabeth Grosz has put it, time is "becoming, an opening up which is at the same time a form of bifurcation and divergence" (1999, 3–4). For others even the constitution of simple sequences of time is in doubt. Benjamin Libet has famously suggested that there is up to a half-second delay between—and complex, nonlinear folding together of—physiological reactions, neuronal impulses, and our conscious sense of an intention in the present (see Massumi 2002, 29).

Henri Lefebvre perhaps sums this up when he writes, "Some people cry out against the acceleration of time, others cry out against stagnation. They're both right" (quoted in Seigworth 2000, 255). Francisco Varela, whose article "The Specious Present" is central to my argument here, writes that "'nowness' is not a point or an object but a location, a field with a structure analogous to the center and periphery structuring of the visual field" (Varela 1999, 278). Varela writes of this field as the "specious present," a term first coined by William James, who suggested that "[d]uration and events together form our intuition of the specious present with its contents" (quoted in Varela 1999, 578n2).

At issue, then, is a present "fallen" into a series of complex ecologies, feedback circuits, or fields. This is a present constituted within dynamic structural couplings (Clark 2001, 127) between brain, body, world, and technologies (different ice platforms, flowing water, polar bears, their hunger, photography, online newspapers, etc.). If this is accurate, network technologies make a huge difference to the mix involved. Before considering this mix, however, I will discuss the obsession with the present in its more regressive form.

The Obsessive-Compulsive Present

How has the sense of a crisis surrounding the present arisen? One of the drives within network culture seems to be a kind of general obsessive-compulsion that attempts to resist the ambiguities of the present as a volatile mix. The response to this volatility is often an ongoing attempt to reinforce the fragile present by recording it, effectively turning it into an archive of past repetitions that will allow control of "future presents" (again performance measures come to mind). This obsession-compulsion involves what Derrida (1996) calls "archive fever." Archive fever is a febrile investment in the technologies and techniques of mediation that always involve the formation of some mix of archives. We find archive fever in the troubled, technological attempt to reassert the construction of the present moment (and the sense of being in this moment—of presence) in the face of its erosion in time. It is in this archive fever—and its mediation of, as Derrida puts it, the "democracy to come" (Derrida and Stiegler 2002, 6)—that the relation of the times of thinking processes to network times and political times is at stake.

Archive fever is troubling, however, because the very use of the technics makes the constitution of presence too obvious as a constitution. In short, the technologies of time control draw attention to an artifactuality, and this threatens the "natural presence" that artifactuality is brought into being to affirm. The resulting insecurity feeds back into the whole process, leading to the kind of destructive obsessive / repetition compulsion found in much of technical culture (checking one's email again and again, measuring performance to the exclusion of actually "performing," staying online for too long, disappearing into a computer game to the point of RSI [repetitive strain injury]).

Derrida is surprisingly political on this point. He writes that there is now an "international artifactuality," a "centralizing appropriation of artifactual powers for 'creating the event'" (Derrida and Stiegler 2002, 5). Contemporary media sacrifices everything here to the fiction of "'immediate,' live presence," to "actuality, to the implacable reality of its supposed present" (6). Yet as I have begun to suggest, the "direct," "real time," or the actual are never pure. Under these conditions Derrida (ibid., 5) suggests that there is the political question of the reality of the virtual "(virtual image, virtual space, and so virtual event) that can doubtless no longer be opposed, in perfect philosophical serenity, to actual [*actuelle*] reality in the way that philosophers used to distinguish between power and act."

Artifactualities as "instruments of archivization" (Derrida and Stiegler 2002, 97), now networked and virtualized archivation, offer "more refined means of producing computer-generated images [*images de synthèse*]" of computed synthesis, yet in this synthesis, "authenticity is both made possible by technics and threatened by it, indissociably" (ibid., 97–98). This provides us with a way to read the dark side of the contemporary fuss over the brain, as well as the faith often placed in cognitive research, as a kind of last bastion of a metaphysics of presence (once God and the soul, perhaps even the social, appear to have failed us). This is what I have called elsewhere "brain-magic" (Murphie 2006), a materialist metaphysics fueled by media technology (brain scanning technologies such as Magnetic Resonance Imaging) and computer models. Brain-magic is, of course, a massive example of archive fever (this is not to say the science involved is invalid—it just explains some of the cultural drive behind it). We build new archives when memory, history, or our feeling of control over our own presence in time fail us. And what better archives than those devoted to "cognition"—to the scientific manipulation of presence itself! Yet the archive only repeats the difficulty. It does not restore our presence / presents—our here and now. To have put something in the archive is to have separated ourselves from it. In this case we separate ourselves from our thoughts, framing them within the archives of cognitivist systems—in educational processes, performance management, "effective communications," or even "personal growth." Far from bringing our presence to life, the archive's distancing systems and its "logic of repetition . . . compulsion" are "indissociable from the death drive . . . from destruction" (Derrida 1996, 11–12). Archive fever's destruction would not be something lost on X-Filers. Any figure or structure that orders, places, and regulates events has already lost those events.

Yet the delayed or deferred time of the archive, although it might not return a simple presence to us, is not just a question of postponement but of an ongoing flow of differentiation (in which any set of connections such as a network immerses us). Networked archives allow a mix of times, spaces, and sequences. Networks constantly undo even their own temporary orders, make any archive's commands redundant as their shouting dies down. In the network, archive fever never settles in one archive, unless this is the meta-archive of the network itself. Here, Derrida (1996, 13) writes, "the radical destruction can again be reinvested in another logic, in the inexhaustible economistic resource of an archive which capitalizes everything, even that which ruins it or radically contests its power." For Derrida the devil is truly at play in the world, via an "unlimited upheaval under way in archival technology" (ibid., 18). In this context Derrida echoes the postconnectionist thinkers of cognitive philosophy. For both it is no longer a question "of simple continuous progress in representation" (ibid., 15) of past-present-future, for example, but rather a constant and unlimited remix of potential connections. As Derrida puts it, "what is no longer archived in the same way is no longer lived in the same way" (ibid., 18). I will now turn to the electronic image in order to understand this ongoing remix.

Remixing the Present

It is well known that Deleuze (1986, 1989) has comprehensively described the cinema's new syntheses of time in terms of a transition from a movement-image, an image of the secondary effects of time, to a time-image, in which we both experience and question time itself. This transition reflects a deep cultural transition. It is seldom noted, however, that the time-image is not where Deleuze stops. He continues on to the electronic image and to its relation to politics and thought.

For Deleuze, thought results from "the shock wave of nervous vibration" (1989, 158). It comes, as Foucault notes, from the outside. Yet this means that one is powerless "to think the whole and to think oneself" (Deleuze 1989, 167). Deleuze complicates this by adding a political dimension. This involves the extent to which "Hitler," and by implication other forms of control via media, work toward the imposition of "psychological automata" (ibid., 264) (in what is often today a series of explicitly cognitivist controls). An appropriate ethics / politics will involve undoing these psychological automata and setting them "free." At this point of *Cinema 2* it is clearly suggested that the movement-image would have to be abandoned "in order to set free other powers that it kept subordinate" (ibid., 264).

These powers were set free when "motor automata, in short, automata of movement, made way for . . . automata of computation and thought, automata with controls and feedback" (Deleuze 1989, 264–265). Power was reconfigured here also, away from Hitler, the emblem of "a single, mysterious leader, inspirer of dreams, commander of actions" (ibid., 265). Yet it was reconfigured toward dilution "in an information network where 'decision-makers' managed control, processing and stock across intersections of insomniacs and seers" (ibid., 265).

It is at this point that we can locate the junction of cinema and new media (Deleuze notes here an "electronic automatism"). Unlike cinema the field involved is all-compassing, and at the same time, as an open network of networks, completely open to its own changes (there is never an identifiable and stable whole). Within these fields or networks electronic images are in "perpetual reorganization"—"a new image can arise from any point whatever of the preceding image" with an image "constantly being cut into another image" (Deleuze 1989, 265). Crucially, even stable and identifiable media forms and processes disappear (Murphie 2003). With the mutability and modularity of digital images "there is no longer a medium properly speaking" (ibid., 331). Electronic images therefore make up a kind of active "table of information, an opaque surface on which are inscribed 'data'" (ibid., 265).

Deleuze raises what might be the central question of the twenty-first century concerning the adequacy of the human brain to these new conditions. He questions the relation between power, knowledge, and our "own" cognition. Seeking, as we have seen, to free thought from any new form of automatism, he suggests that "electronic images will have to be based on still another will to art, or on as yet unknown aspects of the time-image" (Deleuze 1989, 266), and we might say, on a reconfiguration of the basic experience of time. What is the basis for this will to art? It begins in acceptance that "the shot . . . is less like an eye than an overloaded brain endlessly absorbing information" (ibid., 267). This is a new aesthetic that accesses a new constitution of the experience of time. It is one "relaunched" in terms of an enhanced cinematic apparatus, with "a brain which has a direct experience of time, anterior to all motivity of bodies" (ibid., 267). Yet the danger is that psychological automata have become informational, and we internalize "Hitler," who now "exists only through pieces of information which constitute his image in ourselves" (ibid., 269). This means that "it is necessary to go beyond information in order to defeat Hitler" (ibid.). Out of this emerges the political relation of the times of the cinema with the new times of the electronic, in that "[t]he life or afterlife of cinema depends on its internal struggle with informatics" (ibid., 270). The new electronic image, however, also provides a way "beyond information." This is in part because it never quite resolves itself into a full and stable image (or perhaps into a present) and is therefore always open to its own connectedness—we might say to the differential intensity of the networks in which it is immersed.

Deleuze does give an example of this move from relatively stable "images," movement-images and even time-images, to something else. It comes from Antonioni's project *Technically Soft*. Here there is an "exhausted man who is on his back dying and looking at 'the sky which becomes ever bluer, this blue becoming pink'" (Deleuze 1989, 317). This blue becoming pink is the differential image, perhaps the imageless image.

This imageless, differential image is also an image of the fallen, not-quite-fully present, differential present. It is also perhaps an image of a differential thought. Better examples of all of these differential modes of being than Antonioni's exhausted and dying man can be found in the work of contemporary digital artists such as Paul D. Miller (DJ Spooky). As Miller puts it, "the twenty first century self is so fully immersed in and defined by the data that surrounds it, we are entering an era of multiplex consciousness" (2004, 63). He sees himself as "an acrobat drifting through the topologies of codes, glyphs and signs that make up the fabric of my everyday life," flipping things around (Miller n.d.).

DJ Spooky (who is also VJ—or video jockey) quite literally plays out what Deleuze called cinema's "internal struggle with informatics." In a series of performances, *Rebirth of a Nation*, he has remixed images from D. W. Griffith's *Birth of a Nation*, accompanied by a live sound mix. In the process this key film in the history of the movement-image is recreated as an electronic, differential image, one in which the inherent racism of the film begins to unravel in favor of a "multiplex consciousness." It is here that we begin to see the way in which the present as mix opens out from presence, as DJ Spooky "is sifting through the narrative rubble of a phenomenon" (Miller n.d.). DJ Spooky writes here of an "indexical present" served by a "prosthetic realism." This enhances rather than destroys reflection—yet a reflection in which a prosthetically deepened mix of the (not quite present/disrupted) present enables one to work against the weight of given history.

DJ Spooky's flipping things around also opposes itself to the standard ordering of time, "a world of absolute standards of identity, time, regulation" (in Davis n.d.). He also clearly articulates the need for "some sort of intense cognitive break with the psychological/perceptual architecture of what makes you a normal human" (ibid.). This desire to displace regulated times is common among digital artists. Australian digital artist David Haines (2005) puts it this way: "[I]t's like you're just riffing with different time frames. . . . [I]f you can get beyond narrative, it's like all the time compressions are available, and then you've got a choreography of time available to you and this is another good, invisible material . . . the virtual of time . . . and you can play with that." Deleuze, DJ Spooky, and Haines demonstrate that when we think about the present in network cultures, this is not just a matter of cultures of enforced "spontaneity" or "total performance syndrome" within network culture, or worse, one of constant "Reflex Action" as feared by Virilio (2003, 17).

Having briefly analyzed the technical/cultural side of the present in network cultures, it might be useful to rethink the "thinking processes" side of our constitution of the present. Here I will all too briefly summarize some basic principles for alternative models of thinking processes to cognitivist/informational models.

The first of these involves rhythm, and here one could draw on Henri Lefebvre's "rhythmanalysis." For Lefebvre it is to the complex junction of various rhythms in polyrhythms that we should look in order to understand the interaction of different times, different durations. The rhythmanalyst would "'listen' to a house, a street, a town, as an audience listens to a symphony" (Lefebvre 2004, 22). He or she might also listen to a virtual reality environment's times, the lag and fragging of computer games, the mix of a DJ or VJ, in order to understand the way the material movement of various energies (technical, biological, "cosmic," and so on) comes together. This does not necessarily provide a description of a better world—but it might provide a better description of the world, one able to account for the fallen present (which Lefebvre calls a "dilapidated" present [31]). The rhythmanalyst might be more attentive to new technorhythmic ecologies of oppression or freedoms.

Neurologist Detlef Linke has even pointed to the central organizing function of rhythms in the brain. For him the brain "does not come equipped with an original metronomic default setting: the rhythms of cognitive events are situationally determined" (2000, 30). In short, we use the rhythms of the external world to assist our accommodation of the information of the external world to our own internal rhythms. It is not as simple as neat signals traveling along a line of world-body-brain-body-world. Rather there is what we might call a world-brain-body field, formed in the crisscrossing of rhythms and refrains (Guattari 1996) from world, body, and brain. The brain's genius, if any such thing exists, lies in being able to direct the local traffic here—to match up rhythms or to find new mediating rhythms. But it crucially relies on mismatch in order to do this. Thinking arises in the disjunction of rhythms, driven by their differential intensity, in a differential present.

Here the fragmented and contingent nature of the brain—its not-quite-presentness—turns out to be a strength rather than a weakness. For cognitive philosophers such as Tim van Gelder (1999), present-time experience is, in reality, constituted as a shifting differential field, reflecting past states, present states, and possible future states. This can even be expressed via a mathematically modeled "phase space." This describes the complex differential conditions that express the ongoing patterns of becoming at any given moment of past-present-future relations. To oversimplify, we experience the becoming of the interference pattern as a given moment.

This brings us to Francisco Varela's "neurophenomenology" (1999, 267). To sum this up far too simply, Varela sees the "specious present" as constituted—"neurophenomenologically"—in the interaction of at least three levels of duration. These are tenths of a second, a second or so, and longer than this (the level of narrative—and most cultural analysis—which tends to miss the first two levels). What is perhaps the very stuff of our experience of nowness is found in activity among what Varela calls competing cell assemblies (linked, activated neurons across the brain), particularly at the first and second levels of duration, with any given "now" lasting for a maximum of two to three seconds (ibid., 277). These scales provide an important basis for the consideration of the constitution of the present within thinking processes. Indeed, they provide a basis for thinking of the genesis of thought in real terms—and thus for what I will call an ontogenetic politics of thinking processes. As constitutional, they might also be important to our understanding both of the effects of network technologies and of contemporary politics. They draw attention to the need for more critical political analysis of the way in which the fallen present is constituted, before perhaps narratives, interpretations, or ideologies. They point to the need for more work on "neuropolitics" (Connolly 2002b) or, more generally, a micropolitics. Both of these would seem enmeshed with the broader politics of the network society. It is to this politics that I will briefly turn.

An Ontogenetic Politics of Thinking Processes

We can locate an ontogenetic cognitive politics in the temporal extensions (Varela 1999, 280) and contractions between world, body, and brain discussed by many of the thinkers I have discussed. Within human thinking processes this politics would examine the co-constitution of the specious or fallen present and the dynamics of thought itself. This would be a politics of the generation of being/becoming at the very basis of thinking processes (in what Varela [1999, 289] calls the "genetic constitutional analysis of time"). It is these ontogenetic conditions that form a groundless ground for the chronopolitics of network time—of an increasingly complex remix of external time impinging on the remix of endogenous time consciousness. And it is here that a difference in ontological assumptions makes for a very different ethics or politics when it comes to the flow of thinking processes.

For nearly all the theorists I have mentioned this is a flow initiated by affect (Varela 1999, 296). It is not a flow—at least not primarily—initiated by information, representations, or recognitions. These must be regarded as, at best, limited, secondary effects within the technical events surrounding thinking processes rather than their basic "stuff." There is therefore a need for more accounts of affect within new media and the network society—by which I mean the primacy of affect, or what Brian Massumi (2002, 23) has called the "autonomy of affect." There are some examples of these accounts. John Scannell (2001) has given a very good—and to my knowledge unique—account of the role of affect in the network frenzy of MP3 file sharing. Massumi (2002,

2004) has given perhaps the most extensive account of the politics of affect. Tiziana Terranova (2004) has also described the urgency of the need for more such accounts. She describes what might be seen as the network culture correlative to the transient and variable, differential, neuronal constitutions of time—in short the network duplicating and transforming the ontogenetic power of the human nervous system. She writes of the creation of a "common passion giving rise to a distributive movement able to displace the limits and terms within which the political constitution of the future is played out" (Terranova 2004, 156), noting that creation would begin "with intensities, variations of bodily powers that are expressed as fear and empathy, revulsion and attraction, sadness and joy" (157).

The important point about affect as a starting point for an ontogenetic politics of thinking processes is its transience and openness—which in turn account for its complexity and responsiveness. Put simply, affect is about the openness of the mix of the present. Affect is the movement of time as polyrhythm—and of course affect describes the main quality of connectedness within any kind of network. Affective relations, that is, come before discrete packets of information. "Sense"—including the sense of times, of presents—becomes first a matter of sensation, of the dynamic arrangements of the rhythms of bodies (taken in the broadest sense—that is, human bodies, microbes, celestial bodies, technical bodies, etc.). Likewise, code might first be a matter of shifting cuts and flows in relations between bodies—of sensations—before it becomes a matter of symbols (on both these ideas see Bogard 1998). In short, sense and sensation are reconfigured in favor of the latter. Andy Clark (forthcoming) has discussed this reconfiguring of sense and sensation with regard to "perceptual coupling" (an example is watching a ball as one moves to catch it), in which perception acts as an ongoing transformative relation of what we might call microaffective relation: "Instead of using sensing to get enough information inside, past the visual bottleneck, so as to allow the reasoning system to 'throw away the world' and solve the whole problem internally, it uses the sensor as an open conduit allowing environmental magnitudes to exert a constant influence on behaviour."

In this "open conduit" the model of the neat processing of discrete symbols and recognitions is countered by an "asignifying semiotic" (Bogard 2000). For Bogard (after Deleuze and Guattari) the important question is that of an "arepresentational content," even within symbols or signs. This is content that organizes "force relations, rather than . . . a linguistic or 'mental' structure" (Bogard 2000). The present is no longer a "concept." It is not symbolised or represented. It is—per Varela's mix of durations—a true assemblage of rhythms.

John Sutton sums up the problem for the traditional models of mind used within political analyses of media. This is precisely the problem of our ability to acknowledge the complexity and diversity of media-thought contexts (and therefore of different times). The challenge is to "acknowledge the diversity of feedback relations between objects and embodied brain" and not to "too easily neglect the sheer variety of the forms of media and exograms" (Sutton 2002, 138). This suggests that there might be many possible presents, with different "styles" of present made available via the many different media-thought contexts. A network—which could be defined as a series of connections between different media-thought contexts—provides, therefore, the sociotechnical context of many presents, even perhaps different presents that can be constituted at the one time.

Lag and Microtime as the Time of Network Politics

Here, finally, we can formulate how one might pursue effective analyses of time, networks, and new technologies by following William E. Connolly's insight into microtechniques. By "microtechniques" he means the technique involved in micropolitics. For Connolly, technique (often seen as a "dead" support) and thinking (often seen as the mark of life itself) are inseparable, although he does point to the difficulty we have in thinking this inseparability through. So microtechniques are at the heart of the ontogenesis of thought. Connolly (2002a, par. 2) suggests, for example, the "organized combinations of sound, gesture, word, movement and posture through which affectively imbued dispositions, desires and judgments become synthesized."

For Connolly the technique of micropolitics "saturates cultural life," and he opposes the investigation of micropolitics to disciplinary approaches (he mentions psychoanalysis, but any broad discipline based on metanarratives or even textualism, such as media policy approaches, might count here). For Connolly such approaches, dedicated to (Varela's upper level of) narrative and interpretation, resisted the dimension of technique (at Varela's two micro levels of the one-tenth-second and one-second scales).

Connolly goes on to write that one of the consequences of working at this narrative / interpretative level is that it undervalues "the profound significance of multimedia arts to political and ethical life" (2002a, par. 5). In fact, the attention given to narrative only "diverts attention from multi-media techniques that pull viewers into a story line they might otherwise resist" (ibid., par. 15), or researchers and critics into disciplinarities they might otherwise avoid. For Connolly, crucially, these techniques can operate below the threshold of consciousness and can "recode your sensibility," even "re-code the image of time" (ibid., pars. 20, 23). As Lefebvre points out, "codes function durably, more or less tacitly, more or less ritually; they rhythm time as they do relations" (Lefebvre 2004, 93).

So we can see the way in which a consideration of the "fallen present" raises an interesting set of cultural and political problems in relation to network technologies and cultures. These concern first the interference by technics with the very constitution of time. Second, they concern the ability to mix the levels of experience of time—micro and macro—into new forms of control, or new freedoms. The micropolitics and neuropolitics that take place "below" our sense of the present, or within its constitution, become crucial to network politics. It is perhaps at this micropolitical or neuropolitical level that a network politics of time has to be rethought. Technics, time, and thinking processes are intertwined. Only in their relational constitution do we understand not the world but our immersion in the world as an open network.

References

Baudrillard, Jean. 1988. *The ecstasy of communication.* Brooklyn, NY: Autonomedia.

Bogard, William. 1998. Sense and segmentarity: Some markers of a Deleuzian-Guattarian sociology. *Sociological theory* 16 (1): 52–74.

———. 2000. Distraction and digital culture. *CTheory* 23 (3): www.ctheory.net/articles.aspx?id=131 (accessed Jan. 25, 2007).

Clark, Andy. 2001. *Mindware: An introduction to the philosophy of cognitive science.* Oxford: Oxford University Press.

———. Forthcoming. Re-inventing ourselves: The plasticity of embodiment, sensing, and mind. *Journal of Medicine and Philosophy.*

Connolly, William E. 1999. Brain waves: Transcendental fields and techniques of thought. *Radical Philosophy* 94:19–28.

———. 2002a. Film technique and micropolitics. *Theory & Event* 6 (1): http://muse.jhu.edu/journals/theory_&_event/toc/archive.html#6.1.

———. 2002b. *Neuropolitics: Thinking, culture, and speed.* Minneapolis: University of Minnesota Press.

Cooper, Melinda. 2002. The living and the dead: Variations on de anima. *Angelaki* 7 (3): 81–104.

Davis, Erik. n.d. *Remixing the matrix: An interview with Paul D. Miller, aka DJ Spooky.* www.djspooky.com/articles/erikdavis.html (accessed Jan. 25, 2007).

Deleuze, Gilles. 1986. *Cinema 1: The movement-image.* Minneapolis: University of Minnesota Press.

———. 1989. *Cinema 2: The time-image.* Minneapolis: University of Minnesota Press.

Derrida, Jacques. 1978. *Writing and difference.* Trans. Alan Bass. Chicago: University of Chicago Press.

———. 1996. *Archive fever: A Freudian impression.* Trans. Eric Prenowitz. Chicago: University of Chicago Press.

Derrida, Jacques, and Bernard Stiegler. 2002. *Echographies of television.* Cambridge, MA: Polity.

Descombes, Vincent. 1980. *Modern French philosophy.* Cambridge, UK: Cambridge University Press.

Grosz, Elizabeth. 1999. Becoming . . . an introduction. In *Becomings: Explorations in time, memory, and futures,* ed. Elizabeth Grosz, 1–11. Ithaca, NY: Cornell University Press.

Guattari, Felix. 1996. Ritornellos and existential affects. In *The Guattari reader,* ed. Gary Genosko, 158–171. London: Blackwell.

Haines, David. 2005. Interview by author. Not published.

Lefebvre, Henri. 2004. *Rhythmanalysis: Space, time, and everyday life.* London: Continuum.

Libet, Benjamin. 2004. *Mind time: The temporal factor in consciousness.* New York: Harvard University Press.

Linke, Detlef. 2000. The rhythms of happiness. In *Machine times,* ed. Joke Brouwer, 29–43. Rotterdam: NAI.

Mackenzie, Adrian. 2002. *Transductions: Bodies and machines at speed.* London: Continuum.

Massumi, Brian. 2002. *Parables for the virtual: Movement, affect, sensation.* Durham, NC: Duke University Press.

———. 2004. Fear (the spectrum said). *Critique* 13 (1): 31–48.

Miller, Paul D. 2004. *Rhythm science.* Cambridge, MA: MIT Press.

Miller, Paul D. (a.k.a. DJ Spooky that Subliminal Kid). n.d. Notes for Paul D. Miller's "Rebirth of a Nation"—remix of D. W. Griffith's 1915 film "Birth of a Nation." www.djspooky.com/articles/rebirth.html (accessed Jan. 25, 2007).

Murphie, Andrew. 2003. Electronicas: Differential media and proliferating, transient worlds. *fineart forum* 17 (8): www.fineartforum.org/Backissues/Vol_17/faf_v17_n08/reviews/murphie.html (accessed Jan. 25, 2007).

———. 2005. Differential life, perception, and the nervous elements: Whitehead, Bergson, and Virno on the technics of living. *Culture Machine* (7): http://culturemachine.tees.ac.uk/Cmach/Backissues/j007/Articles/murphie.htm (accessed Jan. 25, 2007).

———. 2006. Figures of the brain, technology, and magic. In *Technologies of Magic: A cultural study of ghosts, machines and the uncanny,* ed. Edward Scheer and John Potts, 112–124. Sydney: Power.

Scannell, John. 2001. Renegade refrains: MP3 and the pursuit of affect. *Convergence: The Journal for Research into New Media Technologies* 7 (3): 62–82.

Seigworth, Gregory J. 2000. Banality for cultural studies. *Cultural Studies* 14 (2): 227–268.

Stiegler, Bernard. 2003a. Our ailing educational institutions. *Culture Machine* (5): http://culturemachine.tees.ac.uk/Cmach/Backissues/j005/Articles/Stiegler.htm (accessed Jan. 25, 2007).

————. 2003b. Technics of decision: An interview. *Angelaki* 8 (2): 151–168.

Sutton, John. 2002. Porous memory and the cognitive life of things. In *Prefiguring cyberculture: An intellectual history*, ed. Darren Tofts, Annemarie Jonson, and Alessio Cavallaro, 130–141. Cambridge, MA: MIT Press.

Terranova, Tiziana. 2004. *Network culture: Politics for the information age*. London: Pluto.

Van Gelder, Tim. 1999. Wooden iron? Husserlian phenomenology meets cognitive science. In *Naturalizing phenomenology: Issues in contemporary phenomenology and cognitive science*, ed. Jean Petitot, Francisco J. Varela, Bernard Pachoud, and Jean-Michel Roy, 245–265. Stanford, CA: Stanford University Press.

Varela, Francisco J. 1999. The specious present: A neurophenomenology of time consciousness. In *Naturalizing phenomenology: Issues in contemporary phenomenology and cognitive science*, ed. Jean Petitot, Francisco J. Varela, Bernard Pachoud, and Jean-Michel Roy, 266–314, 577–581. Stanford, CA: Stanford University Press.

Virilio, Paul. 1997. *Open sky*. London: Verso.

————. 2003. *Art and fear*. London: Continuum.

7 Stacking and Continuity

On Temporal Regimes in Popular Culture

Thomas Hylland Eriksen

THE FIRST REAL AMERICAN SOAP OPERA to hit the Scandinavian markets was *Dynasty*. It was introduced to a curious and excited audience in the same year that multichannel viewing appeared in the same countries, thanks to satellite and cable transmissions. The year was 1983, and like many thousands of others, my friends and I went into the kitchen and turned on our old black-and-white set on the first evening of *Dynasty* to find out what this was. After a few weeks we reckoned we had understood the basic message and ceased watching the program since we had other things to do (chiefly wearing black clothes while hanging in the bars of grim concert venues that had been redecorated to look like abandoned factories). The years went by. Six years later, I traveled to Trinidad to carry out ethnographic fieldwork. In Trinidad, it turned out, a considerable proportion of the population followed *Dynasty* (although other soap operas, particularly the lunchtime show *The Young and the Restless*, were even more popular). I rented a TV set and began to watch *Dynasty* again, since a golden rule of anthropology admonishes its practitioners on fieldwork to try to do whatever it is that the natives do.

I had been absent from the series for six years, and it took me about thirty seconds to get into the narrative again. Like other programs of the same kind, *Dynasty* was tailored for the multichannel format. It was being produced in the awareness that the viewers would restlessly finger their remote control while watching, ready to switch channels at the first indication of inertia. It presupposed commercial breaks every seventh minute or thereabouts, so the cliffhangers were overdone and frequent.

The cost of this breathless, accelerated kind of drama is a lack of progression. Like other serials of the same kind, *Dynasty* is a story that stands still at enormous speed. Instantaneous time precludes development. As late as the 1970s, most European countries had one, two, or a maximum of three national television channels. Many were state run and free of commercials. Until the early to mid-1970s, programming in black and white dominated the schedule in many countries. One of the most popular drama series at the time was *A Family at War*, written by John Finch. This fifty-two-episode series, which was a deadly serious narrative about an English family during the Second World War, was characteristically slow and cumulative. If one had missed just one episode, one lost the narrative thread, since the persons and their relationships changed as the story unfolded. It presupposed loyal, patient viewers who did not have to cope with competition from a plethora of noisy alternatives. In this way the series could be based on a rhythm in which particular events slowly reverberated through the cast, leaving their imprint on the future direction of the action. Whereas *Dynasty* was based on the explosive moment, *A Family at War* was based on linear time and organic growth.

I have chosen this example not because it is in itself particularly interesting but because it illustrates a fundamental change in our culture from the relatively slow and linear to the fast and momentary. This change is roughly the same as that which Urry (1999) refers to as glacial versus instantaneous time. Television has become over the past couple of decades an ever-faster medium, and the same change has taken place with radio, which generally seems to become more hectic and breathless the more channels one has to choose between. The relationship between the two TV series is further analogous to the relationship between the World Wide Web and the book. The book is sequential: you begin on the first page and read it in a sequential order. The writer controls the drift of the reading and is therefore at liberty to construct a cumulative, linear plot or argument. The reader reaches ever-new plateaus of knowledge or insight as she or he moves through the text. This, at any rate, is an ideal depiction of the art of reading.

There are several crucial differences between the Web and a library of paper publications. Above all, information on the Web is not really organized, be it alphabetically or in any other way. Different themes and pages are linked together in partly random ways. The Web is not hierarchical either, given that the millions of sites in existence are all accessible at the same level.

Active users of the WWW have for years intuited that it is a dense and cumbersome jungle that grows a little darker and denser every day. When one surfs the Web in search of information that seems not to be there (despite millions of hits on Google), it is tempting to conclude that the Web is a real-world incarnation of Jorge Luis Borges's philosophical fable about the library of Babel. This mythical library contained, apart from all books that had been written, all the books that could have been written—that is, every possible combination of the letters of the alphabet. Everything is available out there, but everything else is also available, and like almost everywhere else, Murphy's Law operates on the Web as well: under normal circumstances, one will find that everything else first. As a cultural sociologist expressed it: the Internet is like the large oceans. They are full of gold, but it costs a fortune to exploit even a tiny fraction of it. The Web is uncensored, democratic, and chaotic. Everything is already stacked on top of everything else there, but it still grows a little every day.

Filters against fragmentation do not remove fragmentation. The most important tool needed to navigate on the Web is neither a superfast computer with lots of RAM, a broadband connection, or the latest news in Web browsers (although all of this helps) but good filters. As mentioned several times already, there is no scarcity of information in the information society. There is far too much of it. With no opportunity to filter away that available information that one does not need, one is lost and will literally drown in zeros and ones.

Many are willing to help Web users to find their way, not least because it can pay off. Several of the greatest economic successes in cyberspace are companies that have specialized in Web searches. The oldest is Yahoo! The currently most popular is Google. It is sometimes said that the home pages of these search engines are the only Web pages that can rival the major pornographic sites for popularity. In their simplest form they function as digital indexes. If, for example, you want to map out the movements of saxophonist Didier Malherbe during the last few months, or you want to read about the current political developments in Kosovo, or you want to find out about the latest operating system from Apple, you type the keywords, and in a matter of seconds you get a list of links to relevant Web sites—usually a useless list containing thousands of links. Then you narrow the search to include, say,

"+ Apple + OSX + download," and soon you will have a manageable list of less than a hundred hits. You have reduced the universe to that microscopic segment you are interested in right now.

Searching with Google or a similar engine is not much more advanced than searching a digital phone book. New methods for filtering information are continuously being developed, however, whether the aim is to help frustrated Web surfers to protect themselves against unwanted information or to sell them goods. The methods used in the latter instance are often inventive and seductive. For a few years I have been greeted regularly by Amazon Web sites in the following way—like millions of other customers: "Hello Thomas! We have recommendations for you!" This greeting is followed by a few "hot titles" in subject areas that fall within my fields of interest (according to Amazon's software). Often, however, filters are less than functional. If you feel the world is not chaotic enough, I recommend an evening of reading with Yahoo's categories as a point of departure.

In the old days most of us tended to accept the information we were offered, whether it came from the daily newspaper or the radio news. Today the freedom of choice is unlimited. Via the Web one can listen to midwestern C&W channels, subscribe to specialized news services—say, one can refuse to take in distressing news about war, terrorism, and natural disasters; one can follow Malaysian weather or the Johannesburg stock exchange daily; or one can read everything about the latest productions from Hollywood and nothing else. These kinds of tailored services are available from several sources and in several formats (email, Web, cell phone). At Microsoft News one may choose one's personal categories from business and health to weather, sports, and travel; America Online has Web centers with material on everything from cars to research and local news. Other kinds of services include UnCover Real, which offers to email you the table of contents of your favorite journals regularly.

In a world where there is a surplus of unclassified information, there is a pressing need for this kind of filtering; it is also evident that if these kinds of filters (and greatly improved versions of them) become sufficiently widespread, there will eventually be little left of the national public spheres. There is, then, no guarantee that the neighbor has heard about the government's latest budget cuts or the most recent plane crash. It may even be that he or she was so busy following software developments at Apple that he or she is blissfully unaware of the perpetually tragic state of the national English football team. Unlike the good old media (such as newspapers and nationwide television channels), news on the Web is placeless and without clear priorities. Everything is in principle equally important as everything else, and besides, distance is bracketed, which entails that it is no more difficult to access the electronic edition of *The Hindu* than the corresponding edition of *The Independent*.

Since everything is available on the Web and there exist no fixed, socially shared routines for distinguishing between wanted and unwanted information, each individual is forced to develop her or his own paths, creating her or his own personal cuts of the world. (In software marketing jargon this is called customization.)

A telling image of the direction developments are taking is the currently popular system for digital storage of music, MP3 (which is about to be replaced by superior successor formats such as AAC). At the time of this writing, most people still buy music on CDs, which are a direct extension of the old vinyl LP. Like a printed book or newspaper, a CD is a finished, completed product with a beginning, a middle, and an end. One cannot cut and paste the content according to whim; even if one is mighty sick of the overexposed first movement in Beethoven's Fifth Symphony, one cannot replace it by an overture from one of Wagner's operas. One may like it or not, but that is how it is.

MP3 is a file format for compressed transmission of music. As is well known, there are both virtual players (for use on the computer) and physical players of the iPod variety, and there is a considerable amount of free music on the Web (much of it accessible via controversial and probably illegal file-sharing applications), which anyone can download. There are also paid services, the most popular being Apple's iTunes Music Store, and one may thus in principle buy, say, Beethoven's Fifth in MP3 format. What one then pays for is a password that allows a single download of the entire symphony (or, if one prefers, one or two movements of it). When one then has the symphony in MP3 format, one can finally evade that tiring first movement, or for that matter the sluggish second movement; one may edit the work just as one wants. Unlike a completed CD, an MP3 playlist contains only pieces that the listener has actively chosen, such as—say—a tune by Oasis, the second movement of Mahler's Fourth, the first movement of Bártok's Second String Quartet, two Beatles classics, and a live recording of Miles Davis with John Coltrane from 1959. Then one may copy the entire thing onto a portable MP3 player for use in the car or on the tube.

MP3 is a concrete example of the logic of the Web. In principle everything is available out there, and each individual user puts together his or her own personal totality out of the fragments. MP3 relates to the CD as the Web relates to the book. The Internet fits perfectly, and is also in at least two ways an important contributing cause, with the prevailing neoliberal ideology. The WWW (and multichannel television, and MP3, and "flexible work") offers freedom and choice by the bucket. On the deficit side of the balance, we have to note, among other things, internal cohesion, meaningful context, and slowness.

Fragments replace coherence. We are slowly moving toward the main point of this essay, and as a prelude I will add yet another facet in the description of the Internet. Marshall McLuhan (1994) once wrote about the difference between a haptic and an optic culture, a contrast that refers to varying usage of the senses under different regimes of information technology. Premodern people lived, according to McLuhan, in a "haptic harmony"—all senses were equal and functioned as a totality, a unity. The "auditive-tactile" senses (hearing and touch) were essential both for experience and for knowledge. With literacy the visual sense gained the upper hand and suppressed the others. (In Plato this has already come about; just think about his cave allegory!) Humans thus became increasingly inhibited and narrow-minded. Writing gave us "an eye for an ear," and to McLuhan this entails something of a fall from grace. To him the pure, linear text is a fragmenting and reductive medium that removes the reader from a total experience with the full use of all his or her senses. In television McLuhan saw an opportunity to recreate that sensory unity that the advent of writing had destroyed, and he had a great—some would say incomprehensible—optimism on behalf of this new medium when he wrote his most important books in the 1960s.

A decade and a half after his death, McLuhan was launched, by the California technology-and-lifestyle magazine *Wired*, as a patron saint for the Internet. Much of what he said in general about new media (especially television) fits the World Wide Web surprisingly well. As far as I am concerned, I agree with the main thrust of McLuhan's argument, but my conclusion is the exact opposite of his. It is not the book but television that functions in a fragmenting way. The book relates to the WWW as single-channel television relates to multichannel television, and linear time is a valuable resource that we cannot afford to waste. In this context it is tempting to propose a whole series of contrasts that may illustrate the transition from industrial to informational society, from nation-building to globalization, from book to monitor. Table 7.1 depicts the dimension of such changes as we have moved from an industrial to an information society.

The tidal waves of information fragments typical of our kind of society stimulate a style of thought that is less reminiscent of the strict, logical, linear thinking characteristic of industrial society than of the freely associating, poetical, metaphorical thinking that characterized many nonmodern societies. Instead of ordering knowledge in tidy rows, information society offers cascades of decontextualized signs more or less randomly connected to each other.

The cause of this change is neither the introduction of the World Wide Web nor multichannel television as such. It is instead the fact that there is rapid growth in every area to do with information but no more time than formerly available to digest it (see Eriksen 2001 for a full analysis). Contemporary culture moves at full speed without moving an inch. Put differently: the close cousins of acceleration and exponential growth lead to vertical stacking. Since the flanks are reserved for small groups with special interests (e.g., progressive rock, theoretical physics, veteran buses, social anthropological method, Greek poetry), more and more of each special interest is stacked on top of others in the middle. Translated from the spatial metaphor to the temporal dimension, this means that since there is no vacant time to spread information in, it is compressed and stacked in time spans that become shorter and shorter. High-rise buildings appear in the center, sprawling bungalows in the suburbs.

TABLE 7.1 Dimensions of the Change from an Industrial to an Informational Society

Industrial Society	Informational Society
CD/vinyl record	MP3
Book	WWW
Single-channel TV	Multichannel TV
Letter	Email
Stationary telephone	Mobile telephone
Lifelong monogamy	Serial monogamy
The era of the gold watch	The era of flexible work
Depth	Breadth
Linear time	Fragmented
Scarcity of information	Scarcity of freedom from

The logic that characterizes *Dynasty* and similar multichannel, commercial-financed television series is the same as that which entails that the most competitive news programs are shorter than the others, that commercials become shorter and shorter—and, yes, I will offer more examples eventually.

The concept of vertical stacking is taken from a book that deals with—of all things—progressive rock, a musical genre that was particularly popular among long-haired and great-coated boys and men in the first half of the 1970s, which was forced more or less underground when punk not only made the dominant youth culture jeer dismissively at anyone daring to go onstage with stacks of synthesizers but also made it a virtue not to be able to play an instrument properly. Like everything else, progressive rock was reawakened by Internet-based retro waves in the second half of the 1990s—sometimes, it must be conceded, with disastrous results. The North American philosophy professor Bill Martin (1997) has tried, in his broad defense plea for rock groups he admires (including Yes, Rush, and King Crimson), to explain what, to his mind, is wrong with the computer- and studio-based dance music of the last decade, including house, techno, drum 'n' bass, and other genres that have little in common apart from the fact that they can be described as varieties of nonlinear, repetitive, rhythmical dance music. This is music that in Martin's view lacks progression and direction, music that—unlike, say, Beethoven, Miles Davis, and Led Zeppelin—is not heading anywhere. Enjoyment of such music is generally undertaken by entering a room full of sound where a great number of aural things are happening, and staying there until it no longer feels cool, like. Martin's preferred music is linear and has an inner development—although it may often be partly improvised. About the new rhythmic music, he has this to say:

> As with postmodern architecture, the idea in this stacking is that, in principle, any sound can go with any other sound. Just as, however, even the most eclectic pastiche of a building must all the same have some sort of foundation that anchors it to the ground, vertically stacked music often depends on an insisting beat. There are layers of trance stacked on top of dance, often without much in the way of stylistic integration. (Martin 1997, 290)

Martin doubts that this music will be capable of creating anything really new. "The vertical-stacking approach implicitly (or even explicitly) accepts the idea that music (or art more generally) is now simply a matter of trying out the combinations, filling out the grid" (ibid., 291). I will not invest my personal friendships with trance adepts in support for this argument, but inadvertently, Martin offers an excellent description of an aspect of the tyranny of the moment: There are layers upon layers on top of each other, every vacant spot is filled, and there is little by way of internal integration. Stacking replaces internal development.

The exceptionally gifted musician and composer Brian Eno is both godfather and pioneer in much of the new rhythmic music. Already in the 1970s he had developed the musical concept "Ambient," that is, nonlinear music that could function as an aural wallpaper but that was also intended to be "as listenable as it was ignorable," as the liner notes of *Music for Airports* put it.

Few know the field of rhythmic music better than Eno. In 1995 he kept a diary, and he published it (presumably an edited version) the following year (Eno 1996). On September 8, 1996, he made a sketch of the "phases" of popular music since the breakthrough of rock 'n' roll. He proposes ten phases plus an eleventh one, which he locates to the near future. What is interesting in our context is Eno's category number 10, that is the period 1991–1995, up to the time of writing. Whereas the other eras have labels such as "synth pop, 4th world" or "Glam," he characterizes the 1990s like this: "See '64–'68, add '76–'78." In other words nothing new, just rehashes of former trends. As a moderately interested bystander, my distinct impression tends to confirm Eno's view: for several years now we seem to have everything at once. Every imaginable retro trend exists, at the same time as the big names of bygone eras remain big today, or—as in the case of the Welsh crooner Tom Jones—are being reawakened by nostalgics. Apart from nonlinear, repetitive dance music, the 1990s saw major breakthroughs of pop groups that sounded roughly like the Beatles, heavy metal groups that took up the challenge where Deep Purple and Led Zeppelin left it in the mid-1970s, "neo-psychedelic" bands that sound vaguely like the Soft Machine of 1968 or the Pink Floyd of 1967—and at the same time, the really big names remain artists like Dylan, the Stones, and Santana, who have been around for forty years.

Just as progressive politics is fueled by a linear faith in progress—a strong, moral idea of development—progressive rock (and many other kinds of music) had an inbuilt faith in progress. The musicians wanted to take their kind of music to new heights, break with the past, create something new and better. Martin discusses the difference between this concept and the new nonlinear music as an instance of the modern / postmodern contrast, which is unfortunate, as modernist contemporary music has been nonlinear for nearly a hundred years.

There are two general points emerging from this idiosyncratic (and far from representative) discussion of trends in popular music that may be linked directly to the issues at hand. First, stacking of trends implies that there is no change but mere recirculation. Rock and pop may be surface phenomena, but they are also barometers. When Beatles clones like Oasis, geriatric groups like the Stones, and chubby crooners of the generic Phil Collins type (who would have believed, in 1975, that this man—at his best he played the drums like an octopus on speed—would turn into Elton John?) are the undisputed masters of the field, this may be symptomatic of a culture unable to renew itself. As Martin (1997) expresses it: no real creativity but a continuous stream of new combinations. As a general point, the filling of gaps characteristic of what I have elsewhere (Eriksen 2001) spoken of as the tyranny of the moment is seriously detrimental to creativity. The new arises unexpectedly from the gaps created by slack in time budgets, not from crowded schedules.

Second, the rock or jazz listener's situation is radically different from that of the listener who opts for the new rhythmic music. The latter's music goes on and on; the former's has a beginning, a long middle (internal development), and an end or climax. Interestingly, Indonesian gamelan music has been a significant source of inspiration to many of those who work with repetitive music, among them the minimalist composer Steve Reich. This is music developed in a traditional, ritualistic culture with no linear concept of development. The link with gamelan music is far from uninteresting, considering McLuhan's (and my own) view to the effect that an essentially nonlinear way of being in time is being strengthened in contemporary culture.

To readers whose relationship to gamelan music, minimalism, trip-hop, and progressive rock is relaxed and perhaps even indifferent, this discussion may seem a bit esoteric. But there is more to say about the matter before we leave it entirely. Somewhere in his enormous work about the information age, Manuel Castells (1996, 1998) has chosen to include a paragraph about new age music. He regards it as the classical music of our era (a debatable assertion, but all right) and describes it as an expression for "the double reference to moment and eternity; me and the universe, the self and the net" (Castells 1996, 308). Desert winds and ocean waves create the backdrop for many of the repetitive patterns that make up new age music. It is a droning, timeless, and lingering kind of music, an antidote to the quotidian rat race but also perfectly symmetrical to it, since it brackets the passage of time.

Put differently: when growing amounts of information are distributed at growing speed, it becomes increasingly difficult to create narratives, orders, developmental sequences. The fragments threaten to become hegemonic. This has consequences for the ways we relate to knowledge, work, and life-style in a wide sense. Cause and effect, internal organic growth, maturity and experience—such categories are under heavy pressure in this situation. The examples from music, which are clearly debatable (many of us have our pas-sions here, don't we?), are chiefly meant as illustrations. The phenomenon as such is naturally much more widespread, and journalism, education, work, politics, and domestic life—just to mention a few areas—are affected by ver-tical stacking. Let us take a look at journalism first.

The law of diminishing returns strikes with a vengeance. In a profoundly pessimistic and critical pamphlet about the misery of television, Pierre Bourdieu (1996) develops a familiar but far from unimportant argument. He claims that the fragmented temporality of television, with its swift tran-sitions and fast-paced journalism, creates an intellectual public culture that favors a particular kind of participant. Bourdieu speaks of these participants as fast-thinkers. Whereas the Belgian cartoon hero Lucky Luke is famous for drawing his gun faster than his own shadow, fast-thinkers are described as "thinkers who think faster than an accelerating bullet" (Bourdieu 1996, 29). They are the people who are able, in a couple of minutes of direct transmis-sion, to explain what is wrong with the economic policies of the EU, why one ought to read Kant's *Critique of Pure Reason* this summer, or how racist pseu-doscience originated. It is nonetheless a fact that some of the sharpest minds need time to reflect and more time (much more, in some cases) to make an accurate, sufficiently nuanced statement on a particular issue. This kind of thinker becomes invisible and virtually deprived of influence, according to Bourdieu, in this rushed era. (In a banal sense Bourdieu is obviously wrong. No contemporary thinker was, until his death in 2002, more influential than Bourdieu himself, and clearly he did not regard himself as a fast-thinker.)

Bourdieu's argument is congruent with the observation that media appeal has become the most important capital of politicians—not, in other words, their political message or cohesive vision. This is not an entirely new phe-nomenon; in the United States the first indication of this development came with John F. Kennedy's victory over Richard M. Nixon. Anyway, a result, in Bourdieu's view, is that the people who speak like machine guns, in boldface and capital letters, are the ones who are given airplay and acquire influence—not the slow and systematic ones.

What is wrong with this? Why should people who have the gift of being able to think fast and accurately be stigmatized in this way? In a word, what is wrong about thinking fast? Nothing in particular, apart from the fact that some thoughts only function in a slow mode and that some lines of reasoning can only be developed in a continuous fashion, without the interruptions of an impatient journalist who wants to "move on" (where?) in the program. Bourdieu mentions an example with which many academics will be able to identify. In 1989 Bourdieu published *La noblesse de l'etat* (The State Nobility), a study of symbolic power and elite formation in the French education system. Bourdieu had been actively interested in the field for twenty years, and the book had been long in the making. A journalist proposed a debate between Bourdieu and the president of the alumni organization of les grandes écoles; the latter would speak "for," and Bourdieu would speak "against." "And," he sums up sourly, "he hadn't a clue as to why I refused."

A topic Bourdieu does not treat explicitly, but which is an evident corollary of his views, is the diminishing returns of media participation following the information explosion. Before the 1990s, if one was invited to contribute to a radio or television program, one appeared well-prepared in the studio. One might shave (even if the medium was radio!), make certain to wear a freshly ironed shirt and a proper tie, and enter the studio in a slightly nervous state, determined to make one's points clearly and concisely. Nowadays, an increasing number of people in the know do not even bother to take part in radio or television transmissions, and if they do, their contributions frequently tend toward the halfhearted and lukewarm. As both viewers and guests on TV shows are aware, each program has a diminishing impact as the number of channels grows, and the higher the number of channels and talk shows, the less impact each of them exerts. It is almost as if Andy Warhol was deliberately understating his point when, directly influenced by McLuhan, he said that in "the future," everybody would be famous for fifteen minutes. (Today, he might have said seconds.)

A related effect of stacking and acceleration in the media world is the tendency that news is becoming shorter and shorter. A tired joke about the competition for attention among tabloids consists in the remark that when war eventually breaks out for real, the papers will only have space for the "W" on the front page. The joke illustrates the principle of diminishing returns (or falling marginal value). In basic economics courses, teachers tend to use food and drink as examples to explain this principle, which is invaluable in an accelerating culture: If you are thirsty, the first soda has very high value for you. The second one is also quite valuable, and you may even—if your thirst is very considerable—be willing to pay for the third one. But then, the many soda cans left in the shop suddenly have no value at all to you; you are unwilling to pay a penny for any of them. Tender steaks, further, are highly valuable if you are allowed to savor them only once a month; when steak becomes daily fare, its value decreases dramatically. The marginal value of a commodity is defined as the value of the last unit one is willing to spend money or time and attention on. Although this principle cannot be applied to everything we do (a lot of activities, such as saxophone playing, become more rewarding the more one carries on), it can offer important insights into the situation Bourdieu describes—how news, and more generally information, is being produced and consumed. In this regard it is easy to see that stronger effects are needed eventually, because the public becomes accustomed to speed and explosive forms of communication.

At the same time—and what is more important here—the people who actually produce news and other kinds of information, the journalists that is, experience the increasing crowdedness of their field. Readers, listeners, and viewers have less and less time to spare for each information snippet. Thus, editors working in every kind of press (from Web and WAP to paper) cut more and more. As an occasional contributor to the press and sometime interviewee, I have never heard an editor complain that particular pieces of journalism are too short. (One may, naturally, daydream about such a scenario: "Look, this interview that you have done, isn't it a bit on the short side? I mean, didn't he say other things as well? He comes through as a man of bombast and one-liners; wouldn't it be better to allow the nuances in his position to come through, in order to avoid his being misunderstood, and then we'll also avoid a stupid and irrelevant controversy in the paper afterwards. Will you give me another hundred lines before lunch tomorrow?")

News on WAP, at the time of this writing the latest vogue in accelerated journalism, offers stories of a length that make *The Mirror* look like Proust. As a compensation they can be updated every thirty minutes. To those of us who are not yet accustomed to this speed and brevity, this kind of journalism is like a persistent insect buzzing around the ear as we try to go to sleep. (Cell phone news = the mosquito problem in equatorial Africa.) Yet there is a marked tendency for such strategies to win, for reasons I have already elaborated. The marginal value of information falls dramatically after a certain amount of images or words; it is pretty high during the first ten seconds, but then what?

The most common objection to this line of reasoning is that slowness seems to enjoy a renaissance in the media, at least in some European countries. For example, dedicated radio channels play classical music twenty-four hours a day, and there is a "perceived need" (the pundits claim) for thorough, decent reasoning and solid journalism providing background information. This may well be the case in the world as it appears from Islington but hardly from Fleet Street. Broadsheets decline, and tabloids (which look more and more like printed television) increase. The people enjoying the "slowness renaissance" can be counted in tenths of percents, and on this scale there may be slight increases here and there; fastness is enjoyed by groups better measured in scores of percents. In Norway a radio program that allowed academics to read thirty-minute talks, called the *P2 Academy*, has been on the air for more than five years, and it covers black holes, juvenile delinquency, the concept of culture, and similar issues authoritatively and well.

The listeners love it. Both of them.

Information lint destroys continuity. Fast thinkers are favored, and the slow thinkers sulk, in some cases reacting through essays like Bourdieu's. He is far from alone; his attack on contemporary journalism stands in a proud lineage of socialist and conservative intellectuals decrying the vulgarity of mass-produced information. This tradition may have begun with Tocqueville's assault on the pragmatic, democratic, and superficial North American settler culture (although, if one reads him closely, Plato had something to say on the matter as well), but it reached its zenith with the Frankfurt School of the interwar years—Marcuse, Horkheimer, and, especially, Adorno. German Jews in the 1930s certainly had their own reasons for pessimism. This does not mean that they were necessarily wrong. When Neil Postman writes that today's students no longer use the word *because* in their exam papers, he points toward the same problem that Bourdieu discusses, which is further illustrated in Table 7.1 above. Coherence and causality slip away when restlessness, flickering gazes, and striking one-liners rule the roost. In his memoir Johan Galtung—otherwise a relentless optimist—writes this about his experiences with students in the 1990s: "And far too many suffer from chronic image flicker, a synchronic experience of reality as images rich in details, not as lines across time, causal chains, reasoning. One needs both, but the way it is today, the ability to think is slowly killed, to the advantage of the ability to see and hear, taste and feel—an orgy of the senses that gives little space for intellectuality" (Galtung 1999, 205, my translation).

In a recent report about the state of higher education in Norway the committee of authors has included a passage about "those students who choose to study full-time." As if studying was not primarily a full-time activity! As a matter of fact, most teachers at the university or polytechnic level in Europe have experienced a gradual change since the 1970s. The cost of living and consumption expectations have gone up, and most students are obliged to take wage work. Formerly, students worked primarily during vacations, eventually weekend and evening work became more common, and presently it is my impression that work and studies are best seen as a seamless whole where it is difficult to tell which activity is deemed the most important. In recent years I have had increasing problems arranging supervision meetings with postgraduate students because they have problems getting away from work. Studying is no longer simply what one does but an entry on the total menu of experiences that composes the life of a young, urban, and unattached person. This result is not, naturally, the students' fault. Like all of us, they are victims of vertical stacking. The range of activities that compete with studying grows every semester. There is always something urgent that needs to be done first, before one sits down with *The Phenomenology of Spirit* for six months or so. As every good academic knows, thorough learning of a complex curriculum requires long, continuous periods of concentration. Insomnia and anxiety. Reduced appetite for sustained periods. Problems in one's love life. Absent-mindedness and aloofness from contemporary matters. (And in the old days, we would have added: Lots of black coffee and tobacco.) This kind of student is still around, but the great majority is of a different kind. When they appear in the lecture room, they are on their way from one place to another; they have a wide spectrum of activities to fill their days with, from clubbing to wage work, television zapping, Web surfing, and being with friends. If they want to be abreast with their surroundings and strengthen their career opportunities, they simply cannot disengage themselves for years of a slow, monastery-like existence. In the labor market attractive applicants have cvs that indicate diverse experience and high speed.

This new situation in academia—the falling marginal value of slowly acquired knowledge—also entails that it can no longer be taken for granted that the most brilliant students will be interested in pursuing a career in research and teaching. Universities may either adapt themselves to the market (which is largely what is happening all over the Western world) and speed up their teaching, or they may redefine themselves as countercultural institutions that embody slowness, thoroughness, and afterthoughts.

The students' situation is comparable to my own, although my research time is not chopped up into useless fragments because of a pressing need for external wage work, cinema and concert attendance, evenings on the town, and so on but because of the prevalence of information lint. This includes tasks like replying to email, taking the phone, filing, responding to letters, booking flights, reading half-baked reports and other kinds of bureaucratic documents, and so on. Before one is finally able to sit down with something that might make a difference, there is always something else that needs to be done first. What is given priority in a situation where one has many tasks waiting to be done is either the first task that comes to mind or that which simply cannot wait. Not surprisingly, quite a few academics plan major works that never get beyond the drawing board. Academic books increasingly look like cut-and-paste collages with snippets of conference papers here and excerpts of journal articles there. We always have five minutes to spare for a given task, often even half an hour, but never five years. Since the growth in information is much, much faster than the population growth, there is inevitably more to relate to for each of us (in particular, those of us who are positioned as information switchboards). The marginal value of new information is nearly zero, and it is therefore easier to attract a crumb of attention if one wraps the information in packages of ever-decreasing size. Little packages that are stacked on top of each other to create wavering, thin towers that are soon tall enough to touch the moon.

The nimble stacking of blocks of decreasing size is a craft that spreads in many directions. Rhythmic dance music, the World Wide Web, multichannel television, journalism, studies, and research are some of the examples that have been mentioned here. One can increasingly combine the blocks according to whim (this is why techno music is such a telling example). This process can only be quantified and "proved" to some extent; its results can only be experienced. More and more of every kind of information is stacked, like gigantic Lego towers where the bricks have nothing in common but the fact that they fit (but they also fit with any other brick). It is not because of the phenomenal global success of Nescafé's main product that the term *instant* is a key concept for an attempt to understand the present age. The moment, or instant, is ephemeral, superficial, and intense. When the moment (or even the next moment) dominates our being in time, we no longer have space for building blocks that can only be used for one or a few configurations with other blocks. Everything must be interchangeable with everything else. The entry ticket has to be cheap, the initial investment modest. Swift changes and unlimited flexibility are main assets. In the last instance everything that is left is a single, overfilled, compressed, eternal moment. Supposing this point is reached sometime in the future, and both past and future are fully erased, we would definitely have reached an absolute limit. To paraphrase Paul Virilio: there would be no delays anymore (see, e.g., Virilio 1996). It is difficult to imagine this happening—there are many universal human experiences that only make sense qua duration. In several fields, however, the tendency toward extreme compression of time is evident, as witnessed in the realms of consumption, work, and the very formation of personal identity. A result is stacking, and stacking is the enemy of logic and coherence.

References

Bourdieu, Pierre. 1989. *La noblesse de l'etat: Grandes écoles et esprit de corps.* Paris: Minuit.

———. 1996. *Sur la télévision: Suivi de l'emprise du journalisme.* Paris: Liber.

Castells, Manuel. 1996. *The rise of the network society.* Vol. 1 of *The information age: Economy, society, and culture.* Oxford: Blackwell.

———. 1998. *End of millennium.* Vol. 3 of *The information age: Economy, society, and culture.* Oxford: Blackwell.

Eno, Brian. 1996. *A year, with swollen appendices.* London: Faber.

Eriksen, Thomas Hylland. 2001. *Tyranny of the moment: Fast and slow time in the information age.* London: Pluto.

Galtung, Johan. 1999. *Johan uten land* [Johan with no land]. Oslo: Aschehoug.

Martin, Bill. 1997. *Listening to the future: The age of progressive rock, 1968–1978.* Chicago: Feedback.

McLuhan, Marshall. 1994. *Understanding media.* London: Routledge. Orig. pub. 1964.

Urry, John. 1999. *Sociology beyond societies: Mobilities for the twenty-first century.* London: Routledge.

Virilio, Paul. 1996. *Cybermonde: La politique du pire.* Paris: Textuel.

3 TEMPORAL PRESENCE

8   Indifference of the Networked Presence

On Time Management of the Self

Geert Lovink

F ROM AN INTERNET PERSPECTIVE it is a banality to complain about the danger of a "global time regime." The Internet is here to stay; understanding its architecture is necessary if we are to make it serve us rather than enslave us. Paul Virilio was right when he said that we no longer live in local time as we did in the past, when we were prisoners of history. We now live in the age of global time. We are experiencing an epoch, which for Virilio, is equivalent to a global accident: "[T]his is the way I interpret simultaneity and its imposition upon us, as well as the immediacy and the ubiquity, that is, the omnipresence of the information bomb, which, at the moment, thanks to the information (super)highways and all the technological breakthroughs and developments in the field of telecommunication, is just about to explode"(Virilio 1996).

Doug Kellner (1998) provides a concise summary of Virilio's thesis on time and the Internet. Cyberspace, Virilio claims, supplies another space without the usual space-time coordinates. This space is disorienting and a disembodying form of experience in which communication and interaction take place instantaneously in a new global time, overcoming boundaries of time and space. As a disembodied space with no fixed coordinates, cyberspace diminishes any sensation of anchoring in one's body, nature, and social community. For Virilio cyberspace is a "dematerialized and abstract realm in which cybernauts can become lost in space and divorced from their bodies and social world" (Kellner 1998). Virilio's social criticism of the network society rarely refers, however, to computer networks or the Internet in particular, let alone to browsers, instant messaging, games, search engines, Voice over Internet Protocol (VoIP), or blogging. Critics from Virilio to Žižek have locked themselves up in a general jargon of 1990s metaphors such as "cyberspace," "the information highway," and "disembodiment," terms that are first and foremost related to the offline "virtual reality" discourse. It is in my opinion exactly because of these mythological terms that we have inherited an apocalyptic mood while reading contemporary theory. Instead of countering skeptical thought with similarly uninformed techno-optimism, I propose to look into the time regimes under which today's Internet users are actually operating.

Going Nowhere Fast: Lost Presence

Instead of focusing on tracing upward or downward trends, it makes sense to practice the art of going nowhere. We all make experiences of getting lost amidst all the open windows and applications on our computer screens, search queries that lead nowhere, emails of friends that got stuck in spam filters, the dead links to closed-down Web sites and disappeared blogs. Instead of conservative complaints about the downfall of civilization because of new media, psychogeography teaches us how to morph lost time into an endless source of imagination and subversion. Let us look into the case of Timi, a self-proclaimed Internet junkie who wrote me about her recent online experiences:

> I enjoy spending time on the Net. From emailing to researching, to playing or just plain googling. I like hanging around in this virtual world. I often miss it, and in the past few years, I couldn't pry myself away from it. First thing I do in the morning is go online. The last thing I do before going to bed is go offline. I've never really devoted too much analysis about my own Internet time, though. (Alcala 2005)

This is what German media theorist Wolfgang Hagen (2003, 11) describes as "Gegenwartsvergessenheit," forgetting the presence, or "topical amnesty," as he also calls it. Time and again media make themselves invisible. Despite free software and open source, the computer experience provokes "blind tactics." We get lost in a technical environment characterized by highly precise transmissions of choices.

But let us go back to Timi:

I'm basically always online. At home, the TV might be on, or I might be cooking, but I remain online. Whether I'm studying or on vacation, time on the Internet is vital for me. I find it difficult not to be online. My Internet time is now so intertwined in my daily life that when my husband and I moved to a new house and were disconnected from the Net, I personally felt "lost" and disconnected from the world. Distress and panic come close to the feeling. Impatience too, and a great curiosity about who had tried to contact me. (Alcala 2005)

What lacks here, Hagen (2003) would say, is "living presence" (lebendige Gegenwart).

What most critics cannot comprehend is the media indifference of today's users. They classify individuals into two categories: users are either complicit or victims—even those that work for the system are in fact also victims. Against this image of the Machine that overwhelms its subjects I propose the "calculating citizen" who builds a harness around his or her daily life in order to cope with the ever-growing demands of society to perform, participate, and communicate. The resource in this context is not money but time (and, as we all know, time is money). What is "calculated" here is the time spent with a certain media device or devices, as particularly women are experts in multitasking numerous channels simultaneously such as phones, text messages, and email, while also minding children, and so on. Getting lost in the media sphere does not stand in opposition to strict time management. It is sometimes a luxury to get lost, and the data dandies who can freely stroll around the Net are the ideal citizen-prosumers.

Time Shifters

No matter how sexy or horrible we judge time management, there is no simple synthesis of the "local" with the "global." Nowhere do we get a better picture of how workers struggle with different time zones than in the IT-outsourcing industry. Rachel Konrad (2005) reports about a Silicon Valley company that collaborates with partners in India. At the end of the working day in California,

managers move into a conference room to dial India, where engineers 12½ time zones ahead are just arriving in Hyderabad. As colleagues on opposite sides of the globe discuss circuit board configurations and debugging strategies for a project code-named "Doppelganger," it's just the start of another endless day for the company. Within twelve hours, Indian workers will end their day with calls and e-mails to California, where managers in the Santa Clara headquarters will just be waking up. "We keep passing the baton between California and India, and that way we can cram a lot more work into a 24-hour period," said Jeff Hawkey, vice president of hardware engineering, who conducts evening meetings from the office or on his laptop at home. "A lot of nights, I go home, tuck the kids into bed and then get on the conference call."

Take Bombay-based consulting powerhouse Tata Consultancy Services, which employs forty-two thousand employees worldwide, including fourteen thousand people in India who handle U.S. projects. Their shifts are from 7 a.m. to 3 p.m., or 2 p.m. to 10 p.m. local time, not including frequent early or late meetings with overseas clients. The human cost of the fifty-plus hours a week is becoming apparent. "'It's one thing to do it for a couple weeks, but it's another to put up with this pain in the neck permanently,'" Konrad is told. "'When executives talk about the efficiencies of offshoring, they're often not factoring in the long-term human toll on management'" (Konrad 2005).

Several years back I published an online polemic against Swiss watch company Swatch's intention to launch its own Internet Time standard (Lovink 2002). Ignoring the developers' community, and Internet users in general, this funky business tried to push through a proprietary time standard and failed miserably. Swatch Time is still around, and even has been installed by a number of Web sites, but it was not endorsed by hackers or early adopters.[1] Most users wouldn't even know it exists. Whereas blogs have bizarre collections of banners and additional functionalities on the left and the right columns, the Swatch Time applet is curiously missing. Rightly so. What is needed is not a Global Standard Time, a "One Time," but rather an enhanced global-time awareness. Are you aware if people in Brazil are still asleep right now, are having breakfast, or are out because it is evening in São Paolo? It is this knowledge that counts if you are participating in online collaborations. A growing number of sites are now announcing their local time, which is extremely useful if you collaborate with a large variety of people dispersed over the planet.[2]

Complaints about "global time" often come from theorists who fail to distinguish between radio and television on the one side, and the Internet on the other. The "real-time" regime that they refer to is actually live global television events that use satellite uplinks.[3] Strictly speaking we have already left the real-time era when BBC News announced that it installed "delay" technology in order to monitor incoming live feeds. From now on "live" television can be controlled without viewers being aware of it. This move happened in response to the uncensored broadcasting of the bloody Beslan school siege in Russia by Chechen fighters in 2004.

Media philosophy professor Sybille Krämer, who recently ran a marathon, told me, "If you're not jogging, you lack time; if you exercise, you do have time." Obviously our experience of time is subjective, while objective time measurement is a mere convention. Mastering techniques that allow one to experience the sense of having "more" time is linked to the quality of life. What I have witnessed over the course of ten to fifteen years of online experience is not time shortage, however, but "time indifference." Most users complain about the computer "eating up" time instead of empowering them to arrange their lives freely. Colleagues that I know typically spend up to five hours "responding to their emails" and then wonder what they have really accomplished. The gnawing feeling of wasting time on what seems to be nonessential or low-payoff tasks is now pervasive. But there are solutions for this most modern feeling of discomfort. The better we understand the architecture of certain media, its interfaces and programs, the less time we have to spend struggling with it. But there are many obstacles to overcome. For example, one problem is that of security threats. Many companies force users to frequently upgrade their software. If this high circulation did not occur, chances would be much more likely that users would drift off or "get lost" in a much more conscious manner. Now, we're constantly interrupted by messages that warn us to download the latest antivirus definition and software patches.

The time spent interacting with media needs to be understood in terms of three distinctively different activities. The first involves the time needed to configure the machine; to install, learn, and operate the software; and to become familiar with the tools for navigation. Second is the time that is spent with certain application-related content such as blogs, email, SMS, and iPods. Only after we have downloaded all the mails, checked intranets and blogs, do we enter the third time—the flat, eternal time of pure communication—be it with humans or machines. Technoilliterate intellectuals have little knowledge about the difference between the metainstruction of the machine and the flows of interaction, once the connection or application is up and running. The "calculating citizen" has an efficient handling of the first time activity and subsequently a rather abundant capacity to engage in the latter.[4] Indeed, it is a pleasure once we can drift off and leave the world of necessities behind to enter the sphere of floating data.

In the "attention economy" value is measured in the amount of time you spend with a certain media object or person. This can be a Web site, watching your favorite show on TV, text-messaging a friend, talking to someone on the phone, or blogging about the concert you attended last night. For a long time the attention economy remained a hyped-up concept, launched during the speculative 1990s to point up the shift from the production of tangible goods to "immaterial" services. What makes attention such an interesting commodity is the fact that it is scarce. As Michael Goldhaber (1996) writes: "Attention is scarce because each of us has only so much of it to give, and it can come only from us—not machines, computers or anywhere else." Attention is another way of saying "time," as in "where I choose to spend my time."

That was more than ten years ago, however. Attempts are now underway to lay the foundation for an actual Web-based attention economy. This is happening as one of numerous initiatives in the "web 2.0"/blogosphere realm. The "attention technology" builds on recent experiences with XML, RSS-feeds, del.icio.us, furl archives (link collections that people share publicly), and so forth. The next development is that users can make the information about the time they visited a site available to others. Because of serious and systematic abuses of privacy by governments and corporations, users have been reluctant to share data related to their surfing behavior. The attention economy heats up once users start "trading" this type of information and sell the metadata of their surf behavior to interested parties. Social Internet entrepreneurs recently set up a nonprofit foundation, the Attention Trust, which will set standards and limits regarding what companies can and cannot do with the collected "attention data."[5] Without trust and transparency the attention economy, no matter how cool and geeky it might look, will not take off. The foundation has also developed its own "attention recorder," built in a browser to capture the click stream of the user.

Whereas the Internet as an information environment elicits observations of timelessness and is perceived as a vast space of never-ending databases and linked sites, most of its users remain locked up in the small tragedies of their everyday lives. Trading data on how many second visitors visit a particular Web page only shows how low we have sunk in terms of the exploration of micro time-related activities. Actually measuring and collecting data on attention as the new currency of the information / time economy may be interesting to gather from a select group of youth, high-end users, and professional knowledge workers, but for the most part it would likely show how little time average users can spend on the Internet. The discrepancy between colossal libraries and the limits of the short-lived individual must have existed throughout time. Even in ancient times scholars must have faced time shortage and information overload. What makes the current data excess so pertinent is the intimacy and everlasting accessibility of such picoknowledge.

Japanese-American venture capitalist and Internet guru Joi Ito wisely keeps sensitive information about his financial deals outside of his blog. Nonetheless, it is relatively easy to trace how he integrates real-world travel (in his case Japan-U.S.-Europe) with his online presence. It is interesting to note how Ito became bored with his hugely successful blog. In the latter half of 2005 Ito became involved in World of Warcraft, a massively multiplayer online role-playing game. In the following blog entry Ito describes how he juggles different media such as PC and cell phone: "I'm sitting in a car on the way home from the airport after arriving in Japan from New York. I had a 14 hour plane trip where I caught up on email and wrote some reports. As it has been noted, the frequency of my posts (as well as the number of blogs I read) has decreased significantly since I started playing World of Warcraft. Originally I was attributing this entirely to the addictive nature of WoW, but I'm wondering if I'm also slightly bored." Ito admits to being an early adopter type: "Reflecting back on my personal early days of blogging, there was something nifty and cool coming out every week. Blogrolls, facerolls, Technorati, etc. My traffic was growing, blogs were becoming global, and it was all new . . . at least to me" (Ito 2005).

Joi Ito describes in detail how applications and platforms are being consumed through the investment of time. But no matter how powerful these "killer apps" are, the nervous innovator has to move on, leaving behind one data ruin after the other. After having abolished email and home pages, it is now time to turn away from blogs.

Ito (2005) goes on: "New things continue to be developed, but more and more of the work seems to involve growing pains like scalability, oversized communities and integration of 'normal people' as we cross the chasm. Also, the new consumer Internet bubble is attracting attention from non-participant investors. This is an important part of making blogs a truly ubiquitous phenomenon, but it definitely feels more and more like real work." And work means dedicating more and more "idle time" to a technology of the past. Prime time is used for private passions, to hack the new. Ito continues:

> When I was in Helsinki visiting Nokia a few days ago, I [was] playing with my phone waiting in line and in cabs. It dawned on me that what I really want is better moblogging. Now, when I am in front of a computer connected to the Internet, I'm mostly immersed in IM for business or Warcraft for fun. When I am mobile, I have idle time that I could spend reading blogs and writing to my blog. I guess this is a sign that, at least for me, blogging has moved from my primary online activity to my idle time filler.

Constantly switching between texting, blogging, gaming, and talking, Ito is in search of further optimizing his "machine time": "Considering how much idle time I have with my phone, I think I could still blog at a relatively consistent rate. Also, I wish there were better ways to read and write when I am with my computer without a connection" (Ito 2005).

To me the issue is not being online from anywhere twenty-four hours a day but to develop an awareness of "other times." This is easier said than done. Even senior Internet scholars and high-profile techies have difficulties remembering if a person on another continent is ahead or behind compared to their own time zone. This confusion only gets worse if you start traveling overseas yourself. It still comes as a surprise to many that the maximum time difference is not twenty-four hours, but in fact only twelve hours. It is important to drop the GMT reference, which suggests that you can have up to twenty-four hours' time difference. For instance, if at Robert Hassan's little desktop World Clock it says Wed 3:43 p.m. in Melbourne and Tue 6:43 p.m. in Honolulu, this does not mean a twenty-one hours' time difference but merely three. Teams in Australia and Hawaii have little trouble working together—except three days a week around Sunday, provided one takes off from work during the weekends.

Developing a sense for local time elsewhere starts with the rather abstract idea that you have to go either forward or backward in time. So it is not global time but time shortage that is perceived as the bigger problem. You haven't even started aimless surfing when you already are aborting the session because your attention has drifted off elsewhere or another technology interferes. It feels as if time reserves are drying up. Bosses are very aware of time management and can closely monitor what individual workers are doing online. New media are renowned for "eating up" time; the *temps perdu* caused by computer games, instant messaging, social networks, blogging, and checking email is astonishing. The crackdown of "lost time" has to begin at some point. Sophisticated surveillance software already exists, not only to monitor employees but also to sanction them: the time you use for private email during work hours is simply deducted from your monthly work time and automatically deducted from your salary.

"Vita brevis, ars longa." Francis Bacon translated this Hippocrates aphorism as "Life is short; art is long." Today's meaning would be that your art outlives your life. Transposed onto the online world we could translate like this: "Art is long and Internet postings are the insects of a day." The amount of Internet sites disappearing is alarming. The fact that all information, up to the speed of touching the keyboard, is recordable flips into its opposite. No medium is as unstable as the Internet. The fact that today's chatter is being stored as digital information doesn't mean that we can compare with historical records. Only technodeterminists, with little experience in computer culture, can state that everything is being recorded, no data will ever get lost, and that is why they now suffer from information overload—das leiden des jungen bloggers.

The Internet is not a time machine that teleports us from here to nowhere and back. Despite its public image as a "virtualizer" and "accelerator," the Net is still not particularly futuristic. No matter how much progress has been made, its interface and speed remain clumsy and slightly disappointing. Compared with virtual reality systems and computer games, the Net is as rudimentary as it was ten or fifteen years ago. Browsers still crash, and connectivity goes down, no matter how much the speed has increased over the years (see, e.g., Lovink 2004). Similar to the usability debate in the late 1990s, we can now start wondering if the measured attention was really spent on that particular content and whether we're not constantly daydreaming. This leads us to the next level of commodification, where our unconscious looking-away and microsleeps get measured, ready to be sold. The construct of the user as a conscious person, who knows what he or she looks for and wants to get in the shortest amount of time, remains questionable.

Jean Baudrillard (2005, 27) writes, "Time itself, lived time, no longer has time to take place." In this pathology of postmodernity the Internet is no doubt the epiphany of the *real-time* power. With regime change no longer possible, we're completely stuck. In this darkest of hours it feels like being locked up in the Soviet Union during the 1970s. "The possible itself is no longer possible. What happens happens, and that's all there is to it." Even the event and its radical discontinuity have come to an end. "All that remains is the blatant self-evidence of actuality." The problem of this outsiders' view on matters digital is its lack of irony and humor. New media are judged as perfect machines, holistic enterprises. The "notworking" is taken out of the daily experience and is replaced with disgust for the perfect simulacrum.

John Holloway (2002) proposes to "break the homogeneity of time." He calls for a world in which "duration is shattered, in which time is not a long railway track or a slice of pizza, but tends towards the intensity of the Jetztzeit (now-time) of Benjamin or the nunc stans of Bloch, towards the timeless-time." Bourgeois thought, of course, will have none of this. Built on identity, on extending what is into what will be, bourgeois thought is obsessed with labeling, with classifying, with fitting things together, with creating neat boxes, with paradigms. We need to revolt against Time itself. "Time becomes stodgy, almost solid, something that can be cut into wedges, into periods, into paradigms, a million miles removed from the timeless-time of intense love or engagement" (Holloway 2002).

Instead of repeating the classic opposition—subversive living / machine time—we can observe, experience, and shape timeless net cultures that undercut capitalistic time logic, even in the midst of surveillance and data-tracking. In this context Robert Hassan (2006) asks, "[W]hat kind of time do we experience online, when we get lost amid dead links, get blocked at restricted access sites, search queries that lead to who knows where? It's not clock time, and it's not Swatch time, it's a time of lags and latencies, of waiting and clicking through, of fast and slow. It is the experience of differing speeds and asynchronicity." But it is not only disruption that characterizes Internet time. We have to find a way to transpose the figure of the flaneur into today's world and take it out of its identity-centered context. Being online exactly is not a lifestyle. This has been the fundamental mistake of the Californian Boing-Boing / Mondo 2000 faction, which dominated cyberculture for a while during the early 1990s, before *Wired* magazine massaged the aggressive business agenda. To get lost is not an exception but the rule. It will be hard to portray the vague user as an outsider or even a rebel. No more relocations. As Bruce Sterling (2005) has suggested: we are past the point of no return. The "gizmofication" of the world makes it impossible to marginalize the Net as a sandbox of microidentities. There is no avant-garde or bohemia anymore that leads us into some radical Wonderland, only "neocrats," the punditocracy that claims to possess knowledge of the latest and coolest functionalities.

Instead of administrating ever smaller (and larger) amounts of time,[6] it is interesting to investigate how, given the current constraints, we can "step out of time," given the digital constraints of what Georg Franck (2005) terms "mental capitalism." It might not be sufficient to criticize linear timetables and introduce the cyclical time model as a way out of time exploitation. Instead of development and progress we would then go in circles—a feeling that we all have anyway. It seems unavoidable to track through the "desert of the real" and to camp here and there for the night, without a promise to ever escape the current time-space capsule. To provide a critical diagnostics of the chronopolitics of our times is one thing, but to inscribe alternative models into the network architectures is another matter. It is not sufficient to delegate quasi-spiritual time experiences into the private realm, a tactic that new age gurus preach and so-called change managers practice. Radical time experiences should not be promoted as compensation for stressful work. Quality time does not save us from quantity misery. Also, we should be careful not to easily adapt the language that talks of "change" and "transformation" of, in this case, time regimes. There is nothing inherently good or bad about what is emerging. What we can do is research, remember, and repeat forgotten concepts that help us to overcome the unbearable lightness of real-time living. What we need are autonomous strategies, what could be called "Time Management of the Self," so we can surf in style, without depicting or glorifying the digital drift. "Self knowledge is power."[7]

Notes

1. For more on Swatch Time go to www.swatch.com/internettime/.

2. See, e.g., www.clocklink.com: "Clocklink provides fashionable clocks that you can easily embed in your web page. All you need to do is simply paste the tag on your web page. Our clock will display the city name of your choice if you choose. You can also choose a time zone for your clock so it will show the correct time."

3. For a discussion of the cultural history of satellites and the first real-time global broadcasts see Parks (2005).

4. The concept of the calculating citizen was developed by Dutch sociologist Kees Schuyt; see Cox (2001).

5. "When you pay attention to something (and when you ignore something), data is created. This 'attention data' is a valuable resource that reflects your interests, your activities and your values, and it serves as a proxy for your attention" (www.attentiontrust.org). The four principles that are fundamental to Attention-Trust are property, mobility, economy, and transparency.

6. As a mirror project of the attention economy, a similar group of technorati (around Stuart Brand) developed the Long Now project, a clock that ticks every ten thousand years: "The Long Now Foundation hopes to provide counterpoint to today's 'faster / cheaper' mind set and promote 'slower / better' thinking" (www.longnow.org/ about).

7. See http://nomediakings.org/vidz/time_management_for_anarchists_the_ movie.html.

References

Alcala, Timi Stoop. 2005. Email to the author. July 12.

Baudrillard, Jean. 2005. *The intelligence of evil or the lucidity pact*. Berg: Oxford University Press.

Cox, Robert Henry. 2001. The social construction of an imperative: Why welfare reform happened in Denmark and the Netherlands but not in Germany. *World Politics* 53 (3): 463–498.

Franck, Georg. 2005. Mental capitalism. www.iemar.tuwien.ac.at/publications/ Franck_2005c.pdf (accessed Jan. 25, 2007).

Goldhaber, Michael. 1996. *Principles of the new economy*. www.well.com/user/mgoldh/ principles.html (accessed Jan. 25, 2007).

Hagen, Wolfgang. 2003. *Gegenwartsvergessenheit*. Berlin: Merve Verlag.

Hassan, Robert. 2006. Personal conversation.

Holloway, John. 2002. *Time to revolt: Reflections on empire*. http://libcom.org/library/ time-to-revolt-empire-john-holloway (accessed Jan. 25, 2007).

Ito, Joi. 2005. *Will more moblog help?* http://joi.ito.com/archives/2005/12/12/will_ more_moblog_help.html (accessed Jan. 25, 2007).

Kellner, Douglas. 1998. *Virilio on vision machines*. www.film-philosophy.com/vol2-1998/n30kellner (accessed Jan. 25, 2007).

Konrad, Rachel. 2005. For some techies, an interminable workday. *India Daily*. May 9: http://indiadaily.com/breaking_news/34689.asp (accessed Jan. 25, 2007).

Lovink, Geert. 2002. Net.times, not Swatch time: 21st century global time wars. In *Dark fiber: Tracking critical Internet culture*, ed. Geert Lovink, 142–159. Cambridge, MA: MIT Press.

———. 2004. *The principle of notworking*. Amsterdam: Amsterdam University Press.

Parks, Lisa. 2005. Interview with Geert Lovink. www.nettime.org/Lists-Archives/ nettime-l-0511/msg00003.html (accessed Jan. 25, 2007).

Sterling, Bruce. 2005. *Shaping things*. Cambridge, MA: MIT Press.

Virilio, Paul. 1996. Global algorithm 1.7: The silence of the lambs: Paul Virilio in conversation. Interview by Carlos Oliveira. *CTheory* (June 12): http://ctheory.net/ articles.aspx?id=38 (accessed Jan. 25, 2007).

9 The Presence of Others

Network Experience as an Antidote to the Subjectivity of Time

Jack Petranker

It is true that the other will never exist for us as we exist ourselves; he is always a lesser figure, and we never feel in him as we do in ourselves the thrust of temporalization. But two temporalities are not mutually exclusive as are two consciousnesses, because each one knows itself only by projecting itself into the present where they can interweave.

—*Maurice Merleau-Ponty,* Phenomenology of Perception

THE SUDDEN, ASTOUNDING GROWTH of the Internet starting in the mid-1990s was heralded by a chorus of predictions that global citizenship in the new world of the Internet would lead to a revolution in human communication and human social structures. Vint Cerf (1999), sometimes referred to as Father of the Internet, wrote movingly of this potential:

> The Internet is a place, an environment, made up of people and their myriad interactions. It is not merely a technology but a new way of cooperating, sharing and caring. Businesses that recognize the human aspect of the Internet will be more likely to find success in the artificial worlds of the Digital Age, for they will understand that the artificial is rooted in reality and reality is rooted in our hearts.

Tim Berners-Lee (1999, 1–2), inventor of the World Wide Web, sounds a similar, though more impersonal, note:

> The vision I have for the Web is about anything being potentially connected with anything. It is a vision that provides us with new freedom, and allows us to grow faster than we ever could when we were fettered by the hierarchical classification systems into which we bound ourselves. It leaves the entirety of

our previous ways of working as just one tool among many. It leaves our previous fears for the future as one set among many. And it brings the workings of society closer to the workings of our minds.

Although the point is not always made explicit, the shift being celebrated here is a shift in the very nature of time and space. The Internet stands in the shoes of that nineteenth-century wonder, the telegraph, whose inventor was toasted for "having annihilated both space and time in the transmission of intelligence" (Standage 1998, 90).

Of course, it is also possible to take a more gloomy view. Robert Hassan (2003, 235–236) describes the network as "a new, empty, detemporalized successor to the clock." Although he acknowledges that in theory this new form of time could be a source of revolutionary change and expanded freedom, his own take is far more pessimistic:

> The asynchronous times of the network may at first glance offer . . . a potential for diversity, for the creation of innumerable original "contextually situated" spaces where difference can flourish, and where new ideas and new knowledges may be produced. However, . . . the network has its own meta-logic. . . . It reflects the social and economic forces that build it and is essentially market-oriented and instrumental. And as it connects, so, too, does the network society tend to isolate and alienate.

Paul Virilio (1997, 10) offers a similar take at a more metaphysical level. He suggests that the network, by creating a form of time that he calls "real time," undermines our ability to be *present* to our own experience:

> Paul Klee hit the nail on the head: "To define the present in isolation is to kill it." This is what the teletechnologies of real time are doing: they are killing "present" time by isolating it from its here and now, in favour of a commutative elsewhere that no longer has anything to do with our "concrete presence" in the world, but is the elsewhere of a "discreet [*sic*: read 'discrete'?] telepresence" that remains a complete mystery.

In this chapter I take a more positive view of the Internet phenomenon. The technologizing of time that the network undoubtedly promotes changes that which would undermine our human potentialities, a possibility I do not want to discount. Nonetheless, the network also allows for new modes of temporal experience—new forms of temporal presence—that serve to promote presence rather than destroy it. At a subtle level, "network presence" can actually deepen our encounters with others and counter the tendencies toward isolation and alienation that Hassan and Virilio identify.

I. A Common Experience

> It's raining sheets of rain;
> Everything is cold and wet;
> Nobody's going out of doors.
> They're all at home,
> livin' it up on the internet:
> I guess nobody's lonely anymore.
> —*Greg Brown, "'Cept You and Me, Babe"*

In the early years of the telegraph a heady conviction spread that the heightened sense of immediate contact this new medium provided could promote feelings of brotherhood and amity. Henry Field, an entrepreneur actively involved in developing the transatlantic telegraph cable, put it like this: "An ocean [telegraph] cable is not an iron chain, lying cold and dead in the icy depths of the Atlantic. It is a living, fleshy bond between severed portions of the human body, along which pulses of love and tenderness will run backward and forward forever. By such strong ties does it bind the human race in unity, peace, and concord" (quoted in Standage 1998, 103). For such enthusiasts it seemed self-evident (based, presumably, on their own experience of the new medium) that presence at a distance—what Virilio dismisses as telepresence—can expand our sense of presence, that shrinking space and time does in fact draw people closer together.

Of course, the hopes of these early enthusiasts were misplaced. The introduction of the telegraph was followed not by a new era of "unity, peace, and concord" but by a century of the worst wars in the history of the world. Indeed, as scholars have been arguing for well over a century (for a review with special reference to the Internet see Hampton and Wellman 2003), there is ample evidence to suggest that the new technologies of communication undermine community and communication at the local level without building it up on the international level.

On a one-to-one basis, however, long-distance communication can certainly promote a sense of presence. Most people have probably had the experience of a heartfelt late-night telephone conversation with a close friend in which there is a strong sense that the one with whom you are speaking is present, that the distance separating the two of you in space has disappeared. More generally, it is not unusual for people to have the feeling that their absent lover is "right there with them" as they go about their lives. Phenomenologically speaking, presence does not always depend on sharing local time and space. Presence-at-a-distance seems an established fact.[1]

With this background, consider the following description of the modest experience on which I intend to build the rest of this essay:

> It sometimes happens that while I am deeply engaged in thinking about some issue or project, I email a colleague or friend involved in the same project or concerned with similar questions, but with whom I am not in regular contact. Knowing how email works, I expect a reply within a few hours, or a day or two at the most. But occasionally my email reaches someone who is online at the same time I am, and who responds immediately. My response is pleased surprise. But that is not all. Looking more closely, I find that on receiving the reply, my sense of personal boundaries undergoes a subtle change. For a while, at least, I feel as though I am in the presence of my colleague, that she or he and I are present together, sharing the same time and space.

This experience of shared presence (which I could also imagine happening in instant messaging, chat rooms, or MMOGs—massively multiplayer online games) may not seem in the telling like anything special. And, indeed, the feeling or shift I am trying to describe is easy enough to pass over if you are not looking for it, not attuned to the issue of presence. Here is why I consider it significant: the sense of shared presence that can happen through serendipitously timed communication with valued others on the network signals the operation of a different temporality from the one that operates in ordinary experience. It is this different temporality—*a temporality of presence*—I turn to now.

II. The Absence of Presence

> [T]he answers of science will always remain replies to questions asked by men; the confusion in the issue of "objectivity" [is] to assume that there could be answers without questions and results independent of a question-asking being.
>
> —*Hannah Arendt*, Between Past and Future

Our understanding of time is socially constructed (Adam 2004; Elias 1992; Nowotny 1994). To function as a community is to share a similar sense of time. A community is bound together by a similar history of events in time, a similar vision of the future, and similar temporal rhythms (Hall 1966). In addition, a community is bound together by a particular understanding of time and temporality, one in which each new generation, as Elias (1992) discusses in some detail, must be socialized.

Contemporary society tends to accept two forms of temporality, the subjective and the objective (Elias 1992; Merleau-Ponty 1962).[2] Objective time is the time of the clock and the calendar, the time of the measured-out grid, in which each second, each minute, each hour has a uniform length. Subjective time is the time of experience, varying as experience varies. A simple example makes the point: If we are governed by subjective time, we eat when we are hungry. If we are governed by objective time, we eat when the clock (or the noon whistle, etc.) says it is time to eat (see Adam 2004; Hassan 2003; Nowotny 1994).

Like clocks and the other instruments that measure it, objective time is a human construct. Still, it is often assumed that objective time is "real," whereas subjective time is "only" subjective. The reasons behind this assumption all come back to the problematic nature of the self in modern thought. The insistence of the natural sciences that matter alone is real is mirrored by the Cartesian turn in philosophy that isolates the self in its own realm. Together, these two bedrocks of our worldview reduce individual concerns, values, and experience to second-order, derivative phenomena. Although thinkers such as Locke sought to turn the isolation of the "punctual self" (Taylor 1989) into a virtue, the fact remains that from the seventeenth century onward, the self was forced to beat a strategic retreat into its own subjective world. It is here that subjective time operates.

The subjectivity of subjective time does not divorce it from objective time. Instead, subjective and objective time are best seen as mirror images of one another (Merleau-Ponty 1962), sharing the same assumptions (Elias 1992, 49). But just what are those assumptions? What accounts for the dominance in this culture of the subjective/objective model of temporality? Hassan (this volume) hints at the answer when he speaks of earlier forms of time reckoning as "embedded" in the natural order of things, embedded, that is, in the way people live their lives (see also Adam 2004; and compare Bluedorn 2002 on epochal time). Before the modern age, temporality expressed the integral unfolding of a world in which we were fully present. It is the loss of presence that accounts for the emergence of the subjective/objective model. When we are no longer present in the world, time becomes an abstraction. Objectively, it is a system of measurement; subjectively, it is a narrative imposed retrospectively by a disengaged self charged with the task of making sense of "the way things are."

Here is an example to help clarify this shift. For millennia the progression of time over the course of a day was marked by the passage of the sun across the sky from east to west, an indisputable fact about the world human beings inhabit. Then scientists discovered that the sun does not move in this fashion at all; instead, the earth rotates around the sun. The appearance of solar movement was based on our subjective impressions; the reality was different. The growing use of clocks helped limit the resulting cognitive dissonance, for around the same time that this discovery began to be widely accepted, we also stopped relying on the sun to "tell" time, turning instead to clocks and other devices. But of course the dissonance remains: we accept as true at one level what we know to be false at another.

What can we say of these two different versions of events? Elsewhere (Petranker 2005) I have written of the difference between lived stories and told stories. The lived story is the truth of our lives, the "way things are." In the lived story the sun glides smoothly across the sky, giving order and sequence to the day. The told story, on the other hand, is an abstraction. Rather than being the embedded truth of our lives, it is an account meant to impose order and make sense.

The told story maintains that the earth rotates round the sun. And because we have learned to discount the experience of the self, we accept that told story as the truth, even though in terms of our lived experience, it is not the way things are. Not that we deny our lived experience or pretend that it is something it is not. Instead, we strip it of its presence, shunting it off into the subjective realm. Subjective temporality, in which the sun rises and sets each day, becomes cut off from reality, from the objective temporality in which the earth orbits the sun, and the sun makes its way through the galaxy, and the galaxy spins its way through the cosmos.

The consequences of accepting this subject/object temporality, which gives the told story priority over the lived story, are momentous. When time reduces to an objective system of measurement on the one hand and a subjective story on the other, meaning and value are confined to the subjective realm. "What is meaningless comes to the fore by default" (Tulku 1987, 33).

In a world that divides temporality into the subjective and objective, we are no longer present to the world but only to our own subjective experience of the world. The lived stories of the self lose their gravity and conviction, as though we were trying to live life on the pages of a novel or the reels of a film. And because we accept the split into subjective and objective temporality as part of the way things are, we have no way to tell that anything has been lost. We live out a temporality that leaves us always already isolated from our own being, never suspecting that it could be otherwise.

The horror of this way of being, in which what is told replaces what is lived, is one we have learned not to recognize, with the result that we do not even find it horrible. But if we do not acknowledge it, if we settle for the simulated as the truth of our lives, we have lost something fundamental in being human. So I will give the horror a name. Invoking the archetypal modern myth of the monster given artificial life by human beings, I will call the time-of-no-presence Frankentime.[3]

Many treatments of time in modern society acknowledge the spread of Frankentime in its objective mode: a measured-out temporality that has relentlessly colonized the whole of human experience (Elias 1992; Hassan 2003; Rifkin 1987) until now, in Hassan's words, it enjoys "overpowering domination." As clocks proliferate on tabletops, computer screens, kitchen appliances, and our wrists; as schedules and plans and to-do lists permeate leisure time in the same way they long ago became the measures of time in factory and office; as cell phones and the Internet give the economic engines of society ongoing access to everyone, Frankentime in these easily recognized forms takes over our lives.

What these analyses miss, however, is that Frankentime has also colonized the inner domain of the self, squeezing out all possibility for meaning in our lives. The reason this is not readily seen is that we do not recognize the distinction between the told and the lived story. It is commonly argued nowadays that meaning enters time through narrative (Bluedorn 2002; MacIntyre 1984; Polkinghorne 1988; Ricoeur 1984). But narrative depends on the told stories that have replaced experience, and the meanings asserted in those stories cannot cross the gap between subjective absence and embedded presence. The stories of the narrator self, the subjective Frankentime self identified by Lasch (1979) as the "new Narcissus," remain nothing but stories: plans and explanations, fantasies and justifications, histories and imaginings. The meanings they assert amount to a fabrication. They lead on the one hand to plays crafted for the theatrified realm of self-presentation (see Nehamas 1998) and on the other to the scenarios hatched in the cubicles of strategic planners.[4]

Cut off from its own experience, the self that lives in Frankentime is itself a mechanistic abstraction (Taylor 1989): the mirror image of the fungible grid of objective time. Just as the monster that Dr. Frankenstein creates in Shelley's famous novel is the doppelgänger of the scientist who brought him into being (Oates 1984), we moderns act out—in our fantasies, role-playing, and plans—inverted variations on the measured-out, abstracted rhythms of objective Frankentime. Small wonder we pass our time yearning for "other" times that will transport us "away" from the emptiness of Frankentime: the times of vacations, shopping, and consuming, the times of recreational drugs, extravaganzas of all sorts, and endless varieties of entertainment.

By accepting as our own reality the abstracted temporality of Frankentime, in which our own experience is reduced to the stories we tell about it, we absent ourselves from our lives. We remain engaged in the lived stories of our own lives (How could we not be?), but our own presence within those stories is nothing but a rumbling in the dark, a movement glimpsed on the periphery; it eludes illumination (Tulku 1987, 175). Bound to the stories we tell instead of those we live, we become simulacra of ourselves (Baudrillard 1998), versions manufactured for consumption by ourselves or others. Sensing that something has gone wrong, we may place great value on our inarticulate desires and feelings, choosing (as Freud would have put it) id over ego. But the more Frankentime colonizes the private realm, the more likely we are to seek comfort in the realms where abstraction feels natural: virtual reality, ironic self-reference, and escapist entertainment.

It helps clarify the alienating impact of Frankentime to compare it to the forms of time that prevailed before the modern era. As Adam (2004) has shown, in other cultures (including some that survive within modern societies) time unfolds in ways that are inherently meaningful, because linked to a divine order. Individuals in such societies are present in a world that is also present to them, a world informed by the numinous presence of transcendent forces or beings. In such a world the Frankentime division of temporality into subjective and objective is literally unthinkable.

Even in modern society there are occasions when this other kind of temporality bursts through the veneer of the simulated. An example is the kind of traumatic event exemplified by the World Trade Center attacks on September 11, 2001; the Kennedy assassination on November 22, 1963; or the bombing of Pearl Harbor on December 7, 1941. It is no accident that these three events are all inseparable from the days on which they happened. On those dates, for a few minutes or hours or even days, ordinary time stood still, and a different temporality operated. The outer world of events and the inner world of meaning were again joined, giving experience, and life itself, a wholly different character.

III. Time of Presence

> Time exists for me because I have a present.
> —*Maurice Merleau-Ponty*, Phenomenology of Perception

We are ready now to return to the modest example I introduced in section I of this chapter. I spoke there of my pleasant surprise on receiving an immediate response to an email I had sent to a colleague. What is happening here in terms of presence? Quite unexpectedly, I find myself in the presence of another. More fundamentally, through the presence of the other I find myself to be present to my own experience. And as I have suggested above, to be present to ourselves is not our usual situation.

In this example I discover through the medium of email and the Internet that I am not alone. The nature of this "not-being-alone" is difficult to describe, and if the reader has not had a similar kind of experience, any description will likely not be wholly convincing. But here is my claim: as the other becomes present for me in this way, the borders of the subjective self are breached. The self is always situated "here" and "now," even if we are not present to that now/here. What happens in the exchange I have described is that the other—my correspondent—is "here" and "now" with me, present for me with a special (because unexpected) immediacy, a special intimacy. Through this presence of the other, the self can emerge from Frankentime into a realm that has suddenly become once again meaningful.[5]

Let me anticipate two objections. The first is that the presence offered by network exchanges like the email I described are themselves only simulacra of presence. The second is that even if such exchanges offer a form of presence, they are nothing out of the ordinary: we are present to others whenever an "I" becomes a "we," and this is an everyday occurrence.

As to the first of these objections, we have already met with it in Virilio's (1997) claim that the rise of the network destroys presence rather than enables it, substituting a weakened, watered-down "telepresence" for our "concrete presence" in the world. But as I suggested above, experiencing the presence of another is possible even when that other is at a distance—even an unbridgeable distance. Consider the following examples, some of which I have already mentioned:

an intimate late-night phone call with a good friend

new love, sleeping in the room next door

an unattained love-object, about whom one obsesses endlessly

a loved one who has passed away, but with whom one still communes

characters in a novel in which one is completely immersed

the presence of a divine being for one who prays with true faith

great thinkers of the past, who seem to speak to one's innermost concerns and questions

Compare these examples to the pseudopresence typical of a commercial interaction between a customer and a salesperson, and the difference is clear. Presence grounded in intimacy depends not at all on physically inhabiting the same "here" and "now," nor is such co-inhabiting a guarantor of presence. I will return to this point below.

Let us turn now to the second objection: that any "presence" evoked by an immediate message from a distant other is nothing special, certainly nothing that rises to the level of intimacy suggested by the examples in the list set forth above and not even as intimate as sitting with your family around the breakfast table in the morning.

Now, it is true enough that love creates its own bonds of intimacy and thus presence. But this misses the point. Living out the rhythms of subjective temporality imposed by Frankentime, the self grows increasingly unable to love, increasingly unable to experience presence. It is natural to seek in the bonds of family or friendship a "haven in a heartless world" (Lasch 1977), but the more Frankentime compels us to see ourselves as subjectively constituted, as "told entities," the more we will be cut off from others, even those we consider closest. And, of course, this will be especially true if those with whom we connect are themselves the victims and fellow perpetrators of Frankentime. To return to the intimacy of presence, we must first find our way out of the linear and lifeless procession of Frankentime.

I have been arguing that Frankentime denies us the possibility of presence. But it would also be possible to put this the other way round: what we experience in Frankentime is precisely *the presence of the reified, measured-out time that Frankentime insists on* in the objective realm. The real difficulty, on this view, is that we incorporate Frankentime into our own self-understanding. We make it the time of our own subjectivity, imposing it on ourselves.

Our complicity in the reign of Frankentime is not easily recognized. Barbara Adam (2004, 113–115) writes: "The clock . . . changed the meaning of time. . . . It became independent from time and space, self-sufficient, empty of meaning and thus apparently neutral. . . . The machine time of the clock is a time cut loose from the temporality of body, nature and the cosmos, from context-bound being and spiritual existence." All this is true and deeply important to acknowledge. But still more important is the fact that we pay a steep price for adapting ourselves to this temporal mode. Slipping from the lived story into the told story, we make of our lives a linear succession of events, ultimately meaningless, from which we ourselves have always already withdrawn. Denying presence, we turn ourselves into something less than we are.

The birth of the network society, governed by network time, offers the potential to escape from this one-dimensional prison. As Hassan (this volume) writes, in the network society "we stand on the brink of a new *engagement with time*." But if my analysis is right, it would be a mistake to view this possible transformation solely in political or social terms, as Hassan tends to do. Before politics, before issues of power and control, there is the issue of presence. If we are not present to ourselves differently, if we do not discover that presence through our interactions with others, the most profound changes in the institutional structures of our age will make little difference. In the end we will live out a way of being that duplicates in its fundamental aspects the temporal rhythms of Frankentime. We will never escape the monster, for in fact we are the monster.

IV. Presence as Intimacy

> To write prescriptions is easy, but to come to an understanding
> with people is hard.
> —*Franz Kafka, "The Country Doctor".*

In the previous section I suggested that presence is available through acts of intimacy and that the network society makes such intimacy available in new ways. To interact with others at "the same time," in the give-and-take of conversation, *and to have this happen unexpectedly*, is to be shocked into presence.

To welcome the other person into one's own private space spontaneously, before barriers can be erected, is to challenge the structures of Frankentime.

The element of surprise is important here. When I walk into my office in the morning, I expect to be in the presence of my colleagues, and as a result their presence lacks the power to move me (absent special circumstances, such as my first day on a new job). Similarly, if I work in a large company and send an email to a colleague, his or her reply in a matter of minutes leaves me essentially unmoved. I am using the technology as it was designed to be used, to facilitate a more rapid exchange of information, more or less as I would use the telephone. Now compare the example I have been working with: I send out an email to a friend or colleague at a distance, on a matter that engages me. I anticipate the distance that separates us: I take it into account, I plan for it temporally, and I expect a reply in due course. Instead, I receive a reply within minutes. I have experienced a direct connection when I did not expect it: the two of us turn out to be in the same place at the same time. Hence the pleasure and the sense of presence. It is like running into an old friend in a foreign city.

Of course, the specifics of this example are not central. But the element of technological innovation in communication is, for it is precisely the changed reality of communicative presence that technology offers that challenges the conventional Frankentime structures.

Consider a different example, from the film *Broadcast News* (Brooks 1987), from an era shortly before the age of ubiquitous email. Tom, an aspiring TV news anchor, has been pressed into service to conduct for the first time a live television interview on a subject about which he knows nothing. Wearing an earphone, he takes suggestions fed to him by the news show's producer, Jane. He proves adept at turning what she feeds him into probing questions and comes away elated:

TOM: You're an amazing woman. What a feeling having you inside my head.

JANE (a bit thrown): Yeah. It was an unusual place to be.

TOM: Indescribable—you knew just when to feed me the next thing, just a split second before I needed it. There was a rhythm we got into, like great sex.

Here the sense of intimacy (intensified by a sexual frisson) traces directly to the technology, which allows someone else to be present in an intimate and unexpected way. In such mutuality of presence the disengaged, self-centered temporality of Frankentime gives way to a different temporal way of being, one in which meaning can again emerge. It is a perfect example of what Hassan (this volume) describes: "In communication with others we can also get to the point where the clock does not matter, so deeply have we shared the flow and rhythms of the constructed time." My point is that this "does not matter" offers a relationship to time whose depths we have not yet begun to explore, a "time of presence" that, as Hassan notes, may in some sense recreate the "embedded" times of presence that operated before the triumph of the clock. Compare Nowotny (1994, 31): "It is no longer predominantly dramatic events, like the fate of the sinking *Titanic* or those ritual moments which serve to strengthen the feeling of solidarity among people, which convey simultaneity, but the course of everyday work, the constant temporal presence, real or virtual, of others."

Of course, the ubiquity of communication technology is not always welcome. We are all familiar with complaints that email and wireless technology make it impossible to escape from work, instilling a sense that we must be always on call. Nor does instant access to others always undermine the subjective temporality that Frankentime encourages; in fact, it may reinforce it. Consider, for example, the impact of role-playing games or virtual realities that start by asking me to create an avatar, a second self, thus confirming and even amplifying the usual structures of identity on which the Frankentime self relies.

Here again the element of the unexpected is crucial. The structures of the self are well established. They come into play more or less automatically in advance of every anticipated situation. It is only with the emergence of the unfamiliar, the arrival of what has not been summoned, that a new form of temporality can emerge.

That is why network time in itself, asynchronous and fragmented though it may be, will not reverse or undermine the circumstances of clock time as they affect presence. Changing the objective structures of Frankentime means little if we do not change the subjective structures of the self that "embody" Frankentime. Network time provides an occasion for change, an opportunity for change, and even the prospect of subverting the existing order (subjective as well as objective). But it does not guarantee it.

On the other hand, the potential for change that networked presence offers operates even away from the network, in those increasingly rare moments when I have left my computer, my cell phone, and my PDA behind me. For if I know myself to inhabit a world in which others are present, their presence casts its glow through the whole reach and range of time, illuminating aspects of my being that would otherwise remain in darkness. Because I have engaged the other on matters of concern to me, because she and I are present together, I am present in the world differently. The world itself is different, and this makes a great difference indeed. In such circumstances Frankentime gives way to a new order, a new timescape (Adam 2004).

What happens in this timescape is less important than what is available to happen. Unlike clock time and network time, unlike even Frankentime, the timescape of presence is not simply a social construct shared by all. When we enter into presence, the timescape of presence manifests itself; it is not owned by a self, not told by a self, not formed by the self's needs and desires.

It may be useful here to compare Adam's (2004, 78) description of mythic time in its relation to ritual:

> When a myth is actualized in ritual, a simultaneity of existence is created. The ritual . . . brings together in the present ritual participants with the sources and forces of reality. We can speak of an active presencing of origin. In this process of presencing, the time of sequence, passage and duration is negated. Time is not abolished, however. Rather, it is rendered non-temporal and ahistorical. In rituals, as in myths, original moments are reproduced, and in their repetition a reality is created where all of time becomes fulfilled in the present.

What does this have to do with the modest example that has inspired these reflections: the simultaneous presence in email conversation of two colleagues, two friends, who thought themselves separate? We can find the hint of a connection in Adam's (2004, 146) observation that "[m]ore like the realm of myths and mysticism, the electronic world of interchangeable no-where and now-here requires knowledge and modes of being that are alien to the industrial way of life." But here I must repeat that the electronic world of asynchronous network time is only a gateway. If we do not accept the unexpected invitations to presence that the network affords, the prospects for a new temporality will never be realized. In the decade or so in which the World Wide Web has been a major social force and the two decades since email began its march toward omnipresence, we have seen again and again how Frankentime-generated structures of commerce and capital, entertainment and escape have established themselves in the new time and space of the network. Change is by no means guaranteed.

V. Presence and Solidarity

> Marriage is not only time, it is also,
> paradoxically, the denial of time.
>
> —*Joan Didion,* The Year of Magical Thinking

Hannah Arendt, that great theorist of political freedom, wrote repeatedly of those special moments in a revolution or political movement when something new is set in motion, when human beings have the rare chance to make a new beginning. In describing the French Resistance during the Second World War, for instance, she writes (1963, 4) that those who joined the resistance "had become 'challengers,' had taken the initiative upon themselves and therefore, without knowing or even noticing it, had begun to create that public space between themselves where freedom could appear."

Putting this in the context of the grand sweep of modern political culture, she goes on to suggest (1963, 5) that "[t]he history of [political] revolutions . . . could be told in parable form as the tale of an age-old treasure which, under the most varied circumstances, appears abruptly, unexpectedly, and disappears again, under different mysterious conditions." In contrast to the great upheavals of politics, the shift that I have been writing of is a modest one, so subtle, as I have repeatedly tried to suggest, that it can easily be missed. Yet in its own way it offers access to the same "age-old treasure" that Arendt is at pains to identify.

I have called this treasure "presence." Arendt, in the passage we have been looking at, describes it as sincerity or authenticity. The resistance fighter, she says (1963, 4), quoting the writings of a French poet who served in the Resistance, "no longer suspected himself of 'insincerity,' of being 'a carping, suspicious actor of life.'" In other words the political actor, like someone discovering a different form of presence in network time, emerges from the disengaged subjectivity of Frankentime into a time of shared presence and solidarity. And this makes all the difference.

Robert Hassan (2003, 235) has suggested that network time, though it does not destroy clock time, gradually displaces and neutralizes it. As I see it, this claim, insightful as it is, goes both too far and not far enough. Whether network time allows us to escape Frankentime will depend wholly on how we make use of it. If we heed the copresencing that the network allows, we move a step closer to the recovery of meaning that Frankentime banishes. But if we approach the network with the same subjective temporality we make use of now, nothing of significance is likely to change. Indeed, the growth of Frankentime, its global dominance, will only accelerate.

At another level, however, to suggest that network time can displace clock time does not tell us enough. If I am right about the time of presence made available through the copresence of another, entering it allows for an entirely different form of temporality. For presence is not something that shifts from moment to moment, unfolding in the linear Frankentime sequence we have learned to equate unthinkingly with time as such. Compared to the flattened, linear temporality that subjectivity mirrors (Tulku 1987), presence is timeless.

If network time allows access to presence, or at least suggests the possibility of such access, it is because it shares with the political movements Arendt describes the sense that something new is underway. In the shared moment of solidarity my time and your time merge, and this fusion loosens the sense of self. The self does not disappear, nor do we forget it; rather, it yields and expands. Having emerged from the meaningless realm of Frankentime, it finds a source of meaning in intimacy with another. As I have discussed elsewhere (Petranker 2005), Hans-Georg Gadamer (1986) wrote with great power of the possibilities for presence and for intimacy that arise in this way, through what he called the "fusion of horizons," whether this happens in the encounter with another, in deep engagement with art or nature, or in moments of insight or of great loss.

My argument in this essay has been that something similar can happen in network time. It does not happen always; in fact, it may happen only rarely. As Arendt writes of political movements, moments of shared presence emerge abruptly and unexpectedly, and they disappear just as abruptly. It is no surprise that pioneers of the Internet, writing of the early days of the communication revolution in which they were caught up, often sound a note of nostalgia for what has been lost. As with all social movements there is a sense that the special times came early on, when people shared a sense of vision and unlimited possibility and when solidarity came naturally. Later, Frankentime enters; later, the subjective self takes over. What was there at the outset is in some sense betrayed.

What makes network time so interesting, however, is that by its very nature it continues to generate opportunities for presence. Provided that we who engage it are ready to proceed with sensitivity and a willingness to challenge our own temporal way of being, it can be a continuing force for change, for openness, and for presence.

VI. The Ongoing Emergency

> Maybe I've never really loved,
> I guess that is the truth.
> I've spent my whole life at icy altitudes.
> And looking down on everything,
> I crashed into his arms.
>
> —*Joni Mitchell, "Amelia"*

The dynamic of presence that network time makes possible may be available in many interactions, both on and off the network. But the moment we look too hard, the moment we take a stand from which to assess it, the dynamic is gone. Once our own position is established, we are caught in the web of subjective Frankentime temporality.

It is the role of the theorist to name the possibility for escaping the established so that it does not disappear from view. But how can one do this, when by definition the theorist is one who stands apart, who takes things in from a distance?

The answer is to look not at the content of what is presented but at the ways of presenting. And here, too, the technology of network time has something special to offer. For it is of the nature of this technology (perhaps of technology in general, but something special seems to be operating when the technology concerns communication) to always be evolving into something different. For the theorist this is a kind of saving grace. It prevents presence from becoming an established position. It keeps presence active and dynamic in the face of theory and names.

I have used as my example in this chapter encountering in the unexpected immediacy of an email response the presence of another. Now, it may be that this kind of event becomes commonplace, based on new hardware or software or new social patterns I cannot now envisage. But even short of that, the very fact that I have named this occasion and gone about it at length means that it no longer has the same quality of the unexpected that made it an occasion for presence to begin with. Having written this chapter, I find that the kinds of email exchanges I have described, though they still take me by surprise, have already shifted toward the expected and the taken for granted. I can still remember the first time I saw a color photograph displayed on a computer screen across the room; after years of green or amber cathode-ray tubes, it was a revelation. Today, of course, I take graphics on the screen for granted, and the sense of beauty and wonder I felt that first time has disappeared. Following Arendt (1963, 169), we could speak here of the interplay between presence and new beginnings, and mourn our inability to sense the presence that is always available:

> Every act, seen from the perspective not of the agent but of the process in whose framework it occurs and whose automatism it interrupts, is a "miracle"—that is, something which could not be expected. If it is true that action and beginning are essentially the same, it follows that a capacity for performing miracles must likely be within the range of human faculties. This sounds stranger than it actually is. It is in the very nature of every new beginning that it breaks into the world as an "infinite improbability," and yet it is precisely this infinitely improbable which actually constitutes the very texture of everything we call real.

The technology of network time offers a way out of the dilemma posed by the taken for granted. For we can predict with some confidence that technology will continue to change with undiminished vigor. As one kind of opening-to-presence turns into the conventional and solid, another emerges. What is familiar loses its power, but something new takes its place. We cannot predict where the next opening will emerge, but if we are sensitive to the possibility of presence, we will be more likely to be open to it when it comes along. True, the contrary dynamic operates as well, for in some respects the technology of communication seems ready-made to replicate the rhythms of Frankentime. But we need not let this second dynamic prevail. We have the power to be present. We can choose.

In investigating the power of presence, Tarthang Tulku (1990, 484) speaks of "points of decision": "The 'decision point' gathers together all that is known and all that presents itself in that 'moment' of time. . . . As a gathering together of all that contributes to its making, each 'point of decision' is the whole. . . . The known world is sustained from moment to moment on the basis of ever-emerging points of decision. In this ongoing 'emergency,' all that is is invariably at stake" (emphasis omitted).

It may seem a far cry from the simple pleasure of an unexpected connection to a colleague or friend to an ongoing emergency in which "everything" is at stake. But the distance is not that great. The question in both cases is whether the subjectivity of the self, in the special sense I have been exploring here, is challenged. And it is just in the unexpected moments of daily interaction, where the self goes undefended, that such challenges are most likely to succeed. If we wish to speak here of revolution, we could call this a revolution of small encounters, each one different from all the others, each one open to presence.

In network time such small encounters will constantly present themselves. Even if the network comes under the control of established structures—political, economic, social—as long as the technology of the network continues to evolve, the next unexpected opportunity will emerge. It is up to us to be aware of it as it arises, to enter it without expectation, and to let it guide us to a different and more fulfilling mode of temporal being.[6]

Notes

1. This notion of presence-at-a-distance may be involved in the phenomenon of cell-phone use contributing to automobile accidents. Starting in 2001, several states in the United States banned the use of handheld cell phones based on findings that their use contributed to higher accident rates. Very soon, however, studies began to show that hands-free cell-phone use was just as likely—and perhaps more so—to contribute to accidents. The issue proved not to be physical impairment as a result of holding a phone in one hand but "cognitive distraction" (Radsch 2005; Strayer and Drews 2004). But what was the nature of this distraction? What makes a telephone conversation more distracting than listening to a radio program? It seems reasonable to say that it is a matter of presence: communicating with others by telephone, I am in their presence, which means I am trying—with only limited success—to be present in two places at once.

2. There are of course many other ways of classifying time, but as Bluedorn (2002, 22–23) points out, they are often binary. Among the examples Bluedorn gives are chronos and kairos, abstract and vital, succession and duration, linear and cyclical. Another pairing closely related to the one I suggest here is private and public (Nowotny 1994). Bluedorn himself classifies temporality into the binary pair of fungible and epochal. My sense is that although these classifications certainly differ in key respects, they are mostly pointing to similar phenomena.

3. I have coined the term *Frankentime* in reference to "Frankenfood," a term used to describe food derived from genetically modified organisms, apparently coined in 1992. For the history of its usage see www.wordspy.com/words/Frankenfood.asp. For more on the nature of Frankentime see, e.g., Rifkin (1987). For a penetrating analysis of Frankentime see Tulku (1987).

4. The possibilities for presence and the overwhelming obstacles to its realization or activation in our own time are prefigured in powerful ways in the short stories of Franz Kafka (1952). "A Common Confusion" portrays in schematic form the failure of subjective and objective time to cohere into a livable whole. "In the Penal Colony" presents a failed, even psychotic, attempt to turn the told story into the lived story and

thus return to a time in which meaning was immediately available, in which the written word could magically be transformed into presence.

Kafka was especially concerned with the potential of the artist to restore to the community a sense of presence. For the most part he presents this capacity as deeply compromised and even incapable of realization. "The Hunger Artist" portrays a circus artist who draws crowds through his refusal to eat. Nourishing them through his own denial, he creates presence out of absence. Yet he suffers from a threefold tragedy. First, he can serve the role of artist only by denying his own nature; second, the audience has lost interest and in the end turns instead to the vital, inarticulate life force of a caged panther; and third, his artistry is based on a lie. In contrast, in "Josephine the Singer, or the Mouse Folk" Kafka offers a glimmer of hope. The story tells of a society of mice who somehow take solace from the songs of Josephine, who continues to sing when the art has been almost lost. The songs are off-key and meaningless, yet somehow they succeed at least a little in restoring a sense of meaning and a deeper temporality.

In more recent fiction nature often replaces art as the medium that can restore human beings to a sense of presence. "A Hunger Artist" sees this shift as a loss, but the short story by Le Guin cited in the next note presents nature as imbued with its own wisdom.

5. For a fascinating fictional riff on the inner truth of such mutual presence see "The Direction of the Road," a short story by Ursula Le Guin (1975). The protagonist of this story is a truly egoless tree, able to be—simultaneously—what all others require it to be. Although Le Guin's tree shares this gift freely with humans, as with others who pass its way, they fail to notice its magic. Another work that explores this theme from the opposite direction is the movie *Groundhog Day*, in which the protagonist finds himself repeating the same day over and over. Through this abolition of linear time, the empty desolation of Frankentime in which he had previously lived gradually gives way to a "timing" shaped by the thriving presence—in precisely the sense I am aiming at here—of a mutually supportive community, one that he helps create by giving it the gift of a present-centered time.

6. Because the shift I describe here is subtle, investigating it requires a certain subtlety as well, a sensitivity to temporal experience and the availability of presence. With regard to this methodological issue, Gallagher (2003) has usefully introduced the term "front-loaded phenomenology"; i.e., using first-person experience to shape the design of empirical studies. Without some such approach, the interactions one is trying to study are likely to get lost in the unremitting stream of data.

References

Adam, Barbara. 2004. *Time*. Cambridge, MA: Polity.

Arendt, Hannah. 1963. *Between past and future: Six exercises in political thought*. Cleveland: World Publishing.

Baudrillard, Jean. 1998. Simulacra and simulations. In *Selected writings*, ed. Mark Poster, 166–184. Stanford, CA: Stanford University Press.

Berners-Lee, Tim. 1999. *Weaving the Web: The original design and ultimate destiny of the World Wide Web by its inventor.* New York: HarperCollins.

Bluedorn, Allen. 2002. *The human organization of time: Temporal realities and experience.* Stanford, CA: Stanford University Press.

Brooks, James. *Broadcast News* [script], 1987. www.script-o-rama.com/movie_scripts/b/broadcast-news-script-screenplay.html (accessed Dec. 13, 2005).

Brown, Greg. 2000. 'Cept you and me, babe. *Covenant.* St. Paul, MN: Red House Records.

Cerf, Vint. 1999. *The caring economy: Business principles for the new digital age.* http://global.mci.com/resources/cerfs_up/reviews/caring_eco.xml (accessed Nov. 23, 2005).

Didion, Joan. 2005. *The year of magical thinking.* New York: Knopf.

Elias, Norbert. 1992. *Time: An essay.* Oxford: Blackwell.

Gadamer, Hans-Georg. 1986. *Truth and method.* New York: Crossroad.

Gallagher, Shaun. 2003. Phenomenology and experimental design. *Journal of Consciousness Studies* 10 (9–10): 85–99.

Hall, Edward. 1966. *The hidden dimension.* Garden City, NJ: Doubleday.

Hampton, Keith, and Barry Wellman. 2003. Neighboring in Netville: How the Internet supports community and social capital in a wired suburb. *City and Community* 2 (4): 277–311.

Hassan, Robert. 2003. Network time and the new knowledge epoch. *Time & Society* 12 (2–3): 225–241.

Kafka, Franz. 1952. *Selected short stories of Franz Kafka.* Trans. Willa and Edwin Muir. New York: Modern Library.

Lasch, Christopher. 1977. *Haven in a heartless world: The family besieged.* New York: Basic Books.

———. 1979. *The culture of narcissism: American life in an age of diminishing expectations.* New York: Norton.

Le Guin, Ursula. 1975. The direction of the road. In *The wind's twelve quarters.* New York: Harper and Row.

MacIntyre, Alistair. 1984. *After virtue.* 2nd ed. Notre Dame, IN: University of Notre Dame Press.

Merleau-Ponty, Maurice. 1962. *Phenomenology of perception.* Trans. Colin Smith. London: Routledge.

Mitchell, Joni. 1976. Amelia. *Hejira.* Los Angeles: Asylum Records.

Nehamas, Alexander. 1998. *The art of living: Socratic reflections from Plato to Foucault.* Berkeley: University of California Press.

Nowotny, Helga. 1994. *Time: The modern and postmodern experience.* Trans. Neville Plaice. Cambridge, MA: Polity.

Oates, Joyce Carol. 1984. Frankenstein's fallen angel. *Critical Inquiry* 10:543–554.

Petranker, Jack. 2005. The when of knowing. *Journal of Applied Behavioral Science* 41 (2): 241–259.

Polkinghorne, Donald. 1988. *Narrative knowing and the human sciences.* Albany: State University of New York Press.

Radsch, Courtney. 2005. "Driver-cellphone laws exist, but their value is disputed." *New York Times*, Jan. 18.

Ricoeur, Paul. 1984. *Time and narrative*. Vol. 1. Chicago: University of Chicago Press.

Rifkin, Jeremy. 1987. *Time wars: The primary conflict in human history*. New York: Simon and Schuster.

Standage, Tom. 1998. *The Victorian Internet*. New York: Berkley.

Strayer, David, and Frank Drews. 2004. Profiles in driver distraction: Effects of cell phone conversations on younger and older drivers. *Human Factors* 46:640–649.

Taylor, Charles. 1989. *Sources of the self: The making of the modern identity*. Cambridge, MA: Harvard University Press.

Tulku, Tarthang. 1987. *Love of knowledge*. Berkeley, CA: Dharma Publishing.

———. 1990. *Knowledge of time and space*. Berkeley, CA: Dharma Publishing.

Virilio, Paul. 1997. *Open sky*. Trans. Julie Rose. London: Verso.

10 CyberLack

David R. Loy

In that unbounded moment, I saw millions of delightful and horrible acts;
none amazed me so much as the fact that all occupied the same point,
without superimposition and without transparency. . . . I saw the populous
sea, saw dawn and dusk, saw the multitudes of the Americas, . . . saw
horses with wind-swept manes on a beach in the Caspian sea at dawn,
saw the delicate bones of a hand, saw the survivors of a battle sending
postcards, saw a Tarot card in a shopwindow in Mirzapur, saw the oblique
shadows of ferns on the floor of a greenhouse, saw tigers, pistons, bisons,
tides and armies.

—*Jorge Luis Borges*, Collected Fictions

A MYSTICAL EXPERIENCE? Another description of that miracle of digital technology, the Internet? Or both? In Borges's "The Aleph" the narrator discovers a mysterious object, only a few centimeters in diameter, that reflects the infinity of things seen from every other point in the cosmos (Borges 1999, 282). Such a fantasy seems, well, rather fantastic, but some netizens have read Borges's 1949 story as forecasting the Internet. "The Aleph, the portal through which one can see every point in the universe, is Netscape Navigator in all but name" (Douglas Wonk). "Mac-and-Netscape is my personal Aleph, in an early T-model form" (Douglas Davis).[1] A fanciful comparison? "You can call for a dual-language text of Marcus Aurelius, or the latest paper in Malay on particle acceleration. Your reading can be interrupted by the appearance of a friend in your portfolio, a look at the actual weather in Djakarta, a film clip of Lyndon Johnson's inaugural, or, for that matter, anything, summoned by voice, available instantaneously, and billed to your central account" (Helprin 2001, 11).

Arthur C. Clarke has claimed that any sufficiently advanced technology is indistinguishable from magic, and certainly there is something magical about a device that can do the above. But is our fascination with these new possibilities motivated by something deeper? Johannes Gutenberg celebrated the religious function of his new technology: "Let us break the seal which seals up the holy things and give wings to Truth in order that she may win every soul that comes into the world by her word, no longer written at great expense by hand easily palsied, but multiplied like the wind by an untiring machine" (Davis 1998, 269). Today we tend to focus less on the salvific function of revealed Truth than on the "side-effects" of the new medium—or rather, the new environment, "corresponding to space-worlds and time-worlds that never before existed in human history" (Holmes 1997, 3). How radically is the new environment changing us? Erik Davis (1998, 96) refers to "the subliminal hunch that our increasingly incorporeal information machines may be altering and expanding consciousness itself"; and Lorne Dawson (2001, 3) agrees that the "very nature and reach of human consciousness and culture are being extended, and hence changed, by the new virtual technologies around us." Do we hope—maybe we cannot help hoping?—that what is involved is some kind of profound transformation of the human condition?

Borges's narrator emphasizes the augmented "unbounded moment" in which the Aleph revealed millions of acts; then the narrator explains that "What my eye saw was *simultaneous*; what I shall write is *successive*, because language is successive" (Borges 1999, 283). A necessary qualification, surely: simultaneity, the nonduality of time and eternity, is something that even the Internet cannot provide us with—or can it?

"Imagine a world in which time seems to vanish and space seems completely malleable. Where the gap between need or desire and fulfillment collapses to zero. Where distance equals a microsecond in lapsed connection time" (McKenna 1999, 3). Regis McKenna calls this "real time," a term that also serves as the title for his breathless book acclaiming our digital conquest of space and time. "The change in our consciousness of time is the creation of ubiquitous programmable technology producing results at the click of the mouse or the touch of the button or key. Real time occurs when time and distance vanish, when action and response are simultaneous" (ibid., 4–5).

McKenna's business book focuses on the implications of real time for e-commerce. Yet his point applies to many of us (and to many of those affected by us) whose lives are increasingly organized around cell phones, email, and the Internet. Before most of us had ever used these media, Helga Nowotny argued that "we are about to abolish the category of the future and replace

it with that of the extended present. . . . The category of the future is shrinking towards becoming a mere extension of the present because science and
technology have successfully reduced the distance that is needed to accommodate their own products" (Nowotny 1988, 14–15). Many other scholars have
been noticing these effects. In *The Condition of Postmodernity* David Harvey
coined the term "time-space compression" to describe the early effects of globalization. Anthony Giddens used the phrase "time-space distanciation" to
describe how the increasing pace of modern life is "disembedding" us by col-
lapsing time / space coordinates. Jean Baudrillard also refers to an implosion
of our time / space axis, and Manuel Castells, in his trilogy *The Information
Age*, discusses how the space of flows has replaced the space of places in what
he calls "timeless time" (Castells 2000, 460).

Insofar as we consciously or unconsciously hope for a transformation of
consciousness, Castells's phrase suggests an intriguing speculation. With the
digital gap between now and then, cause and effect, desire and fulfillment
becoming asymptotically compressed, are we approaching the timeless time
that religious mystics have long sought? If one can believe them, their augmented consciousness has often included an extraordinary transformation
of the present, from a dimensionless line, moving between the infinities of
past and future, to an *eternal present* that contains past and future. Such a
counterintuitive claim is difficult to understand, much less accept, yet there
is ample testimony to it. According to the Neoplatonist philosopher Plotinus,
"There is all one day, series has no place; no yesterday and no tomorrow." The
Christian mystic Nicholas of Cusa made the same point: "All temporal succession coincides in one and the same Eternal Now. So there is nothing past
or future." The Chan (Zen) master Huang-po: "Beginningless time and the
present moment are the same. . . . You have only to understand that time has
no existence."[2] As our new cybernetic present swallows the future—and just
in time, for it is increasingly difficult to have faith in any extended future—
are we beginning to realize something about the eternal, not-falling-away
present? Or is McKenna's "real time" better understood as a digital version of
the mythic scenario that McLuhan believed to be the archetypal scene of all
technology: Narcissus gazing into a pool, mesmerized by his own reflection
(Davis 1998)?

Ronald Purser has criticized McKenna for not discriminating between increasingly compressed clock time and our psychological experience of time
passing. "McKenna not only conflates clock-time with lived time, but he

privileges clock-time and its associative links to technology as deterministic of our consciousness" (Purser 2002). He quotes Paul Virilio: this temporal acceleration means that "there is no more here and there, only the mental confusion of near and far, present and future, real and unreal—a mix of history, stories, and the hallucinatory utopia of communication technologies" (Virilio 1997, 35). We will return to those insights, but, for better or worse, the technological demands of the digital age are restructuring our psychological experience of lived time. With the industrial revolution the need to adapt to the needs of machines made human labor machinelike; today we adapt to computers by becoming cybernetic. Does this mean that human temporality is also digitalizing? Is McKenna's "real time" becoming our real time? And if so, is this transformation simply the conditioning of a new technological environment, or is there something within us that embraces this temporal compression?

The Lack of Time

There is at least a superficial similarity between McKenna's real time and the "*tada!* just this!" recommended in Buddhism, among other spiritual traditions that emphasize the importance of Being Here Now. I first heard the phrase "timeless time" from a Zen teacher, and she wasn't referring to the digital information revolution. When the historical Buddha Shakyamuni was asked why his disciples were so radiant, although eating but a single meal a day, he replied: "They do not sorrow over the past, nor do they hanker for the future. They maintain themselves with what is present: hence their complexion is so serene. Through hankering for the future, through sorrowing for the past, fools dry up and wither away like a green reed cut down" (Bodhi 2000, 93). The contemplative path he taught involves letting go of memories and previous conditioning (the past), as well as desires, intentions, and expectations (the future), in order to realize something about oneself (right now). "Timeless time" could also be used to describe the Japanese Zen master Dōgen's neologism *uji* "being-time": "Each moment is all being, is the entire world. Reflect now whether any being or any world is left out of the present moment" (Tanahashi 1985, 76). Is this what McKenna means when he refers to time and distance vanishing, when action and response become simultaneous?

The short answer is no, because the differences between digital timeless time and Dōgen's timeless time turn out to be more significant than their similarities. Buddhism does not encourage instantaneous gratification of desire (including, we may suppose, desire for immediate information retrieval) but letting go of desire, since craving is the cause of our *dukkha*, and *dukkha*—"dissatisfaction, dis-ease"—is the problem that the Buddhist path is designed to end. To end dukkha we must realize *anatta* "nonself," which does not mean getting rid of the self (since there never has been a self) but rather understanding that one's sense of self is *shunya* "empty"—in modern terms, a psychological and social construct. Dukkha and anatta are the two most important concepts in Buddhism, and what is most distinctive about Buddhism can be expressed in terms of their relationship. That relationship can help us to understand what is problematic about cybertime.

Dukkha is often translated as suffering, but then suffering must be taken in a very broad sense, as including the implications of impermanence (even blissful moments pass away) and nonself (a basic anxiety is built into our delusive sense of self). Existential psychology emphasizes the consequences of repressing our fear of death, but from a Buddhist perspective dread of death still projects our main problem into the future. The Buddhist emphasis on anatta implies that our worst dukkha, and therefore our most troublesome repression, is our groundlessness right now: we do not feel real enough because there is an emptiness at the core of our being. We experience this emptiness—in Freudian terms, the repressed returns in a disguised fashion—as a sense of something missing that haunts us. What is wrong with us? We usually understand the problem as something outside ourselves that we lack: I do not have enough money, or fame, or sex, etc. The problem with those responses is that none of these things can ever satisfy us if they are not really what we want. When we do not understand what is actually motivating us—because what we think we want is only a symptom of something else (the urge to become more real, to ground our groundlessness, which is a spiritual yearning)—we end up compulsive.

This way of understanding spirituality straddles our usual distinction between sacred and secular. If our groundlessness is a constant, and the need to resolve the resulting sense of lack is also constant, and if religion is defined broadly as *how we try to resolve the sense of lack caused by our groundlessness*, then there is no way to avoid a religious understanding of the world. Whether or not we consider ourselves secular, our basic problem remains spiritual inasmuch as the sense-of-self's felt lack of being compels us to seek being some way or another, consciously or unconsciously, in overtly religious ways (e.g., going to church and confessing our sins) or in this-worldly ways (e.g., trying to ground myself by accumulating enough money or fame).

. . .

What does all this have to do with cybertime? This explication of dukkha and anatta has important implications for the ways that human societies experience and conceptualize time, including modern secular understandings and digital "real time." Temporal schemas, like spatial ones, are neither objectively true (e.g., Newton's concept of space as a contentless container) nor simply the reductionistic effects of technological and economic factors. Rather, our temporality always has a "spiritual" dimension in the sense that it is profoundly connected with how we understand our sense of lack and how we attempt to deal with it. As Norman Brown (1961, 277) put it, time is "a schema for the expiation of guilt"—that is, for the resolution of our sense of lack.

This is easier to see with premodern societies, in which religion and the passage of time are almost indistinguishable (Thompson 1996, 4). Temporal schemas are essential to the ways that traditional societies have tried to resolve their collective sense of lack, usually by keeping (or bringing) this world in harmony with a "higher" one. According to this approach our sense of lack is due to their disharmony (or the threat of it), and the solution involves time as a lived pattern that needs to be renewed or reenacted. This is an associative understanding of temporality that does not distinguish history from cosmology, because no distinction is made between time and what happens *in* time. Rituals are performed at certain times because they are needed at those times, which means they do not just happen at those times but as part of those times. The time-obsessed Maya are a good example. They did not just measure time by the sun; rather, each day manifested its own god, and it was necessary to pay close attention to the special demands of each god to maintain harmony with the supernatural. As in most premodern societies, the future was of little interest, for the most important events would recur as long as the balance of cosmic forces was maintained (Aveni 1995, 190).

The Mayans "believed they were active participants and intermediaries in a great cosmic drama. By participating in the rituals, they helped the gods of nature to carry their burdens along their arduous course, for they believed firmly that the rituals served formally to close time's cycles. Without their life's work the universe could not function properly" (Aveni 1995, 252). The Mayans "knew" what their lack was and what they must do to resolve it. They did not feel alienated from nature; on the contrary, the natural world needed them and their rituals. In temporal terms their society did not just happen to be "in" time; they were an essential part of time.

In contrast to its preoccupation with repeating the past, secular modernity emphasizes the future, in the conscious or unconscious belief that our lack will be resolved and we will become more fulfilled (grounded) if and when our projects have been successfully completed. In sociological terms Western cultures emphasize achievement more than affiliation; tradition is less important than the freedom to change and improve our situation. The psychoanalyst Neil Altman realized this when he was a Peace Corps volunteer in India: "It took a year for me to shed my American, culturally based feeling that I had to make something happen. . . . Being an American, and a relatively obsessional American, my first strategy was to find security through getting something done, through feeling worthwhile accomplishing something. My time was something that had to be filled up with progress toward that goal" (Levine 1997, 204–205). Since the goals we accomplish bring no satisfaction (our sense of lack still itches), we always need more ambitious projects. Unfortunately, this same dynamic also seems to be operating collectively, in our preoccupation with never-enough economic growth and never-ending technological development. As Max Weber pointed out, this historical process has become all the more obsessive because it has lost any teleological end point (Brubaker 1991, 10). We feel compelled to grow ever faster because there is nowhere in particular that we are trying to get to. Such a future-orientation, however, no more reflects the "true" nature of time than the Mayan schema did, insofar as it remains motivated by an individual and collective groundlessness that has not been understood.

What does it mean, then, when the future (the "progress" narrative we keep telling ourselves) collapses? The optimism of politicians and advertisers is becoming less persuasive. The environmental crisis no longer merely threatens; ecological collapse and climate change are upon us. The oil age will end in the not-too-distant future. We live in increasing fear of weapons of mass destruction, whether by terrorist groups or by terrorist nation-states. But, of course, we are also unable to revert to a premodern sensibility preoccupied with rituals that will keep the sun on its course. In short, we cannot find security by clinging to the past (traditional ways of doing things), nor do we still expect to build a brighter future (contributing to the march of progress).

That leaves the present, but there are different ways of experiencing it. One reaction is the increasing distractibility that all our new technological devices encourage; cell phones, iPods, etc., are always at hand. Another is the increasing compulsiveness to do more things more quickly, to bury oneself in one's projects, less from the expectation that those projects will achieve very much than from fear of what might happen if we slow down. The basic difficulty with living in the here-and-now is that, when we let go of our temporal strategies for resolving our sense of lack—whether seeking security by reenacting the past or becoming real sometime in the future—we are confronted by our groundlessness in the present. But aren't premodern and modern time schemas also evasive, in their own ways? Perhaps what is special about our postmodern situation is simply that, bereft of past and future, we are beginning to find our inability to cope with our lack / groundlessness more obvious and difficult to ignore. Does that also present us with a special opportunity?

The above reflections offer a "spiritual" perspective for understanding the attraction and function of cybertime. What does this perspective reveal about the digital conflation of now and then, here and there?

CyberBabel

> There will be a road. It will not connect two points. It will connect all points. It will not go from here to there. There will be no there. We will all only be here.
>
> —*MCI television advertisement*

One of the earliest and sharpest critics of cybertime has been Paul Virilio. *Open Sky* identifies a new temporal type of pollution: dromospheric, from the Greek *dromos* "race, running." Instantaneous communication and almost-as-fast transportation are degrading human relationships with the world we live in, diminishing our optical depth of field and creating the desert of a global endless-day time. Virilio's main concern is that remote control and long-distance telepresence technologies are producing "the ultimate state of sedentariness," both terminal and final, "that opens up the incredible possibility of a 'civilization of forgetting,' a *live* (live-coverage) society that has no future and no past, since it has no extension and no duration, a society intensely present here and there at once—in other words, *telepresent to the whole world*" (Virilio 1997, 33). Dromospheric pollution degrades the life of subjects and the mobility of objects by "atrophying the *journey* to the point where it becomes needless" (ibid.). Why make the effort to go anywhere or do anything if everywhere is already here, if every time is now? But then the difference between here and there, now and then, is vitiated and becomes meaningless.

This meaninglessness infects the meanings of our lives, which depend on such differences. Relationships are constructed of meetings and departures, people (and things) who were *there* coming *here*, and then going *somewhere else*, a dialectic of attention and absence. Because we cannot relate to everything and everyone at the same time, we need a spatiotemporal schema to organize those encounters and farewells. As we are beginning to realize, cybertimelessness erodes that schema. Continuous telepresence tends to become indistinguishable from continuous loneliness. "The resistance of distances having ceased, the lost world will send us back to our solitude, a multiple solitude of some billions of individuals whom the multimedia are preparing to organize in quasi-cybernetic fashion" (Virilio 1997, 128). Catie Getches (2004) expresses our gradual realization of what this actually means:

> All it takes is a little time alone, especially late at night, to confirm how much technology has transformed culture and how it has changed the way we relate to each other. That's because being alone is not what it used to be. These days, even momentary solitude seems like something to be avoided at all cost. And technology makes it possible: Thanks to cell phones, no one has to face that stroll down the street, the five-minute commute or the lunch line without companionship. . . .
>
> So it seems as if it should be easier for everyone to connect, late at night or whenever. But the more technology we turn on, the more relationships we have to manage simultaneously—and the more likely we are to ask our best friends if they can hold. I have programmable phone lists and speed dial at my fingertips, and yet I feel more disconnected than ever—somehow, it's easier than ever to be two places at once but nearly impossible to, as my mom says, just "be here now." Yet being in two places at once has become strangely familiar: You don't just go out to lunch with a friend anymore. You go out to lunch with the friend and the friend's cell phone book. . . .
>
> It's so common now to correspond by e-mail alone, it's easy to go for days without actually interacting with a real live human.

The wired way of avoiding solitude reinforces aloneness. The more time people spend online, the higher their rates of loneliness and depression. Repeated studies have shown that increased Internet usage is associated with less family communication and a reduced social circle (e.g., Sanders et al. 2000).

Is that because there is an "economy" to our relationships? In contrast to what might be called the "very high-context information medium" of actual physical presence, telecommunication is a low-context medium that sustains lower-context interpersonal meaning and therefore lower-context relationships. Being able to communicate with so many more people, we find ourselves communicating less with the people most important to us. If we have a limited amount of attention and energy for relating to others, then a profusion of low-context cybercommunications will come at the price of our most important high-context relationships.

Can this point be extrapolated? To be *attentive* to everything telepresent would spread one's awareness so thinly that it would amount to ignore-ance. In terms of my *responsiveness* to that infinity of information, doesn't infinite possibility likewise imply paralytic indecision? How do I decide what to do, what should have priority, when nothing is more present than anything else, physically or temporally?

We are not yet in that situation, but we are close enough to appreciate the problem. For a minor example consider how my CD player and iPod have changed the way I listen to music. Today, when I happen to hear some interesting composition by someone hitherto unknown to me, I usually—often immediately—go online to check it out: to find out what other CDs are available from that performer or composer, and what other listeners think about those CDs. Instead of focusing on the CD I've been listening to, I want to acquire more of the same: I can order other CDs instantly and sometimes do. What happens to those CDs when they arrive? To tell the truth, they tend to pile up unheard for some time because there is not enough time to listen to them. My desire to hear them becomes internalized as another, if more pleasant, aspect of the time-compression that increasingly squeezes me. A decade or so ago my attention would have been focused on appreciating that particular CD, but now it is easy to explore related possibilities—in other words, my interests and desires can effortlessly propagate. The *increasing choice* that Peter Berger (1979) identified as central to modernity has become closer to *infinite choice* today for many of us. Thanks to Amazon and other online services, my problem is not obtaining the CDs I want but finding the time to listen to them with the attention they deserve.

That brings me to my main point. Whenever I do have the time to listen to one of those CDs, often downloaded into my sixty-gigabyte iPod, I'm constantly aware, at some level of consciousness, that if I am not completely satisfied with what I'm hearing, there are a thousand other CDs I could be listening to right now. A century or so ago, someone who loved Beethoven might have only a couple of opportunities, or maybe none, to hear some of his piano sonatas, even if the ticket price of a live performance was not a factor. I can listen to any of those thirty-two sonatas anytime I want. A century ago one was part of a live audience, each member having made efforts to obtain a ticket and gather for that specific event; and once you were there you were *there*, so you settled down *then* and focused on the music being performed. For me, no longer able to attend many live concerts, the decision to listen to any particular *selection* is never completely settled in the sense that I can always change the one that is playing if I become dissatisfied with it for any reason at any time. Like it or not, this aspect of perpetual choice is continually there, at least in the back of my mind, and consciousness of these other possibilities tends to distract me from the music I am actually hearing. I must, in effect, *continually decide* to listen to this particular piece.

What gives this personal example some significance, of course, is that this point applies just as much to many other aspects of our lives: books, TV channel-surfing, DVDs, video games, surfing the net, and so on. Needless to say, this near-infinite choice isn't all bad. I have enjoyed exploring the classical repertoire, discovering obscure composers and new performers. All these options, however, are also affecting our attention and our attention span. I've noticed that I'm listening to fewer symphonies and more short, simple pieces; am I the only one?

Thomas Eriksen (2001) has studied this phenomenon and distilled it into a temporal principle. What we lack most now is lack of information: we are drowning in an info-glut (Eriksen 2001, 19). Our old time-habits were based on info-scarcity, hence the traditional importance of learning how to forage for it. Suddenly, like Mickey Mouse in "The Sorcerer's Apprentice," we find ourselves trying to survive an information tsunami, and the scarcest resources have become *attention* and *control over our own time*. Eriksen formalizes this relationship into a general law of the information revolution: "When an ever increasing amount of information has to be squeezed into the relatively constant amount of time each of us has at our disposal, the span of attention necessarily decreases" (Eriksen 2001, 21–22, 69).

Eriksen's insight can be expanded to include the near-infinite range of consumption possibilities that also attract our attention and proliferate our cravings, giving us the following reformulation:

$$\frac{\text{(same amount of time)}}{\text{(more possibilities [info-glut + digital shopping mall])}} = \text{shorter attention span}$$

Even if we ignore for the moment the omnipresent seduction of infinite consumer alternatives, such an avalanche of information (and therefore shorter attention spans) challenges our ability to construct narratives and logical sequences, putting pressure on traditional ways of thinking that involve cause-effect and organic development. In its very form "the World Wide Web inculcates a strong and almost reflex-like preference for heightened visual stimuli, rapid changes of subject matter, and diversity, combined with simplicity of presentation" (Dawson 2001, 7). Sherry Turkle has noticed that some of her MIT students now reason and arrange their ideas differently: "There is this sense that the world is out there to be Googled," she says, "and there is this associative glut. But linking from one thing to another is not the same as having something to say. A structured thought is more than a link" (Burkeman and Johnson 2005).

A cascading glut of decontextualized signs, with an inelastic amount of attention to make them meaningful, results in association-glut (Eriksen 2001, 109). Is this the personal Aleph that Wonk and David celebrate? Another, less-encouraging metaphor comes to mind, from a different Borges story: "The Library of Babel" (1941).[3] Borges's narrator describes a dystopic world consisting only of a boundless library with endless bookshelves of books containing apparently random letters and punctuation:

> In all the Library, there are no two identical books. From these incontrovertible premises, the librarian deduced that the Library is "total"—perfect, complete, and whole—and that its bookshelves contain all possible combinations of the twenty-two orthographic symbols (a number which, though unimaginably vast, is not infinite)—that is, all that is able to be expressed, in every language.

If it exhausts all orthographic possibilities, the library's books must encompass all linguistic truth and wisdom, including the correct answer to every conceivable question, but at a price:

> When it was announced that the Library contained all books, the first reaction was unbounded joy. All men felt themselves the possessors of an intact and secret treasure. There was no personal problem, no world problem, whose eloquent solution did not exist—somewhere in the hexagon.

We rejoice in having so much information at our fingertips:

> At that same period there was also hope that the fundamental mysteries of mankind—the origin of the Library and of time—might be revealed.

Such a Library will augment our consciousness and transform our lives:

> That unbridled hopefulness was succeeded, naturally enough, by a similarly disproportionate depression. The certainty that some bookshelf in some hexagon contained precious books, yet that those precious books were forever out of reach, was almost unbearable.

Out of reach, because an all-inclusive data-glut turns out to be equivalent to no data at all, if it is impossible to locate any meaningful text—a problem that could not be solved even if the Library had a Google-like search engine, because the basic issue is not how to find the right books but rather the meaningless (because completely decontextualized) nature of the infinite data that the Library's books contain. Is this analogous to the decontextualized moments of our digital "real time"?

> The moment, or instant, is ephemeral, superficial and intense. When the moment (or even the *next*) *moment* dominates our being in time, we no longer have space for building blocks that can only be used for one or a few configurations with other blocks. Everything must be interchangeable with everything else *now*. The entry ticket has to be cheap, the initial investment modest. Swift changes and unlimited flexibility are main assets. In the last instance, everything that is left is a single, overfilled, compressed, eternal moment. (Eriksen 2001, 119)

An eternal now? What makes the mystic's *now* eternal is that it does not repeatedly fall away, replaced by a different *now*, because it encompasses past and future rather than excluding them. Cybertime, however, aspires to a different timelessness. "*When time is chopped up into sufficiently small units,* . . . it ceases to exist as duration (which presupposes that events take a certain time) but continues to exist as *moments about to be overtaken by the next moment*" (Eriksen 2001, 123).

What is the difference between these two types of eternal presence? The cyberpresent results from slicing time so thinly that sense of duration disappears, replaced by accelerating speed. Our awareness usually hops from one perch to the other, but now it hops so quickly that the sensation is more like running on an accelerating treadmill. This is possible, however, only because now-moments—our treadmill steps—are denuded of meaningful content. Each step is no different from the last, or the next. Whatever content there is, is immediately replaced by different content. Without a relationship to previous and following moments, the present becomes dehistoricized, autonomous, fungible, and interchangeable with the next moment—which denudes it of extended meaning. From a Buddhist perspective, the cyberpresent *must* keep falling away insofar as it is still haunted by lack, by the uncomfortable sense of groundlessness that shadows a constructed sense of self. The *dukkha* of having an ungrounded sense-of-self makes us cling to one perch or another, but the inability of any perch to ground us keeps us jumping from one perch to another, seeking something that none of them ever provides us. Cybertime does not escape this problem because it perpetuates the dualism that we experience between things (including ourselves) and the time they are "in." For Buddhism their bifurcation is a delusion, for this perceived split between things and their time is not something real or objective but constructed—which means it can be deconstructed.

Nondual Time

> To define the present in isolation is to kill it.
> —*Paul Klee, quoted in Virilio,* Open Sky

Our basic problem with time is not simply that everything dear to us (including ourselves) will pass away, nor is the solution simply to accept that impermanence. That still presupposes a duality between things and time. As the second-century Indian Buddhist philosopher Nagarjuna emphasized, if there is no permanence then there can be no impermanence either, because the meaning of each term depends on the other: unless there is something permanent to provide a fixed standard of reference, impermanence will not be perceived as impermanence. "So the young man does not grow old nor does the old man grow old" (Nagarjuna 1979). Without nouns (things) there are no referents for verbs (past, present, and future tenses). When there are no *things* that have an existence *in* time, then it makes no sense to describe someone as being young or old.

In his *Shōbōgenzō* the thirteenth-century Japanese Zen master Dōgen deconstructs the usual dualism between time and the things "in" it by reducing each pole to the other. *Objects are time* because they lack any nontemporal existence, having no atemporal essence outside of time, in which case things like apples and cups cannot be objects as usually understood because their impermanent "being" is actually a temporal *process* (easier to see with an apple than with a ceramic cup that might perdure for many years before being broken).

Dōgen also demonstrates that *time is objects*. Temporality for us is inseparable from things because our awareness of time depends on the way things change (for example, the way the hand of a clock circles around a clock face). As Einstein realized, time does not exist in and of itself. It is not an objectively existing "container" of self-existent things; rather, it manifests *as* the temporal processes we call object—in which case time, too, is quite different from how it is usually understood. "The time we call spring blossoms directly expresses an existence called flowers. The flowers, in turn, express the time called spring. This is not existence within time; existence itself is time" (Dōgen, in Masunaga 1958, 68).

Dōgen combines subject and predicate into the Japanese term *uji*, usually rendered into English as "being-time":

> "Being-time" here means that time itself is being . . . and all being is time. . . . Time is not separate from you, and as you are present, time does not go away. . . .
>
> Do not think that time merely flies away. Do not see flying away as the only function of time. If time merely flies away, you would be separated from time. The reason you do not clearly understand being-time is that you think of time as only passing. . . . People only see time's coming and going, and do not thoroughly understand that time-being abides in each moment. . . .
>
> Being-time has the quality of flowing. . . . Because flowing is a quality of time, moments of past and present do not overlap or line up side by side. . . . Do not think flowing is like wind and rain moving from east to west. The entire world is not unchangeable, is not immovable. It flows. Flowing is like spring. Spring with all its numerous aspects is called flowing. When spring flows there is nothing outside of spring. (Dōgen, in Tanahashi 1995, 76–80)

When time flows, there is nothing—no *thing*—outside of it. Paradoxically, then, *if there is only time, there is no time*. I become "being-time" when I no longer situate my activities within a clock time understood as external to me. Then, in place of the present as a thin moving line between the immensities of past and future, I live in (or *as*) an eternal now whenever I *become* what I am doing. If every thing already *is* time—if, for example, the "being" of a flower *is* its gesture of blossoming—then we are freed from the delusion that time is something external to the flower, an outside container that the flower is "in." The same is true for us. If time is what I already am—if, for example, my "being" when I am dancing *is* my dancing—then that dancing-time (one form of my *uji* "being-time") is not something objective that contains me. When I "forget myself" as someone who is *doing* the dancing and become truly one with my dancing, I am living in timeless time. Or, more precisely, "I" realize that I have always been living "in" an eternal present.

In other words, I am not *in* time because I *am* time. What I do and what happens to me are not events that occur in time; they are expressions of my being-time. Insofar as I *am* time, though, I cannot be trapped *by* time (aging, fear of approaching death). Ironically, then, to *be* time is to *be free from* time.

In contrast to such a spiritual resolution, McKenna's "real time" compression aggravates the delusive split between time and the things "in" it, because digital technologies enable us to quantify objectified time and coordinate our schedules more precisely. As clock time became central to modern social organization, life became "centered around the emptying out of time (and space) and the development of an abstract, divisible and universally measurable calculation of time" (Aveni 1995, 135). Cybertime does not provide an alternative to this historical development; it completes it.

The collective objectification of clock time means that now, insofar as we are social beings, we must live according to this commonly agreed-upon standard. The complexities of social interaction require such a mechanism for their coordination, though it alienates us from natural temporal rhythms, including those of our own bodies. In order to get to work (or class) by 9:00 a.m., one has to catch the 8:16 bus. But to live *only* according to that collective construct is to "bind ourselves without a rope," to use the Zen metaphor for a self-imposed mental constriction. In contrast, with Dōgen's *uji* being-time the temporality of an activity is intrinsic to the activity itself. We can sometimes notice this difference in, for example, the way music is played. Often the notes march along precisely following the time signature, but sometimes we become so absorbed in those notes that we do not notice the time signature at all because the music embodies its own time. According to Buddhism, *anatta*—our lack of a substantial self—opens up the same possibility for us: awakening to my nonduality with the world, "I" realize that I am a manifestation of it. This frees me from the self-preoccupation involved in always trying to ground myself. There is no separate self that needs to become real and therefore no need to use time efficiently to do so.

There is another way to make this point—by deconstructing causality rather than temporality—which helps to clarify the problem with digipresence / presents. Mahayana Buddhist philosophy distinguishes three truths or levels of reality.[4] On the first level the world is experienced in the usual way, as a collection of discrete things interacting in objective space and time. Strictly speaking, this is delusive, because their causal interdependence reveals that things are not really separate from each other. To some extent, however, this way of understanding, like the supposed objectivity of clock time, is a necessary fiction: we need to postulate some identity between the person who does the work and the person who collects the paycheck.

The second level of reality denies the substantiality of such things (including us) by emphasizing the interconditionality or "interpermeation" of all phenomena. Nothing has any self-existing reality of its own because everything is cause-and-effect of everything else. The world is composed of an all-encompassing web of relationships. This causal deconstruction corresponds to the temporal deconstruction (e.g., Dōgen's claim, above) that reveals there is *only* time. In this version there are no things, *only* causes and effects. The metaphor of Indra's net is often used to explain this level. In the abode of the great god Indra there is an extraordinary net that stretches infinitely in all directions. At each node of the net there is a jewel that reflects all the other jewels in the net, and if we look more closely, we can see that every one of those infinite reflections in each node is itself reflecting all the other jewels. The point is that each phenomenon in the universe is both an effect of the whole and a cause of the whole, defining and sustaining all the others. What unifies the whole is the web of interpenetrating traces that constitutes each of the myriad jewels. The groundedness we seek is found in the net itself, in the fact that each node, including each of us, is manifesting the whole net.

If that seems far-fetched, consider what the Vietnamese Buddhist teacher Thich Nhat Hanh says about the sheet of paper you are now reading:

> If you are a poet, you will see clearly that there is a cloud floating in this sheet of paper. Without a cloud, there will be no rain; without rain, the tree cannot grow, and without trees we cannot make paper. The cloud is essential for the paper to exist. . . .
>
> If we look into this sheet of paper even more deeply, we can see the sunshine in it. If the sunshine is not there, the tree cannot grow. In fact, nothing can grow. Even we cannot grow without sunshine. And so, we know that the

sunshine is also in this sheet of paper. The paper and the sunshine inter-are. And if we continue to look, we can see the logger who cut the tree and brought it to the mill to be transformed into paper. And we see the wheat. We know that the logger cannot exist without his daily bread, and therefore the wheat that became his bread is also in this sheet of paper. And the logger's father and mother are in it too. . . .

You cannot point out one thing that is not here—time, space, the earth, the rain, the minerals in the soil, the sunshine, the cloud, the river, the heat. Everything co-exists with this sheet of paper. . . . As thin as this sheet of paper is, it contains everything in the universe in it. (Hanh 1988, 3–5)

So there are no discrete things, only conditionality. But then the third truth or level of reality goes on to question causality. The previous discussion of time noted the paradox that, if there is *only* time, then there is *no* time; and if we *are* time, then we cannot be trapped *in* time. Is the same true for causality? "That which, taken as causal or dependent, is the process of being born and passing on, is, taken non-causally and beyond all dependence, declared to be *nirvana*" (Nagarjuna 1979, 25:9). Now the dialectic reverses: after causality has been used to deconstruct the self-existence of things, the lack of self-existing things can be used to deconstruct our usual way of understanding causality. Even as our naive conception of things as separate leaves them dependent on causal relationships to link them together, so our usual conception of causality presumes a (noncausal) thing that becomes different from what *it* was before. The basic problem with such a causal deconstruction is that there is no *thing* left to be caused (or effected). If the person who wakes up in the morning is not the "same" person who goes to bed that night, then it makes no sense to say that "she has changed." As with temporality, if there is no contained, there can be no container. I am not subject to cause and effect because "I" *am* cause and effect. To be nondual with the all-encompassing web of interconditionality is to be free from it, in the sense that I cannot be trapped by "external" circumstances insofar as I am nothing other than a way all those circumstances come together. Like every other node in Indra's infinite net, I am the cause and effect of everything, lacking nothing.

· · ·

Why have I devoted so much time and space to the subtleties of Mahayana Buddhist metaphysics? Because these distinctions clarify, better than anything else I know, what is lacking in cybertimelessness. While McKenna celebrates a new digital world in which time and distance seem to vanish, Virilio laments how telepresence technologies are degrading our relationship with the world into a sedentary forgetfulness that flattens our depth of field, and Eriksen points out how our attention spans are shrinking in response to an info-glut of decontextualized signs. Omnipresent digital relationships nurture a loneliness that knows neither here nor there, a meaningless present unrelated to the past or the future.

The basic point of my Buddhist response is that we already live in an eternal present, but it is an infinitely deep one that escapes Virilio's and Eriksen's critiques because it is nondual with—a manifestation of—the past and future. The challenge is not to achieve such a presence technologically but to realize how that has always been the case. In the piece of paper you are reading right now, the whole world is already present, not as squashed into a flatland of omnipresent video monitors, or as the cornucopia of consumer alternatives that Amazon offers, but as an interconditionality linking us to everything, since we too are expressions of that interconditionality. Each of us manifests an infinite network of relationships, not in the size of our cell phone contact list but by virtue of our intrinsic interdependence. Everything is already here and now, not by obliterating *there* and *then* but in a way that also preserves the necessary distinctions.

Cybertime achieves near-instantaneity by speeding us up, but it still presupposes the basic, problematic duality between time and the supposedly separate things (most problematically, us) that are *in* it. It celebrates that so many more things can happen so much more quickly, yet we remain ungrounded, lack-ridden subjects subject to all the *dukkha* inherent in the delusion of a being trapped in an external, objective temporality. For a solution to that duality, we need to look in a different direction.[5]

Notes

1. The Wonk and Davis quotes, along with references to Borges's "The Aleph," are included in the conclusion to Levy (2001, 201–202).

2. These examples are cited in Wilber (1977, 92–93).

3. In Borges (1999, 112–128); the following quotes are from 114–116. See also Borges's 1944 story "Funes the Memorious" (Borges 1999, 126–132).

4. Although Madhyamika usually distinguishes two (not three) truths, Nagarjuna's analysis of causality—using interdependence to deconstruct self-existing things, and also using that lack of substantiality to deny causal relations—implies such a threefold distinction. This is also the *trisvabhava* "three-natures" of Yogacara philosophy.

5. Eriksen's law—more information means decreasing attention span—can be counteracted by meditative practices that increase our attention span by slowing us down, enabling us to realize something. The Tibetan teacher Tarthang Tulku (1977) offers a collection of exercises to help us realize that the true nature of things is fundamentally "Great Space"; things are nothing other than this Space, which cannot be grasped as an object by a subject. Our more usual way of experiencing static objects *in* space is due to a "freezing tendency," which can be unlearned. For a discussion of this see Purser (2004). There is an obvious parallel with what might be called "Great Time."

References

Aveni, Anthony. 1995. *Empires of time.* New York: Kodansha.

Berger, Peter. 1979. *The heretical imperative.* New York: Doubleday.

Bodhi, Bhikkhu, trans. 2000. *Samyutta Nikaya.* Vol. 1 of *The connected discourses of the Buddha: A new translation of the Samyutta Nikaya.* Boston: Wisdom.

Borges, Jorge Luis. 1999. *Collected fictions.* Trans. Andrew Hurley. New York: Penguin.

Brown, Norman O. 1961. *Life against death: The psychoanalytic meaning of history.* New York: Vintage.

Brubaker, Rogers. 1991. *The limits of rationality: An essay on the social and moral thought of Max Weber.* London: Routledge.

Burkeman, Oliver, and Bobbie Johnson. 2005. Search and you shall find. *The Guardian*, Feb. 2, www.guardian.co.uk/g2/story/0,,1403533,00.html (accessed Dec. 11, 2006).

Castells, Manuel. 2000. *The rise of the network society.* Vol. 1 of *The information age: Economy, society, and culture.* 2nd ed. Oxford: Blackwell.

Davis, Erik. 1998. *TechGnosis: Myth, magic, and mysticism in the age of information.* London: Serpent's Tail.

Dawson, Lorne. 2001. Doing religion in cyberspace: The promise and the perils. *Council of Societies for the Study of Religion Bulletin* 30 (1): 3–9.

Eriksen, Thomas. 2001. *Tyranny of the moment: Fast and slow time in the information age.* London: Pluto.

Getches, Catie. 2004. Wired nights: In the 24-hour universe, there's no winding down. *Washington Post*, Oct. 17.

Hanh, Thich Nhat. 1988. *The heart of understanding.* Berkeley, CA: Parallax Press.

Helprin, Mark. 2001. The acceleration of tranquility. In *Big issues: The examined life in the digital age*, ed. *Forbes ASAP*, 9–21. New York: John Wiley and Sons.

Holmes, David. 1997. Introduction: Virtual politics—Identity and community in cyberspace. In *Virtual politics: Identity and community in cyberspace*, ed. David Holmes, 1–25. London: Sage.

Levine, Robert. 1997. *A geography of time.* New York: Basic Books.

Levy, David M. 2001. *Scrolling forward: Making sense of documents in the digital age.* New York: Arcade.

Masunaga, Reihō. 1958. *The Sōtō approach to Zen.* Trans. and ed. Reihō Masunaga. Tokyo: Layman Buddhist Society.

McKenna, Regis. 1999. *Real time: Preparing for the age of the never satisfied customer.* Cambridge, MA: Harvard Business School Press.

Nagarjuna. 1979. *Mulamadhyamikakārikā* 13:5. In Candrakīrti, *Lucid Exposition of the Middle Way.* Trans. Mervyn Sprung. Boulder, CO: Prajñā Press.

Nowotny, Helga. 1988. From the future to the extended present: Time in social systems. In *The formulation of time preferences in multidisciplinary perspective,* ed. G. Kirsch, P. Nijkamp, and K. Zimmerman, 17–31. Aldershot, U.K.: Gower.

Purser, Ronald. 2002. Contested presents. In *Making time: Time and management in organizations,* ed. R. Whipp, B. Adam, and I. Sabelis, 155–167. Oxford: Oxford University Press.

———. 2004. Putting Great Space at the center: A commentary on the TSK space exercises. In *A new way of being,* ed. Jack Petranker, 131–158. Berkeley, CA: Dharma Publishing.

Sanders, Christopher E., Tiffany M. Field, Miguel Diego, and Michele Kaplan. 2000. The relationship of Internet use to depression and social isolation among adolescents. *Adolescence* (summer): www.findarticles.com/p/articles/mi_m2248/is_138_35/ai_66171001 (accessed July 20, 2005).

Tanahashi, Kazuaki, ed. 1985. *Moon in a dewdrop: Writings of Zen master Dōgen.* San Francisco: North Point.

Thompson, Damien. 1996. *The end of time.* London: Minerva.

Tulku, Tarthang. 1977. *Time, space, and knowledge: A new vision of reality.* Berkeley, CA: Dharma Publishing.

Virilio, Paul. 1997. *Open sky.* Trans. Julie Rose. London: Verso.

Wilber, Ken. 1977. *The spectrum of consciousness.* Wheaton, IL: Theosophical Publishing House.

4 TIME IN THE NETWORK ECONOMY

11 Time Robbers, Time Rebels

Limits to Fast Capital

Ben Agger

M ARX WELL UNDERSTOOD that capitalism operates through time. This is time in two senses: capitalism has a past, present, and future; and capitalism utilizes time in order to produce and reproduce itself. Marx's final book, *Capital*, brilliantly analyzes the role of the clock in exploiting workers. It is precisely through the time of the working day that capitalists have figured out how to extract what Marx called surplus value from workers. There is a time each workday during which workers are uncompensated for their labor; this is the time from which profit flows. There is also a possible time, ahead, in which people free themselves from managed and exploiting time and begin to experience the passage of time as unencumbered experience, what Bergson called duration. As I explore below, free time can function as a utopian imagery.

Time helped Marx understand how the seemingly fair exchange of daily labor for a wage was in fact unjust. He theorized that the worker labors for a portion of the working day in order to transfer enough value to the commodity that, if the workday ended then, the sale of the commodity would produce enough value (exchange value in Marx's terms) that the owner of the company would recover his or her investment—in materials, plant, spoilage, advertising, transportation to market, overhead, and, of course, wages. Everyone would "break even." But the bourgeois political economists insisted that capitalists must receive an additional return on their investment, moral compensation for taking the desperate risk of starting a business in the first place. Where does this "profit" come from?

It is tempting to view capitalists as Scrooges who dole out a meager shilling or two a day, purposely depressing wages so that they can live in opulence. But that would risk workers' resistance and revolt. It would also impoverish them so much that they could not consume the commodities they and other workers produce. Capitalism, as Keynes well understood, needs workers to view themselves also as consumers, negotiating the balance between their public (work) and private (leisure / consumer) roles so that consumption can match production. Only if consumption matches production can capitalists retrieve from commodities otherwise languishing as inventory not only their original investments but also the portion called profit. Capitalism, in fact, as Henry Ford brilliantly understood, wants to keep profit margins relatively slender, relying on mass production to help amass large profits (Aronowitz 1992; Braverman 1974).

Indeed, mass production, to be matched by mass consumption, would have been impossible had Ford priced his Model Ts too high. He wanted to put working- and middle-class Americans on wheels, allowing them to escape the din of the early-twentieth-century city in order to picnic in state parks on the weekend. Of course, this assumes a pristine wilderness carefully compartmentalized as "nature" and not part of urban sprawl—a tenuous assumption today. Indeed, Ford voluntarily doubled his workers' wages in order to enhance their ability to buy his cars and to engender loyalty to his company. He also gave them a two-day weekend, both in order to shop and to recreate themselves for the grueling stint of the workweek. (Marx, too, advocated a five-day week, as Tom Hayden reminded me in our discussions about the legacy of the Port Huron Statement of early SDS, which, I contend, is firmly grounded in early Marx.)

Marx and Ford identified two complementary parts of the same process of time theft. Marx identified the need for time to be regimented and controlled in the workplace so that workers would work without compensation for a portion of the working day. Ford identified the need to free people from work time so that they could spend money and restore themselves after the drudgery of factory labor. This is not to suggest that "leisure" is really free. It is precisely my point that it is not in a fast capitalism in which leisure time is as severely regimented as work time. Many people watch television after work (see Miller 1988). The television schedule is rigidly structured and displayed in newspapers and available online. If people cannot manage to find time for their favorite shows, they may tape them and watch them later. Television on demand, via taping, has become a major industry, first for manufacturers of VCRs and now for the brand name TiVo.

Marx stressed time theft in order to demonstrate the origin of profit in workers' uncompensated labor. Ford stressed the need for time management as workers were, in a somewhat later stage of production, able to enjoy a few more hours of apparently "free" time. Ford was advancing beyond Marx as capitalism in the 1920s and 1930s entered the era of mass production, which cheapened commodities such as the first mass-produced automobiles and inserted technology into the production process, especially with the advent of the assembly line, later to be followed by robots and computers (see Mandel 1978). Ford was working and strategizing nearly half a century after Marx. In the interim, people's rudimentary needs could be more readily satisfied, and they were encouraged to work and shop beyond those basic needs. As mass production evolved through both twentieth-century world wars, the primary challenge for capitalism was to persuade people to work and shop beyond the level of mere subsistence. As the Frankfurt School recognized, beginning in the 1930s, capitalism had to produce "false" needs, or wants, for the latest technologies, which were planned to be obsolescent (see Marcuse 1964). In this context time became a more significant factor in capitalism, as people were manipulated not only in the workplace but in after-hours spheres of their existence and experience (see Agger 1989). The culture industries (see Horkheimer and Adorno 1972) were designed precisely to bring about the total administration of time, blurring the boundary between the economy and entertainment.

For Marx, writing in the mid-nineteenth century, urban penury was so oppressive that he did not have to theorize consumption, for example distinguishing between true and false needs (or between needs and wants). People wanted bread, clothing, housing. The leisure class had not yet appeared on the horizon. For Ford, and of course much more for post–World War II theorists such as Veblen and the Frankfurt School, leisure time (*time* is the key word) needed to be theorized and administered so that people shopped sufficiently and in ways that did not harm their work performance, such as overindulgence in alcohol (see Ewen 1976; Leiss 1976). Although time was always a central issue in capitalism—for it is through unpaid time that capitalists derive profit from labor—in an era of potential affluence, at least for the majority of people in industrial countries, time became even more important as capitalism needed to control not only work time but all time. It was in time away from work (or, now, at work using ICTs) that capitalists could ensure that people were kept busy shopping, both fueling the profit machine and remaining distracted from larger questions (see Dyer-Witheford 1999).

Total Administration of Time

Ford couldn't be certain that his workers would handle their doubled wages and an extra day of weekend time responsibly. In a stunning and prescient move—anticipating the total administration of time more than half a century later—Ford created a "sociological department" staffed not by degreed academic sociologists but by people who functioned as social workers, truant officers, and union busters to supervise workers' use of time and money. Members of the sociological department went door to door and canvassed Ford workers to make sure that they were not absent from work and were not drinking away their wages. The sociological department also forcefully resisted Walter Reuther's attempts, during the 1930s, to unionize auto workers. Well before Foucault, Ford understood that people needed to be supervised (or believe that they are being supervised) so that they "spend" (in both senses of the term) their leisure responsibly.

There is a telling dialectic at play here: as people enjoy shorter work hours, they must be encouraged to use those hours in ways that benefit capital. Hence, we watch television and surf the Internet, bombarded by advertising images of the "goods" life. Yet the intensification of time robbery and time administration robs people of the time and space in which to recreate themselves, reproducing their selfhood and identity in ways that allow them to function during "public" time.

Where Adam Smith preached abstinence and thrift in the mid-eighteenth century, by the twentieth century Keynes recognized that capitalism could only survive and thrive if people and government spend beyond their means. Saving was to be replaced by shopping, a process rapidly accelerated after World War II with the advent of personal credit (see Packard 1957). Endless shopping was to match endless production, a process first understood by Marx, where he analyzed workers simultaneously as consumers. To achieve endless consumption, post–World War II capitalism, using information and communication technologies such as the telephone, fax machine, cell phone, and now the Internet, enabled round-the-clock shopping. This was accompanied by a blurring of the boundary, heretofore inviolable in modernity, between the public and private spheres. The Frankfurt School recognized that privacy was imperiled by what I am calling the total administration of time or, as I have called it elsewhere (Agger 1989, 2004), fast capitalism. The problem is that the total administration of time breeds massive discontent and psychic rebellion—alienation, to use an earlier vernacular.

Ford envisaged people leaving crowded cities in their vehicles and achieving communion with nature. Early-twentieth-century environmentalism assumed the distinction between unsavory urban life and unsullied nature. Of course, with the malling and suburbanization of America, that image is a thing of the past. Instead of driving to nature, people have to fly to it, if "it" is to be found anywhere at all. The automobile has become not a means of escape but a home and an office. Women rushing to work in the morning apply their makeup while stopped at the red light. People of both sexes talk to the office and to their kids on their cell phones while driving. People drive to work, as they did before, but now they also drive everywhere else. Americans walk much less than their European counterparts, which may explain in part why obesity is a much more serious problem for Americans. The era of Walter Benjamin's flaneur, walking unhurriedly and with curiosity around great cities, has long passed, at least in the United States.

Part of this story about the management of leisure as well as work time is also, implicitly, a story about space. Critical theory, with a few notable exceptions (e.g., Adam 1995, 1998; Harvey 1989; Hassan 2003; Soja 1989), has neglected both space and time. Time has compressed in fast capitalism largely because things are so far apart and because the only way to get to them is by driving over urban, regional, and interstate roadways. And the malling of suburbs, coupled with the decline of urban cores, has usurped even more time for interurban commuters and shoppers. Jane Holtz Kay (1997) tells this story nicely.

Ford was such an important figure, if not a trained social theorist, because he understood the connection among the automobile, cities, nature, and time use. Ray Kroc and Walt Disney, World War I compatriots, had a similar sophisticated understanding. The era of mass production, which involved the administration of work time and space on the assembly line, cheapened cars and made them available to workers who formerly went to work on foot or by streetcar. Although initially people went on picnics away from the city to escape their urban alienation, the road less traveled was quickly overrun by streams of weekend commuters. Think of the exodus to and from Long Island on a New York City summer weekend.

Initially, the automobile helped people escape their alienated urban lives. And weekends could be spent recreating the self and the selves of one's family members. But gradually this "time" became compressed (not enough of it) and administered (managed by stewards of the culture industries). Images abound from the post–World War II period in America of people sitting in highway gridlock, privatized, their vehicles guzzling gas and polluting the atmosphere. They are going nowhere fast. The REM music video "Everybody Hurts" bespeaks this posturban alienation, which was certainly not intended by Ford. This video captures the lived experience of a post-Fordist, Los Angeles–like sprawl in which time and space have broken down, connoting the imagined experience of the aftermath of a nuclear holocaust in which both cities and norms dissolve (see Davis 1998). Ford's utopia of the five-day workweek, tea-totaling families, and picnics on the weekend has become a dystopia of compressed and managed time and gridlocked, polluted space, disrupting capitalism in ways unimagined by Marx, whose depiction of alienation might have been understated.

Horkheimer and Adorno (1972) argue that Marx's critique of capitalism was not sweeping enough. Indeed, they argue that civilization began to erode as early as the Greece of antiquity, whose philosophers, with hubris, attempted to master nature without considering the repercussions for humanity. What the Frankfurt theorists call "domination," borrowing a Weberian term, is actually more encompassing than Marx's "alienation," referring to all Promethean projects that seek total control as a way of validating the externalizing, conquering self. They would have readily theorized the total administration of time in this way, noticing that the compression and acceleration of time produces a dialectical backlash, much as the domination of nature triggers nature's revolt. This revolt of nature is captured in cultural works all the way from Rachel Carson's (1999) *Silent Spring* to the recent blockbuster movie *The Day after Tomorrow*, in which the world is beset by meteorological catastrophes caused by global warming.

Truth can be stranger than fiction. The 2005 tsunami that pounded Asian coastlines is stunning testament to nature's apparent malevolent agency. And the destruction of the World Trade towers could have been depicted in a Hollywood horror movie starring Bruce Willis. The total administration of time belongs to the same dialectic of domination and disruption, stemming from Greek effort to conquer nature and having matured in a cybercapitalism (Dyer-Witheford 1999) that makes global instantaneity possible.

Reproduction of Selves Thwarts Reproduction of Capital: A Port Huronized Slowmodernist Critical Theory

The total administration of time saved capitalism from itself, given its internally contradictory nature, first recognized by Marx. But it also threatens to thwart capital formation and accumulation as the administration, colonization, and intensification of time runs up against its outer limits: the working and shopping day cannot be expanded beyond 24/7, given people's needs for sleep, recuperation, recovery. The reproduction of the self slows and stymies the reproduction of capital and creates a fertile ground for rebellious, transforming projects and movements. Capitalism cannot afford to let people rest, and it cannot afford not to.

As I discuss in the concluding section, time robbery breeds time rebels, who could become political rebels once we theorize time as an essential political category in fast capitalism. Time robbery also deprives people of sleep, affect, the vestiges of autonomy with which to theorize and strategize about their system-serving use of time. Time robbery, when taken to its limit, robs the object—fast capital—of a subject, the self. Eventually, the system will shut down as people reach overload, deprived of time, family, leisure, nature, self, identity with which to make informed choices. Even if they don't become rebels and revolutionaries, they cease to function productively. The only means available is to medicate them with alcohol, speed, anxiety drugs. It is not clear that this is a viable long-term solution for time robbery, as Huxley (1954) well understood.

Marx explained the basic contradiction underlying or, perhaps better, inhabiting capital as the fateful conflict between labor and capital. The former produces value for the latter, which as a noun refers to both a class and to amassed productive wealth. Labor expends itself through time, which becomes a means of depriving labor of a portion of value, thus allowing for private profit. Labor is not allowed to either possess or manage time during the working day. Now, in fast capitalism, time management extends beyond the job site into private downtime and even into nighttime. Influenced by Hegel, early Marx argued that the protean human project is work, which allows us to externalize ourselves in nature, fulfilling our desire to make, create, produce, build. I wonder if a better way to say this now is to argue that the fundamental human project is to have and use time freely, unbound from clocks, schedules, supervision, and now the rapid information and communication technologies tethering us to work, entertainment, and shopping.

Building on Petrini's (2003) image of slow food as a metaphor of slow life, I have argued that we can conceptualize utopia not as the fulfillment of modernity but as a "slowmodernity" in which we blend modern and premodern in a dialectical synthesis that forgoes neither useful (Schumacher's [1973] appropriate) technologies nor the social relations and pleasures of preindustrial *Gemeinschaft*, such as Petrini's slow dining. This is not Luddite per se, nor antiscience. It is a version of Marcuse's (1955) Nietzschean / Freudian critical theory that implants a "rationality of gratification" in "new sensibilities" who choose everyday lives no longer governed by capitalist principles of productivity and performativity. At issue in a critical theory reformulated as a theory of time is the idea of *free time* as an equivalent of social and political freedom, a latter-day version of early Marx's concept of disalienation.

Writing in the mid-nineteenth century, Marx could not foresee the welfare state, culture industries, post-Fordism, or the Internet; thus he did not imagine how administration could become total. This is the point made by both the Frankfurt School and Foucault. Neither Adorno nor Foucault conceived of an exit strategy for selves whose lives were accelerated and administered, now nearly 24/7. The Frankfurt theorists, in books such as Marcuse's (1964) *One-Dimensional Man*, Adorno's (1973) *Negative Dialectics* and Horkheimer's (1974) *Eclipse of Reason*, emphasized the negative tendencies of the total administration of life in late capitalism. I include time robbery on their list of usurpations of humanity and freedom. With the possible exception of Marcuse, especially in his 1960s writings, the Frankfurters did not also emphasize the dialectical—potentially positive—implications of total administration, such as the implosion and possible reconstruction of the social system and everyday life. They had a particularly pessimistic view of capitalism after the Holocaust, and with good reason.

Marcuse (1964, 203–248) concludes *One-Dimensional Man* with comments on what he calls "the chance of the alternatives." In 1969 he published *An Essay on Liberation*, which earlier had the working title "Beyond One-Dimensional Man," stressing the emancipatory possibilities opened during the social movements of the 1960s. None of the Frankfurt theorists emphasized time robbery, or perhaps better said time fascism, as an element of one-dimensionality and total administration, although their analysis of the closure of the universe of political discourse would certainly include my discussion of time.

Here I want to stress the positive potentials opened by time robbery carried to such an extreme that time compresses into sheer nothingness, preventing any life from shining through. These are the moments when people feel crushed by their accumulating and sometimes conflicting obligations, roles, schedules, stimuli. Although the effects on the self are always damaging, people can be turned into rebels as they theorize—think through—why this is happening to them and what they can do about it. This is dealing with domination (a Frankfurt term) at the level of the lifeworld, of everyday life (*Lebenswelt*, Husserl's term). There is another possible positive outcome of time fascism: people simply cease to function as diligent workers, consumers, and citizens at the high level necessary for fast capitalism to thrive. As people resist the total administration of time, they enter a timeless zone of retreat and reflection in which they turn off their electronic prostheses, put away their credit cards, and cease working overtime—anytime, anywhere. Even if they don't fully understand what is happening to them, and what their options are, retreat from total administration is equivalent to, in Mario Savio's New Left terms, placing one's body on the apparatus, slowing it down.

In these seemingly post-Marxist, postmodern times it is very difficult to convince people that socialism and what Marcuse called a rationality of gratification have any meaning for them. Neoconservatives and postmodernists meet on the ground of their rejection of Marxism, even if their argumentation is different. I am suggesting that a reformulation of early Marx's utopian goals—slowmodernity instead of socialism, even if their meaning is nearly identical—would help invigorate the left project. Other metaphors can be marshaled as well. The American New Left, stemming from the 1962 Port Huron Statement, argued for "participatory democracy" as a ground-level device for countering bureaucratic hierarchy, of both the corporate capitalist and state socialist kinds. Indeed, the SDS's critique of cold war–era capitalism was forged out of Tom Hayden's and Dick Flack's readings of early Marx and of C. Wright Mills, both of whom would probably have embraced a critique of time robbery had they paused to theorize the relationship between clocks and capitalism. (That only came later in Marx's work.)

A Port Huronized version of slowmodernist critical theory—risking a jumble of metaphors and slogans!—is especially apposite in these times of

American military adventurism, right-wing evangelical Christianity, gay bashing, and the othering of foreignness. These times feel like the 1960s, especially with Bush's reelection and the quagmire of Iraq, which is costing thousands of lives and billions of dollars, not to mention galvanizing the Arab world in potential jihad against the modernist West. Although critical theorists and postmodernists alike abandoned talk of the self or subject as inadequate in an era of late-modernist gigantism, not to mention talk of a collective subject, the times are right for return to a Marcusean vocabulary of the new sensibility and its attempts to create new life and new social structure in the gestures of a gentle everyday life. Time would be central to this agenda. A "new" New Left would retain from early Marx and Marcuse the urgency of disalienation on the ground of everyday life, and it would speak a somewhat new vocabulary of slowmodernity and participatory democracy, playing on people's experiences of the crushing weight of accelerated daily life and their feeling of utter powerlessness in their everyday worlds (see Agger forthcoming).

All of this is possible because ICTs, especially the Internet, have changed our world in significant ways since the late 1960s, when Marcuse was temporarily optimistic about the New Left. The world is now global, even if Marx had already anticipated globalization as an outcome of the logic of capital. But it has become global via mechanisms of instantaneity utterly unimaginable to theorists of the nineteenth century and early twentieth century such as Marx, Durkheim, and Weber and even to those of the mid-twentieth century, when Frankfurt theory was composed. Instruments of instantaneity such as the cell phone and the Internet compress time and make the administration of time more relentless and inescapable. Email is a paradigm of time theft. One must disentangle spam from serious stuff and then compose considered responses. We are almost always "behind" in our management of email, which leaves even less time for serious writing and living. This is not to deny the amazing efficiencies of electronic communication—again, the positive/negative dialectic of slowmodernity—which open the world to us, and us to the world, producing serendipitous intellectual, social, and political connections. I was recently invited, via email, to a conference in China by a Chinese scholar who spent time at my former university, SUNY-Buffalo. In response I am sending him some books in English. I recently started an electronic journal (www.fastcapitalism.com) that considers the social and psychic impact of the Internet. The journal would not have been possible without email, which made submitting, responding, editing, and proofing much more efficient.

Marx anticipated globalization as he suggested that the "logic of capital" causes capital to ignore national boundaries and colonize the planet wherever it can find fertile ground for production and consumption. One doesn't even need Lenin's concept of imperialism to explain the near-identity of Americanization and globalization, given Marx's own analysis of the compulsive, invasive tendencies of capital (see Hardt and Negri 2000). Habermas (1984, 1987) refers to all this as the colonization of the lifeworld, blending Marx, Durkheim, Weber, and Parsons. Habermas argues that we must protect everyday life from imposed meanings, strictures, and structures. Time is certainly in play as ICTs allow people's uses of time to be bent to the purposes of capital, bureaucracy, and nation, colonizing people's circadian rhythms.

Time Rebels: What People Can Do to Reclaim Time and Their Lives

Theory confronts practice on the grounds of everyday lives. Phenomenological and existential leftists such as Paci (1972) and Sartre (1976) converge with Freudian "new" leftists such as Marcuse in agreeing that change is worthless, and probably counterproductive, if it doesn't pass through the self. The model of a long road to radical change is ultimately endless, also sanctioning short-run sacrifices and liberty and life itself. The theft of time, and its totalitarian administration in a fast stage of capitalism, can be matched and bested by time rebels, people like you and me who think through these issues and decide to live differently, prefiguring and working toward a different world.

In *Speeding Up Fast Capitalism* (2004) I close by discussing ways of slowing it all down; my final chapter is entitled "Slowmodernity." I offer not only desiderata but accounts of what people are already doing to reclaim time and, thus, their lives. As I argue there and here, this does not in itself transform capitalism but is a beginning, a necessary way for people to carve out space and time to become thoughtful and caring people. These choices are aspects of what Marcuse in 1964 termed the Great Refusal, the decision of protean selves, illuminated by theory, to reject the quotidian and to live differently. In the 1960s these choices often resulted in communal and quite preindustrial living arrangements, even in cities. Action provoked reaction and repression. The Berkeley police action against the architects and occupants of People's Park refracts conflict over the proper uses of the public sphere and nature. The New Left ran up against the repressive machine of Nixon's White House and the FBI, which launched an organized effort labeled COINTELPRO to rid America of young leftists. The right "won" the 1960s politically by launching a successful and long-lasting counterrevolution—first Nixon, then Reagan, now Bush Jr.

In a recent interview I conducted with Todd Gitlin, he argued that although the right "won" politics during and after the 1960s, the left "won" culture. One needs a differentiated analysis of the 1960s to understand the boundary, often quite permeable, between political and cultural rebellion. Gitlin (1987) argues that the baby-boom generation (those born between about 1947 and 1960) assimilated the cultural politics and styles of the time—self-expression, music, attitudes toward nature, sexuality—but did not sustain their radical politics. Another way to say this is that people remain committed to change on the local level but do not have ways to extend this globally. This is because they lack "theory," a big-picture view that helps them understand possible connections between changes in everyday life and changes wrought by mass movements. This is not to suggest that the 1960s were entirely politically un-successful. Young people and even some of their parents stopped the war in Vietnam, won important civil rights for black people, and began the women's movement. In any case we learn from the 1960s generation—ourselves!—that change must begin "at home," even if it cannot end there.

The problem with orthodox Marxism, and especially the Soviet variant, as Marcuse (1958), his Frankfurt colleagues, and Sartre and Merleau-Ponty well understood, is that the long road to socialism never seems to end. And it is a road whose map is dictated by elites who never seem to wither away.

So baby boomers and their children today can become "time rebels" and thereby, much as we did in the 1960s, use an issue to bring about important social change. The issues then were civil rights and Vietnam, and today it is time fascism. We experience time fascism in our daily lives, much as black people and their white allies were radicalized by the rage of Bull Connor and the Klan and draft opponents and resisters were galvanized by the threat of going to Vietnam. This experience of being crushed by time pressure can be a politicizing one, as I am suggesting. It can lead to time rebellion, augur-ing other rebellions, all designed to change the entire social and economic system.

Time rebellion avoids Luddism. My "imaginary" of slowmodernity blends anti- and protechnology postures in a twenty-first-century synthesis. We can use the Internet instead of being used by it. We can continue to drive, but in hybrids and hydrogen-driven vehicles. We can further automate industrial production. But we need to break the clocks—a metaphor—where we purposely slow down our lives as a way of becoming more human and of effecting a prefiguring radical change. By prefiguration I am returning to Marcuse's Freudianized image of new sensibilities making different and better choices, armed with a Hegelian-Marxist "reason" (see Marcuse 1960), a rationality of gratification, according to *Eros and Civilization*. Marcuse makes it clear in his study of Freud and Marx that we need not abandon high technology as long as we use it for human purposes. He borrows from Schiller and Nietzsche in positing a gay or new science and technology that would play with nature and with concepts instead of dominating them.

Marcuse suggests that false needs perpetuate domination far beyond what is historically necessary for survival. By keeping people in the shopping malls, false needs keep people in political check, a basic argument of the Frankfurt School. Although Marcuse doesn't talk much about time, acquiescence to time robbery is clearly a false need in the sense that people feel unnecessarily pressured and thus pressure themselves to spend inadequate time—and therefore freedom—in reflection, enjoyment, noninstrumental activities. Clearly, early Marx and Marcuse would include time among the most important political variables and values. And Marcuse would suggest possible "times" that break with domination and do not succumb to the Weberian rational calculations at the heart of capitalist logic. In this sense I believe that Marcuse would have endorsed the notion of slowmodernity as a blend of premodern and modern that, in dialectical synthesis, takes them to a higher level and thus provides a much-needed utopian imagery just when utopia seems a remote possibility (see Jacoby's [1999] work on utopia).

Time, therefore, needs to be at the center of critical theories that attempt to understand people's servitude today, much of which is self-imposed. This is not to blame people for rushing around and courting the dangers associated with high blood pressure but simply to recognize, with Marx and Marcuse, that people must be involved in their own liberation, making better choices that prefigure utopia for all.

People already resist and refuse the theft of time, their time, and hence their lives. They must configure their time differently, where possible. Although singular protean "agency" cannot change the world by itself, without people exercising agency nothing will change and time will only accelerate and compress. It will accelerate until such "time" that people can no longer function in their waking lives but implode, simply unable to handle so much stimulation and deal with so little sleep and "downtime." In the mean"time" people can shut down electronic prostheses, such as email, cell or mobile phones, television, all of which dictate both pace and content. They can throw away their calendars and planners, turn off their alarm clocks, and banish clocks and watches, where possible, refusing (and thus reconfiguring) the "timescapes" of an accelerated capitalism that equate time and money, punctuality and duty.

Sexuality, for the Frankfurt School and especially Marcuse, was at once irreducibly intimate and transparently political, providing a medium of resistance and liberation. Time is equally intimate and political, both private and public. Without time management capitalism couldn't function. But the self requires time off the clock in order to restore itself, both asleep and awake. In fast capitalism there is no time off the clock; all time is sucked up and made performative, productive, and reproductive. Advertising is a perfect example: people watch television to escape, but, while watching television, they are stimulated to turn off television and shop. They can do this using the Internet or 800 numbers. If they call "just in time," they will receive a discount, which might be applied to the next purchase.

Marcuse (1969) theorized a "new sensibility," borne of the New Left and counterculture, which would choose a different life and thus model different living for others. Twenty-first-century new sensibilities will experience, organize, count, theorize time differently, unhinging time from production and performance and choosing to live unencumbered by imposed schedules and acceleration that compress and crush.

Time is thus an essential component of potential political agency, as the original existentialists such as Sartre understood. Bergson captures this well in his concept of time as *durée* "duration," not as a functional, divisible unit. But to experience time this way, as a moment of everyday sensibility that neither compresses nor crushes, is difficult, if not impossible, under a regime of time fascism. It could be said that an agenda of time liberation, which is central to a contemporary critical theory dealing with globality and instantaneity, is a reformulation of early Marx's communal utopia and of Marcuse's rationality of gratification. We must incorporate time, just as we incorporate space, into the emancipatory project, especially because time, like sexuality, is such an important medium of domination today.

My concluding observation is that time robbery cannot continue without running up against the limit of sunrise and sunset, the solstices, growing old—sheer scarcity. The problem with capitalism, now as before, is that its logic is utterly colonizing, refusing limit. But, as Heidegger recognized, our time is limited, and people naturally resist and refuse overscheduled, sleep-deprived, anxiety-ridden existence as symptoms of what Adorno called damaged life. People escape, resist, shut down; for them—us—time becomes political. We simply don't have enough time, affect, money (always money) to soak up the commodities they and their mechanical prostheses ceaselessly produce. We require sleep; we need to unplug. For capital not to recognize this, nor resolve it, is the real limit to capital.

References

Adam, Barbara. 1995. *Timewatch: The social analysis of time.* Cambridge, MA: Polity.
———. 1998. *Timescapes of modernity.* London: Routledge.
Adorno, Theodor W. 1973. *Negative dialectics.* New York: Seabury.
Agger, Ben. 1989. *Fast capitalism: A critical theory of significance.* Urbana: University of Illinois Press.
———. 2004. *Speeding up fast capitalism: Cultures, jobs, families, schools, bodies.* Boulder, CO: Paradigm.
———. Forthcoming. *Hey, Hey LBJ: Generation and identity among sixties people.* Boulder, CO: Paradigm.
Aronowitz, Stanley. 1992. *False promises: The shaping of American working class consciousness.* 2nd ed. Durham, NC: Duke University Press.
Braverman, Harry. 1974. *Labor and monopoly capital: The degradation of work in the twentieth century.* New York: Monthly Review Press.
Carson, Rachel, 1999. *Silent spring.* London: Penguin.
Davis, Mike. 1998. *Ecology of fear: Los Angeles and the imagination of disaster.* New York: Metropolitan Books.
Dyer-Witheford, Nick. 1999. *Cyber-Marx: Cycles and circuits of struggle in high-technology capitalism.* Urbana: University of Illinois Press.
Ewen, Stewart. 1976. *Captains of consciousness: Advertising and the social roots of the consumer culture.* New York: McGraw-Hill.
Gitlin, Todd. 1987. *The sixties: Years of hope, days of rage.* New York: Bantam.
Habermas, Jürgen. 1984. *The theory of communicative action.* Vol. 1. Boston: Beacon.
———. 1987. *The theory of communicative action.* Vol. 2. Boston: Beacon.
Hardt, Michael, and Antonio Negri. 2000. *Empire.* Cambridge, MA: Harvard University Press.
Harvey, David. 1989. *The condition of postmodernity.* Oxford: Blackwell.
Hassan, Robert. 2003. *The chronoscopic society.* New York: Peter Lang.
Horkheimer, Max. 1974. *Eclipse of reason.* New York: Seabury.

Horkheimer, Max, and Theodor W. Adorno. 1972. *Dialectic of enlightenment*. New York: Herder and Herder.

Huxley, Aldous. 1954. *The doors of perception*. New York: Harper and Brothers.

Jacoby, Russell. 1999. *The end of utopia: Politics and culture in an age of apathy*. New York: Basic.

Kay, Jane Holtz. 1997. *Asphalt nation*. Berkeley: University of California Press.

Leiss, William. 1976. *The limits to satisfaction*. Toronto: University of Toronto Press.

Mandel, Ernest. 1978. *Late capitalism*. London: Verso.

Marcuse, Herbert. 1955. *Eros and civilization*. New York: Vintage.

———. 1958. *Soviet Marxism*. New York: Columbia University Press.

———. 1960. *Reason and revolution: Hegel and the rise of social theory*. 2nd ed. Boston: Beacon.

———. 1964. *One-dimensional man*. Boston: Beacon.

———. 1969. *An essay on liberation*. Boston: Beacon.

Miller, Mark Crispin. 1988. *Boxed in: The culture of TV*. Evanston, IL: Northwestern University Press.

Paci, Enzo. 1972. *The function of the sciences and the meaning of man*. Evanston, IL: Northwestern University Press.

Packard, Vance. 1957. *The hidden persuaders*. New York: David McKay.

Petrini, Carlo. 2003. *Slow food: The case for taste*. New York: Columbia University Press.

Sartre, Jean-Paul. 1976. *Critique of dialectical reason*. London: NLB.

Schumacher, E. F. 1973. *Small is beautiful: A study of economics as if people mattered*. New York: Harper and Row.

Soja, Edward. 1989. *Postmodern geographies: The reassertion of space in critical social theory*. London: Verso.

12 Finding Time and Place for Trust in ICT Network Organizations

Hans Rämö

T HE GLOBAL NETWORK ECONOMY is all-embracing in ways never before possible. This is a fact that is at once fascinating and intimidating. The ceaseless flow of information that we try to avidly absorb has, paradoxically, contributed to an increasing lack of attention regarding, for example, the differences between physical place and abstract space and between clock time and experienced time. These spatiotemporal differences may be somewhat neglected, but they cannot be lost. Contemporary networking methods based on electronic information and communication technologies (ICTs) frequently lack the experience of what Hallowell (1999) calls "the human moment"—the encounter where people share the same place in a meaningful moment of conversation. How can we create trust in electronic networks without face-to-face contact? In traditional networks, when we see and speak to each other, at least occasionally, trust or distrust emanates from connection and dealings between persons or groups. To create and uphold trust in electronic networks is somewhat different in that our direct counterpart might be unknown to us. In some cases our "counterpart" may not be human but a substitute in the digital form of genetic algorithms that creates individualized responses for human receivers.

What, then, has time and space to do with an analysis of trust in network organizations? In ICT network organizations the boundary between the

I would like to thank Ida Sabelis and the volume editors for their helpful comments.

physical here and now and the virtual there and now is erased by the computer's interface. For example, ordering merchandise or communicating over the Internet is an exceedingly easy operation. Behind the Internet's apparent dissolution of time and space, however, we often find an increasing amount of physical transportation of goods takes place via complicated distribution networks. If our counterpart is distant—and perhaps even unknown—to us, how can we trust and rely on the people delivering the services and goods we have ordered? Issues of trust in ICT networks have clear spatiotemporal implications, but it is important to state that it is insufficient to consider these through only a singular aspect of spatiotemporality, that is to say, through either clock time or abstract space.

This chapter takes an explicitly spatiotemporal approach; the central question that will be explored is how the rise of increasingly sophisticated ICT-based networks influences trust in human and nonhuman communication environments. I begin with a section examining the various forms of trust and network prevalent in the contemporary management literature, with a particular focus on ICT-based networking. Next comes a section showing why the study of different forms of time/timing and space/place is a relevant topic for analysis of trust in networks. This is followed by a presentation of trust in four different but archetypical network settings, and their temporal and spatial assumptions are highlighted. I conclude with a section discussing the conditions of trust in ICT network settings in which the (human/nonhuman) status of the counterpart is becoming increasingly unknown.

Trust and Network Organizations

The notion of trust has been the object of continuous interest in economics, sociology, and organization studies since at least the 1970s. Nevertheless, few studies have specifically explored both the temporal *and* spatial factors of trust. I contend, however, that adequate understanding of the different conditions for trust-based cooperation and management in traditional office settings and in virtual networks requires an explicit focus on different forms of trust in conjunction with (and interactions of) aspects of *time/timing* and *space/place*.

The complex nature of trust in human interaction has generated a vast literature from various disciplines. By way of a basic working definition it can be postulated that trust involves aspects of wisdom and judgment by the person who depends on the other's ability to reciprocate implicitly promised actions.

Such a suspension of disbelief between actors does not develop instantaneously. It is most likely developed through actions between parties in contractual or noncontractual relations that gradually become implicit and trustful. Trust, on the analysis proposed by Baier (1986), involves elements of judgment and discretionary power beyond instrumental specifications (e.g., beyond contracts). In many ways Baier's analysis corresponds with Luhmann's (1979), in that they both acknowledge that trust reduces complication and enhances the effectiveness of agency. Almost all accounts of trust revolve around situations of reducing risk and uncertainty in ways that contracts cannot—either as implicit background factors of human action or as explicit forms of risk reduction. Based on Granovetter's (1985) classic argument that economic behavior is "embedded" in informal social and trustful relationships, many socially oriented management scholars have stressed the importance of embeddedness in social network relations (Brass, Butterfield, and Skaggs 1998; Gössling 2004; Uzzi 1997). Moreover, there are some examples in the literature of both "swift trust" and high initial trust levels based on "hidden" favorable factors that question the need for longtime cooperation for creating trust (McKnight, Cummings, and Chervany 1998; Meyerson, Weick, and Kramer 1996).

Spatiotemporal Forms of Trust

To provide a starting point for further exploration, I will divide the concept of trust into four broad categories that correspond to a level of abstraction. By distinguishing between different aspects of abstract and concrete representations of trust—and time / timing and space / place—I provide the means to understand what goes beyond the reified objectivization of not only time and space but humans as well. The four categories may be defined in the following way:

Trust in Abstract Time and Abstract Space   Purely abstract conceptualizations in attempts to build formal models of cooperation, competition, and trust have replaced humans with actors or agents moving in decontextualized situations. The objective is to determine rational and optimal conflict-free maneuvers (motions) to build models of trust, while taking into account the fact that agents tend to have conflicting priorities (e.g., game theory, transaction cost, functional analysis).

Trust at a Desired Instant in Time and Place   The antithesis to the above is our time-honored ability to act judiciously and wisely at a concrete and opportune occasion in real-world settings. In such moments trust is an intentional mental phenomenon in relations of intimacy, loyalty, friendships, and in other acts of nurture and care not necessarily instrumentally purposive (e.g., family, friends, nurse-cum-caretaker).

Trust Just in Time and Just in Place   Forms of trust that include weak and/or instrumental modalities in competitive market settings, where the presumption typically is that trust should be related to enhanced profitability in fast-moving industries (e.g., time management).

Trust and Timing in Virtual Space   Forms of trust in a category that have particular relevance for the understanding of trust in ICT-based network organizations. This category embraces communication based on human "right moments" to act judiciously in "virtual spaces," such as in ICT-based networks. Such a virtual setting, in comparison with most time-management concepts in production-line settings, is more likely to contain trust that appears to be very fragile and temporal. Online network communication entails greater uncertainty than face-to-face communication in physical interdepartmental settings. Virtual organization settings also direct demands for timely and judicious online communication among the participants in order to encourage both task information and social information (see Järvenpää and Leidner 1999).

. . .

Just as the concept of trust has been a subject of continuous interest in different disciplines, the growing field of research into network organization studies is also well developed, not least in contemporary management studies (e.g., Borgatti and Foster 2003; Freeman 2004; Smith-Doerr and Powell 2004; Van Alstyne 1997; Varamäki and Vesalainen 2003). The question of trust in network organizations has attracted many scholarly commentaries, but few studies have examined the relation between time, space, and trust in networks. Some social network researchers have primarily focused on the temporal aspects (Doreian and Stockman 1996; Moody 2002; Snijders 2001; Snijders and Van Duijn 1997; Suitor, Wellman, and Morgan 1997; Weesie and Flap 1990). Others devote their attention to spatial analysis, particularly in studies of diffusion and clustering of innovations, knowledge, and technology (Kavanagh and Kelly 2002; Powell et al. 2002). What is most important when considering these theories and methods is that almost without exception they still rely on a specific understanding of time and space—of time as chronological clock time and space as abstract space.

Before considering examples of trust in different network settings, there is something further to be said about when and where, so to speak, this trust-building exercise is taking place. In other words a fuller understanding of what is meant by time and space is necessary. Fundamentally, this involves a distinction between abstract and concrete representations of both time / timing and space / place.

From Clock Time and Space to Timing in Place

Nowadays time is frequently reduced to clock time, which is equated with speed and is regarded as an important yardstick against which we measure the value of our activities at work. Action and communication based on right and timely moments to act judiciously in unique situations are also encouraged virtues in management. Such timely judgment-based decisions, however, cannot be depicted by using clocks only; impromptu situations do occur irrespective of the clock. In a similar fashion attention to the spatial aspects of management has ranged from economic models of exchange, distribution, and allocation in "abstract" geometrical extensions to more nuanced and contextual understandings of space and place in, for example, relationship building ICT network strategies. The dual time and space focus in this chapter is based on a belief that analyses in social science settings remain crippled if there is a partisan focus on either time or space only. As much new work in this area attests, including the present volume, the mutual implication of both time and space must be the ontological basis of any investigation in the social sciences (May and Thrift 2001).

To comprehend the notion that time is something beyond the successive reading of a clock is intuitively easy because a human's ability to coordinate his or her activities has a history that is much older than the history of mechanical clocks. This nonchronological understanding of time is also discernible in our ability to act judiciously and wisely at an opportune occasion.

Parallel to different aspects of human time, spatial notions of space and place are also important aspects of everyday life. Alfred Marshall already asserted in his 1890 treatise, *The Principles of Economics*, that in economic life the influence of time is more fundamental than the influence of space. Nevertheless, a study that chiefly considers trust building and ICT-based

networking as concepts being constantly negotiated in interactive information exchange between individuals requires some form of elucidation of
the spatial assumptions involved in these settings. ICT-based networking
is sometimes claimed to operate independently of space and time in creating worldwide sources of information-based products and processes. This
is, however, only partially true in the sense that, despite being a network
communication "existing" in a virtual space, it is still dependent on situated
persons exercising a clear sense of timing with each other. Even in recent
situations when (nonhuman) genetic algorithms are creating individualized
online communication messages to a (human) receiver, a sense of timing is
important in order to gain attention over numerous ads and Internet pitchers
that pop up unbidden on the receiver's computer screen.

Situations that develop under the influence of clock time can be characterized as *chronos time*, a notion that has a long history. As early as Aristotle's
Physics (4.11.219b), *chronos* is defined as the "number of motion with respect
to the before and the after," which is a classical expression of the concept of
(chronos) time as change, measure, and serial order. Therefore, despite Aristotle's antiquated understanding of physics—and a possible circularity in the
definition—in this chapter I use *chronos* as a definition of an exact quantification of time (e.g., passing time expressed in successive readings of a clock). In
studies of managerial performance in network organizations this clock time
of chronos is the ruling factor, particularly in terms of efficiency, time management, administration, and the improvement of what already exists and is
already known in different industrial settings.

This omnipresent characterization of time as clock time (i.e., chronos
time) is, however, only one delimited way of understanding time. Although
an important and inescapable aspect of modern life, the clock time of chronos eventually creates blinders. Analyses of the theory of time and its different representations include a vast field of ontological studies (see, e.g., Macey
1994). With reference to C. P. Snow (1964) there is subdivision after subdivision also within the field of time study, and it soon becomes meaningless to
discuss not only two theories of time but a hundred and two or two thousand
and two theories of time. For the sake of practicality, therefore, I will discuss the concept of *chronos* together with a more timely and nonchronological
aspect of time, namely *kairos*. These two ideas of time, chronos and kairos,
should not be seen as sharply distinguished classifications but rather as a
complementary pair of human time concepts.

This second and more obscure Greek notion of time, kairos, and its *kairic*-stem, is little used in the social sciences. Terms such as *due measure, proportion*, and, above all, the *right moment* are some of the English translations of *kairos* that connote ideas of wisdom and judgment in timely situations (e.g., Kinneavy 1986; Kinneavy and Eskin 1994; Smith 1969, 1986; White 1987; on chronos and kairos in organizational settings see, e.g., Bartunek and Necochea 2000; Berman Brown and Herring 1998; Jaques 1982; Kirkeby 2000; Rämö 1999, 2002, 2004a, 2004b).

In addition to working with (or to) the clock in terms of what already exists and is already known, all managers are expected to seize new opportunities, in "windows of opportunities," that exist for a finite period of time. Furthermore, all managers face timely situations characterized as "moments of truth," which might imply judicious actions beyond the mechanically learned and beyond timetables. Understanding timeliness is also crucial in dealings with effectiveness and trust in relationships. The chronological time of chronos, whether it is described as clock time, linear, circular, or spiral, remains inadequate in such timely situations. Chronos—and most notably clock-time manifestation—must be augmented by the nonchronological practice of time as kairos.

Concrete Places and Abstract Virtual Spaces

We move now from time to space. What is it that distinguishes place from space? Perhaps understandably, the difference is not very clearly delineated. Whereas space is a three-dimensional geometric extension, place is a specific contextual setting. Next to a virtual space that is mediated through different computerized boundaries, there are always concrete places that we as humans exist in all the time. The difference between space and place was already emphasized in ancient Greece, where the two concepts *chora* and *topos* were (roughly) used to refer to space and place, respectively (though a strict framing into abstract / concrete is more restricted than they were for the ancient Greeks). Certainly, the concept of space has shown its dominance over the concept of place in the natural sciences for more than three hundred years; however, the question is brought to a head when the virtual spaces of the Internet have come in on the side of the physical spaces.

The difference between the two ancient Greek spatial notions of space (chora) and place (topos) is that whereas the former is an abstract geometric or cartographic extension, the latter is a concrete contextual localization, without sharp demarcations. Thus, the two notions serve as a useful distinction between abstract and virtual space (chora) and concrete place (topos) (e.g., Casey 1993, 1997; Rämö 1999, 2002, 2004a, 2004b).

The temporal and spatial notions proposed here make a distinction between two ideas of time / timing and space / place. Chronos time relates to the "exact" quantification of passing time expressed in successive readings of a clock. This idea is complemented by kairos time, the nonchronological timely moments in which we manifest abilities to act judiciously and wisely at a concrete and opportune occasion. A similar distinction is made between the abstract spaces (chora) of theory and virtuality and concrete human lived places (topos).

In the next section of this chapter I examine these mutually implicating notions of time and space in terms of their organizational aspects of trust within ICT-based network organizations.

Spatiotemporal Forms of Trust in Network Organizations

To capture the spatiotemporal aspects of trust in different network settings, some archetypical examples are illustrative. By merging the notions of trust, time / timing, space / place, and network organizations discussed in the previous sections, four analytical categories emerge:

Inanimate Network and Trust   In this categorization clock time (chronos) and abstract space (chora) are expressed as infinitesimal slices, such as in mathematics. In terms of trust in network organizations, such an abstract course of action is used in attempts to build formal models of cooperation, competition, and trust (for game theory see, e.g., Axelrod 1984; Friedland 1990; for transaction cost see, e.g., Freeman 1984; Hindmoor 1998; Williamson 1975, 1993; and for functional analysis see, e.g., Bhattacharya, Devinney, and Pillutla 1998; Buskens 2002). Formal models of network and trust tend to remain close to abstract reasoning and barely resemble personal acts of trusting someone. Instead, these formal models are calculations based on existing policies (such as trust) and on informed opinion about the implementation environment in which an application is intended to execute (the network). Explaining network optimality and efficiency is more in focus, rather than attempts to understand social aspects and effectiveness. The attention to formal trust and abstract spatiotemporality (clock time and space) also entails a focus on artifacts and actors devoid of nuanced and contextual understanding of trust in human-network relations.

Trustful Networking in Context   This category comprises situations when a "kairic" feeling for the right moment merges with being in the right place—when one has to act judiciously and wisely at a concrete and opportune occasion. Studies of network organizations populated by human beings reveal situations when new opportunities have to be seized, opportunities that exist for a finite period of time in a specific place. Furthermore, timely situations characterized as "moments of truth," which imply intelligent actions beyond clocks and timetables, happen in all organizations. Gaining and upholding trust in such timely situations requires strong demands for trustworthiness. Chronological clock time (chronos) and abstract space (chora) remain inadequate representations in such timely occasions. In terms of trust in network organizations, the interpersonal situation can also be an example of trustworthiness between fellow human beings in networks when goodwill is esteemed beyond its usefulness. Thus, in such will-based accounts the value of trust is not exclusively instrumental (see Baier 1986). The much-recognized importance of trust in social settings, however, whether in economic, political, legal, or organizational relations, quite frequently includes clear goals such as profit, number of votes, administration of justice, and efficiency. Consequently, trust in (social) network organization settings with instrumental goal-directed overtones has attracted much attention in recent years (e.g., Abrams et al. 2003; Buskens 2002; Koniordos 2005; Monge and Contractor 2001; Oliver and Ebers 1998; Van Alstyne 1997; Weesie and Flap 1990).

Instrumental Trust in Networks   In the growing litany of managerial fads *time management* became one of the most influential buzzwords during the 1990s (e.g., Stalk and Hout 1990; Stern and Stalk 1998; Womack, Jones, and Roos 1990). By using the terminology specified in the previous sections, it becomes clear that time-management ideas in general are equal to situations when clock time and deadlines inform our daily activities from place to place. Time-management concepts such as "just-in-time" are based on the idea of conjoining different production stages within the organization to those in sequence outside its boundaries, in networks of subcontractors and suppliers. The common denominator among these management ideas is ultimately to create a smooth, swift, and thrifty flow of goods and services from the supplier via the manufacturer to the customer. This places inordinate stress on (chronos) clock time and (topos) place, for instance, when issuing an order with the delivery date for the next day at exactly 3:00 p.m. to a specific place. Clock time, efficiency, deadlines, and working by the book are strong imperatives in networks of manufacturing companies. Yet the notion of a concrete place (topos) remains crucial since this kind of thrifty production flow relies heavily on on-time delivery to accurate places (just-in-time and just-in-place). In terms of trust in industrial network organizations, some explicit studies are available on this spatiotemporal topic (e.g., Cullen, Johnson, and Sakano 2000; Das and Teng 1998; Gulati 1995, 1998; Lane and Bachman 1998; Ring 1997; Van Alstyne 1997). Implicitly, however, the bulk of the debate on trust in multilateral cooperations, joint ventures, supply chains, and so forth refers to situations that can be characterized as clock-time control of manufacturing networks in different locations (i.e., concrete places).

Trust in Virtual Net-Work(ing)   These examples of generally known situations when clock time guides our daily activities from place to place (e.g., time management) have, however, recently been complemented with a notion of timely situations in abstract/virtual space (kairos and chora). This spatiotemporal category is characteristic of another well-known management concept with a clear focus on time, the ICT-based network organization, a term typically used to refer to systems that are interlinked by advanced information technology (Clases, Bachmann, and Wehner 2003; Davidow and Malone 1992; Grabowski and Roberts 1999; Grenier and Metes 1995; Grundy 1998; Handy 1995; Järvenpää and Leidner 1999; Nohria and Eccles 1992). This category includes all forms of networking methods in intra- and interorganizational settings based on electronic information and communication technology.

· · ·

The online world of ICT-based network organizations differs from the physical organizational setting in ways that have implications relevant to trust. In particular, the loss of interdepartmental dynamics obscures the physical dimensions of character and personality, nature of relationships, and the institutional character on which we normally rely to form decisions about trust. Different forms of ICT-based networking have recently created sophisticated systems of human cooperation in global virtual networks. Such a form of global virtual organizational development places strong demands for trustworthiness among the participants because spontaneous physical interaction between the actors, as in an office setting, is no longer possible in virtual communication (Monge and Contractor 2001). From this question of trust, especially in global and virtual settings, follow further questions of wisdom and judgment in actions undertaken since trust does not emanate from rules and regulations only but also from action in concrete and timely situations. Upholding a trust relationship in virtual and impersonal ICT communication networks, in which we frequently interact with persons unknown, unseen, or distant to us, calls for timely forms of discernment.

The key difference between trust in networks of manufacturing industries using time-management concepts and trust in virtual network organizations is that whereas the former has a clear site-consciousness, the latter is not bound to either flows of physical goods between proximate human beings or to any particular place. Certainly, ICT-based network organizations are ruled by rational and decontextualized clock time (chronos) as well. But the virtual form in an ICT-based network organization still gives new possibilities to break the iron law of time clocks, watch and ward, and the time-wasting friction of distance. But this nonetheless presupposes delicate forms of trust at a distance, beyond the physical distribution of goods in manufacturing networks.

A key question presents itself: is it still meaningful to speak of trust in situations when we never meet or know our counterpart, or in situations when it becomes unclear whether our trustful counterpart is a human or a machine?

Trusting Her, Him, or It?

As has been described above, the spatiotemporal multitude of trust in networks can be categorized in concrete and abstract representations of time and space. From its etymological origin in Old Norse, *trust* has been associated with questions of making and breaking cooperative relations in human face-to-face interaction and in errands to companies and authorities (Shamir and Lapidot 2003). In doing so, the implicit assumption is that the contact is between two or more human counterparts. Therefore, traditional forms of trust, based on personal acquaintance, are both timely and local. The introduction and growing ubiquity of ICT-based networking, however, will increasingly call into question the assumption that a human counterpart in the communication process is actually present. There are, of course, numerous examples in history of faceless bureaucracy and elusive business representatives without vested interest in human interaction. But we still know that behind the faceless bureaucracy resides a human being referring to legal texts and practices. Everyday trust in technology, with, for instance, air travel, is also taken for granted. Advancements in the automation of sophisticated technological systems have blurred the already less-than-clear relationship between humans and machines (Collins and Kusch 1999). The perennial question of whether the humans control machines or vice versa is made yet more complex (Goldberg 2000; Latour 1996). Sophisticated technological systems are controlled, or at least monitored at some level, by humans; we continue to fly in planes that still have pilots, and most trains still have an engineer onboard. This has implications for our understanding of trust. We trust that the people in charge of the automated system know what they are doing and that they are being supervised by authorized officials. One way of promoting (global) trust in technological systems is therefore the use of standards, institutions for investigation, regulation, and sanction of particular types of behavior (e.g., IATA in air transportation, ISO in technical standards). The difficulty, however, is that the growing ICT-based networking has a very sparse institutional structure, and trust regulation is particularly negligible. Therefore we increasingly have to (quickly) trust counterparts who are not only unknown but distant to us. In some situations our counterparts are no longer even human but have been replaced by machines that simulate and synthesize human actors and may exist beyond the reach of effective legal systems.

Over time, some of our trustful counterparts in ICT networks will therefore become only remotely associated with direct human action. Not only is our human counterpart distant or unknown to us, but the entrusted real-time communication from the counterpart might be created, instrumented, and mediated through, for instance, genetic algorithms, devoid of human input. In today's formal, institutionalized ICT networks of organizations, non-human counterparts can be found in systems such as automatic identification technology (AIT), which perform logistics tasks like tracking inventory and locating equipment, and in geographical information systems (GIS). ICT-based networking is changing the conditions of competitiveness even within traditionally slow-moving process industries (such as metals, chemicals, petrochemicals, and minerals). Seemingly intelligent network models have moved from the control of individual pieces of equipment to the management of entire lines and factory entities. As a consequence even the small and medium-sized industry can deviate from the "economy of scale strategy" and look for integration with fast-moving networks.

A more profound elusive facelessness in elaborated ICT network communication is now emerging. We are therefore increasingly dealing not only with human actors but with nonhuman actors, which are creating new sources of power, trust, and legitimacy, particularly in adaptable fast-moving ICT-based information networks.

In financial and manufacturing machine network interactions, the value-adding (clock) time processes remain a question of (physical or recently virtual) compatibility. In human-machine network interactions the question of compatibility becomes a question of finding user-friendly interfaces that are controlled by clocks at a specific place (situated interactions). In human ICT networking, however, the sense of time and place cannot be reduced to functional (but inhuman) momentary spaces of entering commands and monitoring execution, as in making finance transactions and controlling manufacturing operations. Instead, ICT-based networking is trying to mimic the instantaneous impression of real time and real place, here and now. On the one hand, abstract accounts of clock time and space reduce humans to agents in decontextualized network spaces. Time-management objectives, on the other hand, easily reduce humans to instrumental objects operating in asymmetric network services of agents-patients, buyer-seller, and service provider–service receiver. In contrast, virtual ICT-based timely collaboration tries to mimic the real-world settings of here and now—increasingly with interactive, real-time, 3-D simulacra and eventually with tactile-sensing elements creating both ambience and milieu (see, e.g., Baudrillard's [1981 / 1994] theory of the simulacrum). Over time, such virtual network simulacra should be able to provide artificial experiences mimicking some of the richness and complexity of the real-world closeness and togetherness in time and place. It remains to be seen how this interaction with machines mimicking humans will influence our views of, for instance, trust and kairic timely situations. But at a minimum it provides a cautionary reminder that concepts traditionally associated with human behavior cannot be taken for granted in increasingly sophisticated ICT-based networking.

Is a hyperreal "reality by proxy," a limbo between what "exists" and what does "not exist," the eventual fate for the concept of trust in ICT-networks settings? In what is called "massively multiplayer online role-playing games" (MMORPG) players experience such virtual trust-building situations with both their characters and coplayers. But the players are acting inside enclosed ICT-induced illusions of community, separated from the world of nature and from human nature. People interacting in ICT-based network organizations will also increasingly experience trust-building situations with people they have rarely met and even with nonhuman collaborators. The safe enclosure of disembodied trust in swift virtuality unfortunately cannot replace trust in timely and real-world settings of friendship, loyalty, and intimacy. Trust mediated through increasingly sophisticated interfaces remains only a simulacrum of real-world trust relationships.

While the prospect for trust building in ICT networking looks promising, much optimism is based on lofty sentiments and grandiose claims. Regardless of increasing virtualization and ICT-based networking, questions of management in (old or new) economies are still a matter of trustful management of scarce resources—ultimately about cooperation over time in habitable places.

Conclusion

This chapter has sought to explore two well-noted concepts in contemporary management, namely trust and networks, in conjunction with dual forms of time/timing and space/place. Four types of spatiotemporal network depictions were examined in this analysis, and their underlying implications in terms of trust were outlined.

First, the purely abstract and generally applicable form of *inanimate network and trust* is based on a depiction of time and space expressed as infinitesimal slices: clock time (chronos) and abstract geometrical extension (chora). In terms of trust in network organizations this theoretical category has no concrete bearing on trust beyond formal conceptualizations (e.g., game theory or transaction cost).

Second, *trustful networking in context* is a concept embracing the ability to act judiciously and wisely at concrete and opportune occasions. Such timely moments (kairos) reveal concrete impromptu situations when opportunities have to be seized, here and now, beyond clocks and timetables. Gaining and upholding trust in such timely situations in networks (and otherwise) directs demand for credibility and judgment.

Third, *instrumental trust in networks* is a concept based on the abstract chronos time of clocks in conjunction with a conception of concrete and meaningful place—most notably in the time-management ideas of just-in-time and just-in-place manufacturing. From a network organization point of view this category of trust has been noted particularly in studies of industrial and manufacturing networks (e.g., joint ventures and supply-chain networks).

Fourth, *trust in virtual net-work(ing)* is a communication based on human right moments to act judiciously in "virtual spaces" such as in ICT-based network organizations. Such a virtual setting is more likely to contain trust that appears to be very fragile and temporal. Online communication in virtual network organizations simply entails greater uncertainty than face-to-face communication in physical network settings. Eventually, however, the growing sophistication in ICT technology renders it increasingly difficult to determine the status of the actors in the network; can we trust a machine counterpart mimicking humans? The meaningfulness of the traditionally human concepts of trust and kairic timeliness will therefore eventually decrease in ICT-based networking with artificial actors.

· · ·

To err is a human predicament, to forgive a human achievement, and the willingness to trust is a question of timely discernment. However sophisticated a human-mimicking counterpart might ever be, we have little or no indulgence for nonhuman shortcomings. As users, we require stable and reliable ICT network software systems at levels that cannot be achieved by humans alone. When the level of uncertainty is barely perceptible, questions of timely trust or distrust will be replaced by questions of building reliable and robust network systems. Such technical matters are, however, beyond the realities of human shortcomings in personal relationships.

In the early 1970s the American philosopher Hubert Dreyfus wrote a perceptive book entitled *What Computers Can't Do*. In it he argues that computer-driven artificial intelligence (AI) rests on the assumption—an assumption that underlies computer science more generally—that the human mind functions, logically, like a computer. This is a fallacy, he argues, and the instrumentalization and formal mathematization of human behavior deny the fundamental essence of human thought-processes and behaviors that are shaped by context, by illogic, by culture, and by the social and natural environment. It is an argument he has related more recently to questions of trust and computer mediation, and it is worthwhile quoting him here at some length (Dreyfus 2000, 62–63):

> [I]t is only on the background of our indubitable faith in the perceptual world that we can doubt the veracity of any specific perceptual experience, so we seem to have a background predisposition to trust those who touch us, and it is only on the basis of [t]his *Urtrust* that we can then be mistrustful in any specific case.

But if that background trust were missing, we might tend to be suspicious of the trustworthiness of every mediated social interaction and withhold our trust until we could confirm its reliability. Such skepticism would cease to be academic and would complicate if not poison all human interaction. As we spend more and more time interacting remotely, we may erode our embodied sense of a risky yet trustworthy world that makes physical or human contact seem real. As this sense is weakened, even our daily "local" experience may take on an illusory quality and so seem to be in need of justification.

Finally, we also have to recall the linguistic difference between *network*, as a noun, and *networking* as a verb (and perhaps also the intermediate infinitive *to network*). A network can be both inanimate, such as a depiction of a transport network, as well as an animate network of interacting groups of people. The first case is obviously instrumental, a means for achieving something else (swiftly moving from A to B). Even the latter case, however, with groups of people networking, has instrumental overtones (e.g., in so-called business card exchanges). Networking therefore has a (covert or overt) purpose of gaining something, or selling something, sometime, to someone. To this extent networking is purely instrumental and commercial in intent (thus a buzzword without benign purposes). Commercial networking is about doing it all faster, and ICT-based networking aims at eliminating costly time and space-consuming friction. *Networking* is also an unfortunate term because it implies connections (nodes) but underrates the importance of trustful relationships between humans (not machines). Undoubtedly, speed and ease of connection determine technological progress, but people trust other people they know, and getting to know someone tends to take time. Focusing on relationships, rather than on networking, reveals integrity and patience. People who have taken that time are usually worthy of trust. Therefore, relationship building for the sake of building relationships is hardly a question of networking but of building and maintaining circles of friends (with or without ICTs). That is what makes a really good circle (or network?) of people so difficult to become a part of. It is also what makes it so desirable to belong to.

References

Abrams, L. C., R. Cross, E. Lesser, and D. Z. Levin. 2003. Nurturing interpersonal trust in knowledge-sharing networks. *Academy of Management Executive* 4:64–77.

Axelrod, Robert. 1984. *The evolution of cooperation.* New York: Basic Books.

Baier, Annette. 1986. Trust and antitrust. *Ethics* 96:231–260.

Bartunek, Jean M., and Raul A. Necochea. 2000. Old insights and new times: Kairos, Inca cosmology, and their contributions to contemporary management inquiry. *Journal of Management Inquiry* 2:103–112.

Baudrillard, Jean. 1981. *Simulacres et simulation.* Paris: Galilée.

———. 1994. *Simulacra and simulation.* Trans. Sheila Faria Glaser. Michigan: University of Michigan Press.

Berman Brown, Reva, and Richard Herring. 1998. The circles of time. An exploratory study in measuring temporal perceptions within organizations. *Journal of Management Psychology* 8:580–602.

Bhattacharya, R., T. M. Devinney, and M. M. Pillutla. 1998. A formal model of trust based on outcomes. *Academy of Management Review* 3:459–472.

Borgatti, Stephen P., and Pacey C. Foster. 2003. The network paradigm in organizational research: A review and typology. *Journal of Management* 6:991–1013.

Brass, D. J., K. D. Butterfield, and B. C. Skaggs. 1998. Relationships and unethical behavior: A social network perspective. *Academy of Management Review* 1:14–31.

Buskens, Vincent W. 2002. *Social networks and trust.* Hingham: Kluwer.

Casey, Edward S. 1993. *Getting back into place: Toward a renewed understanding of the place-world.* Bloomington: Indiana University Press.

———. 1997. *The fate of place: A philosophical history.* Berkeley: University of California Press.

Clases, C., R. Bachmann, and T. Wehner. 2003. Studying trust in virtual organizations. *International Studies of Management and Organization* 3:7–27.

Collins, Harry, and Martin Kusch. 1999. *The shape of actions: What humans and machines can do.* Cambridge, MA: MIT Press.

Cullen, J. B., J. L. Johnson, and T. Sakano. 2000. Success through commitment and trust: The soft side of strategic alliance management. *Journal of World Business* 3:223–240.

Das, T. K., and Bing-Sheng Teng. 1998. Between trust and control: Developing confidence in partner cooperation in alliances. *Academy of Management Review* 3:491–512.

Davidow, William H., and Michael S. Malone. 1992. *The virtual corporation.* New York: HarperCollins.

Doreian, Patrick, and Frans Stockman. 1996. *Evolution of social networks.* New York: Gordon and Breach.

Dreyfus, Hubert L. 2000. Telepistemology: Descartes's last stand. In *The robot in the garden: Telerobotics and telepistemology in the age of the Internet,* ed. Ken Goldberg, 49–63. Cambridge, MA: MIT Press.

Freeman, Linton C. 2004. *The development of social network analysis: A study in the sociology of science.* Vancouver: Booksurge.

Freeman, R. Edward. 1984. *Strategic management: A stakeholder approach.* Boston: Pitman.

Friedland, Nehemia. 1990. Attribution of control as a determinant of cooperation in exchange interaction. *Journal of Applied Social Psychology* 4:303–320.

Goldberg, Ken, ed. 2000. *The robot in the garden: Telerobotics and telepistemology in the age of the Internet.* Cambridge, MA: MIT Press.

Grabowski, Martha, and Karlene H. Roberts. 1999. Risk mitigation in virtual organizations. *Organization Science* 6:704–721.

Granovetter, Mark. 1985. Economic action and social structure: The problem of embeddedness. *American Journal of Sociology* 3:481–510.

Grenier, Ray, and George Metes. 1995. *Going virtual: Moving your organization into the 21st century.* Englewood Cliffs: Prentice Hall.

Grundy, John. 1998. Trust in virtual teams. *Harvard Business Review* 76 (Nov.–Dec.): 180.

Gulati, Ranjay. 1995. Does familiarity breed trust? The implications of repeated ties for contractual choice in alliances. *Academy of Management Journal* 1:85–112.

———. 1998. Alliances and networks. *Strategic Management Journal* 4:293–317.

Gössling, Tobias. 2004. Proximity, trust, and morality in networks. *European Planning Studies* 5:675–689.

Hallowell, Edward M. 1999. The human moment at work. *Harvard Business Review* 77 (Jan.–Feb.): 58–66.

Handy, Charles. 1995. How do you manage people whom you do not see? Trust and the virtual organization. *Harvard Business Review* 73 (May–June): 40–50.

Hindmoor, Andrew. 1998. The importance of being trusted: Transaction costs and policy network theory. *Public Administration* 1:25–43.

Jaques, Elliott. 1982. *The form of time.* New York: Crane Russak.

Järvenpää, Sirkka L., and Dorothy E. Leidner. 1999. Communication and trust in global virtual teams. *Organization Science* 6:791–815.

Kavanagh, Donncha, and Seamus Kelly. 2002. Sensemaking, safety, and situated communities in (con)temporary networks. *Journal of Business Research* 7:583–594.

Kinneavy, James L. 1986. Kairos: A neglected concept in classical rhetoric. In *Rhetoric and praxis*, ed. Jean D. Moss, 79–105. Washington, DC: Catholic University of America Press.

Kinneavy, James L., and Catherine R. Eskin. 1994. Kairos in Aristotle's *Rhetoric. Written Communication* 1:131–142.

Kirkeby, Ole F. 2000. *Management philosophy. A radical-normative perspective.* Berlin: Springer.

Koniordos, Sokratis M. 2005. *Networks, trust, and social capital: Theoretical and empirical investigations from Europe.* Aldershot, UK: Ashgate.

Lane, Christel, and Reinhard Bachmann. 1998. *Trust within and between organizations: Conceptual issues and empirical applications.* Oxford: Oxford University Press.

Latour, Bruno. 1996. *Aramis, or, The love of technology.* Trans. Catherine Porter. Cambridge, MA: Harvard University Press.

Luhmann, Niklas. 1979. *Trust and power.* Chichester: John Wiley and Sons.

Macey, Samuel L., ed. 1994. *Encyclopedia of time.* New York: Garland.

May, Jon, and Nigel Thrift, eds. 2001. *Timespace: Geographies of temporality.* London: Routledge.

McKnight, D. H., L. L. Cummings, and N. L. Chervany. 1998. Initial trust formation in new organizational relationships. *Academy of Management Review* 3:473–490.

Meyerson, D., K. E. Weick, and R. M. Kramer. 1996. Swift trust and temporary groups. In *Trust in organizations: Frontiers of theory and research,* ed. R. M. Kramer and T. R. Tyler, 166–195. Thousand Oaks, CA: Sage.

Monge, Peter R., and Noshir S. Contractor. 2001. Emergence of communication networks. In *The new handbook of organizational communication,* ed. F. M. Jablin and L. L. Putnam, 440–502. Thousand Oaks, CA: Sage.

Moody, James. 2002. The importance of relationship timing for diffusion. *Social Forces* 1:25–56.

Nohria, Nitin, and Robert G. Eccles. 1992. Face-to-face: Making network organizations work. In *Network and organizations,* ed. Nitin Nohria and Robert G. Eccles, 288–308. Boston: Harvard Business School Press.

Oliver, Amalya L., and Mark Ebers. 1998. Networking network studies: An analysis of conceptual configurations in the study of inter-organizational relationships. *Organization Studies* 4:549–583.

Powell, W. W., K. W. Koput, J. I. Bowie, and L. Smith-Doerr. 2002. The spatial clustering of science and capital: Accounting for biotech firm-venture capital relationships. *Regional Studies* 3:299–313.

Ring, Peter S. 1997. Processes facilitating reliance on trust in inter-organizational networks. In *The Formation of inter-organizational networks,* ed. Mark Ebers, 114–145. Oxford: Oxford University Press.

Rämö, Hans. 1999. An Aristotelian human time-space manifold: From chronochora to kairotopos. *Time & Society* 2:311–330.

———. 2002. Doing things right and doing the right things. Time and timing in projects. *International Journal of Project Management* 7:569–574.

———. 2004a. Spatio-temporal notions and organized environmental issues—An axiology of action. *Organization* 6:849–872.

———. 2004b. Moments of trust: Temporal and spatial factors of trust in organizations. *Journal of Managerial Psychology* 8:760–775.

Shamir, Boas, and Yael Lapidot. 2003. Trust in organizational superiors: Systemic and collective considerations. *Organization Studies* 3:463–491.

Smith, John E. 1969. Time, times, and the "right time," *chronos* and *kairos. Monist* 1:1–13.

———. 1986. Time and qualitative time. *Review of Metaphysics* 1:3–16.

Smith-Doerr, Laurel, and Walther W. Powell. 2004. Networks and economic life. In *The handbook of economic sociology,* ed. Neal Smelser and Richard Swedberg, 379–402. 2nd ed. Princeton, NJ: Princeton University Press.

Snijders, Tom A. B. 2001. The statistical evaluation of social network dynamics. *Sociological Methodology* 31:361–395.

Snijders, Tom A. B., and Marijtje A. J. van Duijn, 1997. Simulation for statistical inference in dynamic network models. In *Simulating social phenomena,* ed. R. Conte, R. Hegselmann, and P. Terna, 493–512. Berlin: Springer.

Snow, Charles P. 1964. *The two cultures; and, A second look: An expanded version of "The two cultures and the scientific revolution."* Cambridge, UK: Cambridge University Press.

Stalk, George, Jr., and Thomas M. Hout. 1990. *Competing against time: How time-based competition is reshaping global markets.* New York: Free Press.

Stern, Carl W., and George Stalk Jr., eds. 1998. *Perspectives on strategy.* Chichester: John Wiley and Sons.

Suitor, J. J., B. Wellman, and D. L. Morgan. 1997. It's about time: How, why, and when networks change. *Social Networks* 19:1–7.

Uzzi, Brian. 1997. Social structure and competition in interfirm networks: The paradox of embeddedness. *Administrative Science Quarterly* 1:35–67.

Van Alstyne, Marshall W. 1997. The state of network organization: A survey in three frameworks. *Journal of Organizational Computing and Electronic Commerce* 2/3:83–151.

Varamäki, Elina, and Jukka Vesalainen. 2003. Modelling different types of multilateral co-operation between SMEs. *Entrepreneurship and Regional Development* 1:27–47.

Weesie, Jeroen, and Henk Flap. 1990. *Social networks through time.* Utrecht: ISOR.

White, Eric C. 1987. *Kaironomia: On the will-to-invent.* Ithaca, NY: Cornell University Press.

Williamson, Oliver E. 1975. *Markets and hierarchies: Analysis and antitrust implications: A study in the economics of internal organization.* New York: Free Press.

———. 1993. Calculativeness, trust, and economic-organization. *Journal of Law and Economics* 1:453–486.

Womack, J. P., D. T. Jones, and D. Roos. 1990. *The machine that changed the world.* New York: Macmillan.

13 The Clock-Time Paradox

Time Regimes in the Network Society

Ida H. J. Sabelis

Time is an essential feature of social and organizational life. It is our prime organizing tool. People use time in order to create, shape, and order their worlds. And yet, despite its importance, we take our time values and uses of time largely for granted.

—*Barbara Adam, Richard Whipp, and Ida Sabelis,* Making Time

THE RISE OF THE NETWORK ORGANIZATION seems to be radically altering our values toward time and, subsequently, the patterns of our daily lives. The underlying values and patterns of time use, however, are largely taken for granted, even in the midst of the rapid changes brought about by the new information and communication technologies (ICTs). Drawing from the interdisciplinary field of time studies, my aim is to make the invisible visible (Adam 1995, 1998, 2004), connecting seemingly "fragmented" (Handy 1990) phenomena in contemporary society, enabling theorists and practitioners to better understand the long-term effects of postmodern organizational practices that suffer from a too-narrow time view and use.

In the introductory chapter of *Making Time* (Adam, Whipp, and Sabelis 2002), the authors provide an overview of the history of organization and management and the current problematic relationship of management studies with time. Not only can contrasting intellectual traditions be distinguished in the history of management studies, but also a rather paradoxical development in the study of organizations emerges from a temporal perspective. Mainstream studies of organization and management subscribe to the understanding of time as linear, plannable, and therefore a controllable mode of clock time, or industrial time. Although clock time has enabled organization in our modern society in the first place (Bluedorn 2002; Karsten 2003; Thompson

1967), it has also created dilemmas and problems that become visible only when we manage to switch focus from the smooth ideals of control, planning, and organization to the everyday experience of people trying to cope with the reality of this in practice. Such a shift in focus requires a concomitant change in research methods: from an exclusive reliance on quantitative time-budget studies to more qualitative research utilizing ethnography, fieldwork, and discourse analysis in order to contextualize industrial, clock-time use and its implicit effects. Such methods can provide a more complete picture of the sense-making routines that are employed in network organizations, showing how structural issues are linked to underlying norms and values. From an empirical view, we face key questions about the types of coordinating and synchronizing mechanisms used within and between organizations vis-à-vis ICTs. What determines the expansion of a clock-time orientation, both in and beyond the boundaries of organization, in terms of care, reproduction, family life, and the ways in which people experience their daily lifeworld? These questions guide the analysis of time complexity in the context of the network society, with its growing web of communication devices.

As an organizational anthropologist I focus my research on uncovering the unintended effects of (imposed, fast, and recurrent) organizational change, as experienced, for instance, via struggles with boundaries between organizational and private life, the accelerating effects of globalizing bureaucracy or automation (Virilio 2002), and the occurrence of ambiguity related to identity issues and acceleration (Rosa 2002). The workings of the networked organization can be made visible by problematizing the temporal restraints people face when, for instance, rhythmicities in organizations are violated and the boundaries between work, care, and private life become blurred (see also Menzies 2005; Paolucci 1996; Ylijoki and Mäntylä 2003). These restraints become explicit mainly in terms of coping with one's professional identity, workload, burnout-related issues, and discussions about "work-life balance," in short: the tensions between the organization and "other times."

Questioning people directly about their time use often produces rather shallow answers concerning time-schedule problems. This is manifest in, for example, complaints about being "busy, busy, busy," or being always short of time, or the need for better time management. Almost without exception, when asked about time-related issues, people frequently report a general feeling of being stressed, or, if not stressed yet, they anticipate becoming stressed in their attempts to cope with the "acceleration of just about everything," to borrow a phrase from James Gleick (1999). Inevitably, use of the Internet adds to feelings of acceleration. Given the unavoidable necessity of being online, the top-level managers I interviewed expressed annoyance about having to respond to information faster and more frequently, compared to when letters were delivered to their desks in the morning. Similarly, email communication has fundamentally altered the nature of work for middle-level managers. These managers reported that a greater portion of their time is now spent with and via "computerization," dealing with corporate policy issues, leaving less time for being involved in day-to-day operational realities and consultation with subordinates (Ybema and Sabelis 2006). In another study I concentrated on how the work of academics is changing with the introduction of email and the Internet. ICTs have presented both more opportunities for cooperation and an increase of bureaucratic intrusion into the daily work of academics.

Are such changes in the nature of work simply a matter of a change in technology and the mode of communication, or can we also gain deeper insights into such changes by incorporating a time-study perspective? This chapter focuses on how the experience of "being networked" influences people in their daily work routines and how the introduction of ICTs is actually an extension of the bureaucratic organization. To explore these questions, I draw on two case studies. One is a study of the coping strategies employed by top-level managers (Koot and Sabelis 2002); the other is a workload study of academics in a selection of European and Canadian universities (Menzies and Newson 2005; Sabelis 2004a; Schouteten 2005; Ylijoki and Mäntylä 2003). Taken as explorative examples, these cases show the different ways in which professionals at work are dealing with the network society. Importantly, they offer ground for reflection and discussion of the underlying temporal patterns in everyday working life. In order to make explicit how these studies are interpreted, it is necessary to say something about the theories of time, organization, and management that underpin the analysis.

Time, Organization, and Sense-Making

Recent reviews in management studies show that clock time is taken for granted as a prime organizing tool and that temporal complexity is ignored in everyday *practice* (see, e.g., AMJ 2002). In the first case, studies tend to be limited to time-budget or time-use studies that do not go beyond the long-standing tradition of Fordist-structuralist perspectives on organization and management; these studies merely reinforce the assumption that clock time is the ruling device for organizations. Such studies fail to address the implicit values incorporated in the application of a rationalist, clock-time understanding of organizational processes. In the second case more theoretically nuanced studies may manage to provide a wider understanding of the complex temporalities that encompass the clock-time orientation—by revealing, for instance, the lack of understanding of *rhythmicity* in contemporary management studies or the diversity of time orientation in global or transcultural organizational networks. A significant drawback, however, is that such research is rarely based on empirical findings and usually has an orientation toward the philosophical. The result is that there may be a great deal of inspiring reflection but little practice-oriented guidance. Consequently, the aim of my research is to find a position between these two poles in order to question the implicit time understandings in the clock-time perspective and to combine this with an overarching theoretical perspective that deals with empirical data. To illustrate the tension implied in this endeavor, I have constructed a schedule of time perspectives in which the current debates are ordered according to their contribution to the different foci or time views (see Figure 13.1).

First, there is the clock-time view, in which an orientation toward scheduling and control emerging from a specific rationality of planning and temporal linearity is most prominent. Second, we find the more nuanced, cultural perspective, in which differences in time use and time perception are acknowledged. Seen from an organizational point of view, the fundamental divergence here has an inherent political quality. It implies a dichotomization of temporal qualities, which usually leads to an implicit or explicit appreciation of certain norms and values (with their concomitant expression in clock time, for instance fast versus slow, long-term versus short-term orientation, monochromic versus polychromic) (see also Hall 1983; Sabelis 2004b). And third, there is the "timescape" (Adam 1998) perspective, which emphasizes the holistic or *holographic* (Keenoy 1999) qualities of time. The timescape perspective suggests time as encompassing, pervasive, and especially focused on interrelations over the long term. It further suggests the development of temporal interrelations that are not present in the other perspectives and very difficult to interpret from the short-term horizons usually present in studies of management and organization.

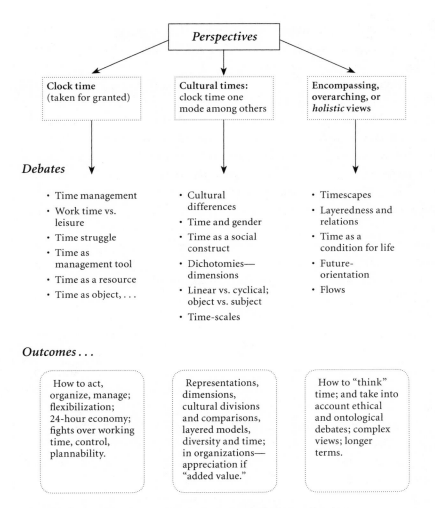

FIGURE 13.1 Overview of Time Debates and Their Implications

In the top-level managers' time study (Sabelis 2002) I utilized the time-scape perspective as a theoretical model for interpreting the cultural values and habits in dealing with time that were identified as most important. The study offers insight into the contradictory, sometimes paradoxical, patterns and schemes of time use, time views, and the managers' assumptions of how time is "spent" by themselves and their subordinates. Indeed, the concept of timescapes proved useful for revealing the interconnectedness of times in organizational life and served to address some of the usually implicit expectations that trigger temporal acceleration and colonization of the future within organizational structures.

Although there is a growing acknowledgment that clock time is a one-dimensional, virtually "empty" category (Adam 1998), current organization studies still tend to reinforce the idea that organizational life should be based on temporal planning and control. Indeed, it is an assumption regarding time that has become an implicit *ideological device* for organizations, with uses that go beyond the original goal of coordination. From the perspective of the theoretician, or even the empirical sociologist, it may be at least intuitively more attractive to attribute more value to the "timescape" perspective, as this seems to offer a more fruitful way to consider time complexity. On the other hand, from the managerial perspective this logic runs precisely in the opposite direction. Clock time is the ruling device, and other time perspectives are considered only if there is value to be gained, efficiencies to be made, and flexibilities to be achieved.

A useful strategy to reconcile this tension is the inclusion of temporal sense-making routines, both during the research (be it in interviews, observation, or surveys) and reflexively in the analyses (Alvesson and Sköldberg 2000). The concept of timescapes serves to link the disparity between assumptions of measurement in quantitatively oriented studies and the inspirational promises of holistic, theorizing studies. The dimension of "making sense," or attributing value and meaning to organizational life, is often ignored in the rationality of the debates, whereas to my mind it is the connecting undercurrent in organizational life, enabling exemplification of the "webs of meaning" (see Geertz 1973). At some level of consciousness we may recognize that there are other "sorts" of time (see Gell 1992; Gurvitch 1964; Hall 1983), but the theoretical notions of time dimensions (McTaggart 1908), timescales (Kümmerer 1996), or timescapes (Adam 1998) have not yet provided an extensive empirical analysis for the paradoxical role of clock time in modern organizations.[1] The ways in which we study temporalities in and between organizations calls for further development and more empirical analysis of how time "works." The combination of perspectives with acknowledgment of the paradoxical role of clock time allows for the development of a "new vocabulary" (Whipp 1994) that can contribute to a greater understanding of the role of temporality in management and organization studies. The following cases can be taken as examples of this endeavor.

Executive Level Acceleration

> I strongly feel that acceleration is a pivotal thing in life for all of us—I
> can't tell you what causes what, but it is so obvious in notions of how
> fast things have to be achieved, that everything has become faster.
> —*Anonymous executive*

As part of a biographical study of *coping strategies* (Pahl 1995; Watson and
Harris 1999) in managerial lives, I developed a specific focus on the temporal
aspects underlying the daily routines of top-level managers (Koot and Sabelis
2002; Sabelis 2002). The aim was to provide insight into who these "top-level"
managers are, what motivates them on a daily basis, and what types of managerial insights they use (and struggle with).[2] The variant of the biographical, constructivist method applied in the research allowed for the insertion of
time-related topics via thematic topic lists used for the discussions with the
managers. This provided the opportunity, together with elaborate observation reports, to link themes of time use to time perception and gain a more
comprehensive view on both working patterns and the meanings (tensions,
paradoxes, norms, values) attached to those.

At first glance, the term *coping strategies* might suggest that such processes
operate on the conscious level. Acceleration within the network society is now
so taken-for-granted, however, that such coping strategies have simply become routinized and are not always made explicit in managerial interviews.
Given that so much of the work executives do involves being online, simply
asking direct questions about the accelerative effects of "being networked"
would be akin to asking a watchmaker if the clocks he is working with are
supposed to tell the time. Instead, I found that the theme of networks occurred when discussions turned to the managers' views on recent societal
developments. Almost without exception the executives we interviewed and
observed noted that acceleration and speed are the core organizational challenge that has emerged over the last twenty years. In conjunction with temporal acceleration, executives also stressed the fact that their spatial horizons
have expanded, requiring greater attention to international developments
and geopolitical change. The impact of networks was understood on two
levels. First, executives recognized that their firms are inextricably linked to
multinational or global organizational networks, as the result of mergers or
by developments in the professional context of their organizations, such as
being a partner with other firms in innovation projects. Second, networking

was viewed within the context of ICTs, which were seen as enabling fast and frequent communication. Both of these ways of understanding networks were identified by executives as presenting both opportunities and constraints in their organizations.

Consider, for example, the chief technology officer (CTO) of a global electronics firm who stressed how shifting alliances in international business have fundamentally changed the ways in which he deals with partners and competitors. The shift in focus from managing a production firm to being a partner in the processes of innovation has brought about changes in the ways in which he works with people both in the company and across the world. This executive's job has changed from promotion and supervision of product lines to seeking partners and bonding shifting alliances in order to safeguard patents and research teams. The complexity of the changes has increased work demands; this executive finds himself engaging in more tasks during any given twenty-four-hour day now that he has the capability of being instantly aware of the latest information regarding competitors around the globe. Complexity has also increased. For example, competitors may become partners in short- or medium-term projects. This CTO noted that ICTs have allowed him to expand his range of personal contacts, enabling him to acquire the latest information on innovation in the field and potential research and development partners. To maintain and develop these contacts, he has to be constantly online.

The CTO's story seems typical of most managers employed in global industries. Similar stories were found for managers in the ICT businesses, in food enterprises, and in the chemical industry. For example, a female manager of a multinational ICT organization in my study illustrates the life of a cosmopolitan traveler and an ICT addict. Based on fastidious time management, an analysis of her weekly planner revealed that the majority of her time was devoted to travel and teleconferences on a continuous basis. Teleconferences were scheduled during the day and after hours in order to synchronize with Asian and American partners in *real time*. She describes a typical day: "I get up at five in the morning and sit behind my desk, well-dressed of course, to catch one partner finishing a working day and the others just starting. . . . [T]his is a regular pattern, and on my days off I tend to restrict my working time to a maximum of two hours."

While it is obvious that her daily schedule is structured by tight time management, the rhythmicity of her life—the recurrence of traveling patterns, the constant use of ICTs, and particularly her private life entrained to the global demands of her work—is of most importance. Her case shows how the assumed linearity of time management forces the delegation of "other times" to her surroundings, her private inner circle as well as the administrative systems of the organization. Her good home planning increasingly requires the times of others, spreading the idea of rational plannability into areas of life where it was not intended to be applied. The technological devices used (and offered) by the organization soon turned into indispensable needs, to be used at formerly nonworking times and preventing her from reflection about alternatives to the speeding up of the pace of her life. As soon as she had the connection for teleworking, she started to work at home more than before, developing "new routines." Within months, or weeks, "the firm" relied on the new practice, including the "loops" (recurrent and almost rhythmic delegation of tasks and time use) this caused for secretaries and staff: email, for instance, tends to invite quick answers to "small" questions and for communicating to and fro.

Another example was provided by the head of a chemical firm. During the interviews he expressed his frustration at "having lost control of the organization." This executive's story is not unusual; he spent most of his adult career striving to "be at the top." Yet he now finds himself actually "caught in the middle" between shareholder pressures, potential mergers, and the constant demand for instant performance. As he confesses: "I always wanted to be the boss, but now that I'm here, the shareholders' economy forces me to deal with facts and figures, instead of actualizing the vision and social ideas I once had for my organization." His daily planner is computerized and organized by his secretary ("ask her my schedule, she always knows"). One of the threats in his current position is emerging mergers and opportunities for outsourcing: "if I don't do it [reorganizing], somebody else will." He faces constant demands for instant performance—the "market" is always "about the need to act now"—no matter what the long-term effects may be.

A paradoxical pattern arises from the accounts of these executives: communication technologies have enabled them to acquire more contacts, but they are then expected to maintain such contacts over time. Accordingly, maintenance of contacts via email, teleconferencing and "online schedulers" has grown, as has the need periodically to meet partners and competitors in person. The net outcome of this is that online time for executives has increased, along with their face-to-face meetings with stakeholders. This change implies not only more virtual contacts but also more traveling than before. Furthermore, via the speed of virtual contacts, these executives find themselves in a situation of fragmentation: both inside and outside the organization, the habits of sending and responding to short messages (questions, queries) increases, which results in decision making based on partial information, in which the "speed of the action" becomes more important than thorough reflection. Simultaneously, as ICTs provide more possibilities, the traditional rhythmicity in having meetings (meeting during what is regarded as "working hours") has expanded into what once was considered "free time." Most executives report variations in their adaptation to global times, which in practice means availability on a 24/7 basis.

For these executives, being online implies being embedded in the network society. That is to say they are perpetually en route—whether in the virtual space of network communication or in real space via modes of physical transport such as the car or jet. The most common reason for complying with this trend is expressed in the phrase "If I didn't do it, someone else would." To some extent this is reality. But in another sense it is illustrative of the "mental split" these executives have when reflecting on their work. They make a clear distinction between their own values and desires and those of the external world of international networks. Some executives report that the network also provides them with a sense of technical omniscience, of being in control across the boundaries of space and time. As in the case of one executive, ICTs have created a "pace that is addictive" and that enabled him to feel as if he was "always on top of it all."

The intense pace, the continuous striving for efficiency, acceleration of global competition, and the demand to be online at all times are also colonizing the private lives of executives and managers. Times outside of network time are, in effect, being delegated to their families, secretaries, and friends. This phenomenon of technological extension is an example of acceleration in the classical sense, that is, using technology-as-it-is-available because growth and speed are the core aspects of competition in the context of a free-market economy. As space seems to have become compressed via the networks, these executives are running out(side) of time, which in turn has to be compressed in order for them to cope with the flow of events: "the art of leaving things out is called compression." With compression as temporal experience, the emerging norm is to forget the past—there is not enough storage space nor time for memories, and the future is nothing more than a luxury of afterthought. One of the executives expressed it in these terms:

> "I'm very much a here and now person—I don't carry memories with me. . . . I know it just takes half an hour to get over a disappointment. . . . I don't look back".

And he doesn't look forward either:

> "You can't predict the future anyway, so why bother? In the seventies there used to be futurologists—you don't see those nowadays. No—long-term is two years, that's quite enough to deal with."

Temporal acceleration and compression are the realities for these executives. Obviously, ICTs and global networks have radically changed the organizations that they manage, as well as the nature of their work. With such profound change comes anxiety. To cope with their daily demands, time pressures, and increased workload, executives have embraced rationality to promote compression ("leaving things out"). The compression of tasks in time and space, augmented by rational systems of computerization, demands that again more time is spent online. ICTs, however, also pose the problem of information overload. Executives may be spending more time online, but a lot of that time is wasted in sorting through essential from nonessential information.

The effect of temporal compression via ICTs is so pervasive that little time is left for serious reflection of management practices. Temporal momentum generated by the technological demands of the network society seems inexorable. Is this another form of technological determinism that is but a postmodern expression of clock-time rule?

Academics, Workload, and ICTs

Unlike executives in the private sector, academics rarely have staff and administrative support assigned to them. Faculty in universities utilize ICTs for structuring work processes, scheduling, and the control of core activities (teaching, research, and administrative tasks), as well as to enable swift contact and exchange between colleagues. In this section I draw on a study that examined the workload of faculty in the School of Social Sciences at the Vrije Universiteit, Amsterdam. Similar studies (Keenoy 2005; Schouteten 2005;

Ylijoki and Mäntylä 2003) have shown that academics are struggling with time pressure that is a result of increased dependence on ICTs.

Traditionally, academics have enjoyed a high degree of autonomy over their work and time; they do not conform to the standard nine-to-five work routine. The academic calendar allows faculty to self-manage their own tasks around their teaching schedule. Most academics allocate their time between teaching, research, and administrative / service activities. Research typically consists of reading, doing fieldwork, thinking, and writing. Teaching is scheduled and usually leaves time slots that are then attributed to research time. Irregular periods of intensive overwork are considered normal.

Over the last decade universities have been facing increased pressures for relevancy, accountability, and marketability. Many public universities have suffered from decreases in state support, with a demand to increase the growth of external and entrepreneurial funding. Such external pressures, often argued for in terms of the imperatives of globalization, directly affect academics who are now confronted with frequent and externally imposed changes to their work.

In the Amsterdam workload study, the majority of faculty reported that mainly external pressures were contributing to their feeling of "being constantly behind one's schedule."[3] Faculty are now subjected to *efficiency measures* that are applied to various academic tasks. For example, time allocated to teaching courses is now calculated using an economic model where a certain monetary value is budgeted to individual faculty and departments based on contact hours in the classroom. This economic model fails to account, however, for the ancillary time associated with teaching, such as course preparation, advising students, grading papers, and so forth. Instead, teaching time is viewed as a fixed quantity subject to economic rationalization and temporal compression. By compressing teaching time, administration could justify increases in faculty teaching loads. While this economic model fits well with the ideas of planning and control, my interviews revealed that compression of teaching time for pure efficiency reasons actually resulted in a degradation of quality time spent teaching and a reduction of time available for research.

To enforce the rational calculation of teaching hours and output criteria, additional bureaucratic rules and policies had to be implemented. Ironically, such efficiency measures made the delivery of education less flexible, with a subsequent decline in quality. Faculty who prided themselves on serving students found themselves investing more of their own personal (unpaid, "free") time to maintain acceptable levels of quality. Faculty frequently complained of "never having enough time to finish" (68 percent), of "having to leave work before finished" (66 percent), and "worrying about work while at home" (62 percent). Moreover, 55 percent reported that they would always (7 percent), often (24 percent), or regularly (24 percent) be "too tired after a working day to be able to do the things they wanted." More surprisingly, 61 percent of faculty reported suffering from health problems that they attributed to increased workload. In the focus groups that I conducted, these issues were explicitly addressed to find out more about the assumed causes of the survey findings. As one might suspect, position in the hierarchy (academic and staff, but also hierarchies within the groups) made a difference in terms of autonomy over work and in the time spent (regardless of working hours) between members. For older staff and for academics now in managerial positions, however, there seemed to be a tendency toward less autonomy, because of perceived increases in workload, over the last five to ten years. There was strong agreement among academics of lower rank (and age) about the fragmentation of their work. Among this group of academics, 70 percent reported that they were frequently interrupted by administrative changes and unexpected organizational demands, which either caused tiredness or compelled them to start working more at home.

One coping strategy developed by academic staff to avoid frequent interruptions was to try to fix problems by themselves instead of engaging in what they considered to be potentially lengthy and time-consuming procedures. For example, if procedures for administrative work were considered too complex, subject to frequent changes, or simply "not effective," many academic staff would simply try to "fix it myself." It was a reaction that paradoxically added to the complaint, broadly expressed, that "disturbances while in the office" are putting pressure on the daily workload. Simultaneously, attempts to bypass set procedures caused more work for others in the organization: "fixing the fix" and not communicating this to others added to the amount of "disturbances" elsewhere in the network. It is not that set procedures were not considered necessary but that they were applied to all problems. This example might be considered a symptom of what the analysis gradually saw as "time loops" in the system: when the striving for rational efficiency clashes with the limits of what people can manage on a daily basis. Interestingly, this phenomenon in the university setting parallels the habit of top-level managers to engage in quick responses to fragmented demands, adding to the delegation of time overflow to others in the organizations.

Superimposing and pervading all activities in this context is the use of email and the Internet by all faculty members and staff. Over the last ten years ICTs have helped to deal with growing organizational complexity, that is in terms of fast communication, but they have changed the (expected) speed at which the work is done. ICTs have exacerbated faculty irritation and miscommunication, especially as staff and academics develop different, task-related habits for their use. Staff expects instantaneous responses to administrative demands, and academics postpone replying because of the different working times. For the academics, autonomy over working time is highly important and has led to increased teleworking, doing research and other tasks while at home or while traveling and conferencing. Staff, usually working on a nine-to-five basis, use ICTs to obtain and spread important information for the bureaucratic system. This study illustrates how the habits of working with the new ICT devices exposes the difference in rhythmicities between the two professional groups.

More rules and regulations tend to prevent the "in-between" space and time for improvisation (Peters 2005). Disturbances to daily routines via email messages were considered to have a far more structured character than just "the odd intrusion on a working day." And working at home more to avoid the combination of email and physical disturbance is a double-edged sword: working at home more tends to make them invisible, sometimes unreachable by staff colleagues, causing irritation and suspicion. In turn, this leads to more pressing messages to react to, the imposition of deadlines, on so on. Teleworking thus tends to lead to desynchronization (Paolucci 1996), where private time and working time become blurred.

Being networked and being online thus plays a specific role in the everyday working life of faculty. Online communication suggests fast answers. As with the example of top managers, this tends to create habits of communication in which parts of problems are transferred to and fro: unripe decisions, part decisions, and "small" ("tiny") questions are spread and cause confusion. Organizational response to this problem is the desire for "better communication." Typically, in both the Amsterdam and Nijmegen studies, one of the solutions for the problems of workload was better communication. For example, in Amsterdam a new intranet was put in place (remarkably not accessible externally, via the Web) because some of the higher management was convinced that this would help to decrease the pressure caused by lack of information. Over time, however, communication turned out to entail mainly more "messages of information," usually in a top-down manner, which served to irritate professionals. Increase in email usage substitutes for face-to-face meetings within the organization, and this serves to strengthen the tendency for one-way communication.

Exploratory research by Tom Keenoy (2005) in the United Kingdom and the Netherlands focuses on the use of email by academics and provides some possible explanations for the change in academic work that is related to "being networked." Besides suggesting that being networked has some parallels with addiction, Keenoy argues that the possibilities of "being wired" have brought about several new intrusions to the daily flow of work. Although email "seems to function as a socio-digital circadian rhythm" (Keenoy 2005, 9), his data indicate that a large portion of work is added by being online. The out-of-time quality, or rather the quality of email being there (popping up, often checked) all the time, can be considered an intrusion as such. This largely parallels the top-level managers' fragmented decision making. Email, however, also motivates academics to communicate and react to questions in "a private space in between teaching, research and administration . . . usually without the aid of a secretary" (ibid., 10). Based on the findings of the workload study, it may also be argued that a fair proportion of work previously done by secretaries is now carried out by academics themselves because of the possibilities offered by computerization and ICTs. The speed-enabling function of computerization produces a work flow in which academics simultaneously gain a new sense of autonomy (doing many things themselves out of efficiency considerations), as well as a dependence on IT systems and IT professionals.

This emerging-dependency thesis has been investigated by Heather Menzies and Janice Newson (2005), who researched the effects of being networked among (Canadian) academics. The results of their study show that, for female academics in particular, the Internet provided a structure for international support and debate—as well as a means to escape from one's own faculty politics through developing a virtual network of colleagues. This online community contains its own problems, however, in the sense that "being online" can sometimes be addictive, as users seek to develop the new possibilities inherent in ICT processes and applications. The "urge to achieve" at an increasingly accelerated rate can militate against reflection and the deepening of analyses and thought. And of course, *being productive* is precisely the dominant trend in academic life under the influence of the new public management (Parker and Jary 1995). ICTs have changed the ways in which people "naturally" develop inspiration, creativity, and innovation by direct communication and using "loops" of different temporal qualities, that is, rhythmicities in the process of creative thinking impeding the production of "output"-related products.

A question that arises is how being networked relates to the changes in academic life. Doing more in less time *and* expanding one's intellectual range adds to the daily pressures and illustrates the paradoxical struggle of compressing and intensifying at the same time. In a context in which predominantly managerial ways determine the attributed times, this leads to the phenomenon of not just having to cope with issues of work-life balance (working at odd hours) but also with what we might term "work-work" balance as a cause of problems. We see this in the struggle with frequent shifts in work-related rhythms (answering emails, writing, preparing classes, and trying to think while often being interrupted). Administrative staff experience workload and pressure but apply "working to rule" and "follow the designated tasks" as coping strategies. Because of the fact that they do mainly office work, the visibility of their work and occurring problems with workload are relatively easily perceptible for the organization. By contrast academics, especially when working at home, are seeking a new rhythmicity by individually coping with the overflow of compression practices in a totally different manner. And as noted before, their work is, apart from formal teaching, mostly invisible to the organization.

In the attempt to label the differences in experience between support staff and academics, it was revealing that implicit differences in time perception related to the temporal orders in their daily tasks, to which very diverse values were attached. This produced the idea of *time regimes*: under new public management the tasks of professionals implicitly are designed based on the assumption of traditional office hours, which causes industrial-time budget views to dominate the working time of all organizational members. When time is money, those "in-between-times," with their variation and unpredictability, can at most be "estimated" (Peters 2005). Under the pressure of the market economy, compression first and foremost causes work based on "estimations" to be cut out. The compression of working times causes academics to extend their working times, which ironically becomes even less visible and adds further to the workload.

The compression of tasks in many state service organizations through widespread computerization (Sabelis 2002, 163–164) illustrates how rationalized views of work in these sectors systematically render the "human-sized scale" to a matter of rational, economically based design: the overflow of what has been "left aside" by compression seems to spread to irregular working hours and other periods of the year, that is, the time otherwise designated to research and writing. For academics the output demands of research become, in turn, subject to compression also, causing even more pressure, eventually leading to the conclusion that academics "use the new technologies to enable them to 'keep up,' 'link up' and 'speed up' in their increasingly competitive and production-oriented work environments, [and] they also help to bring into being the fast-paced, productivity-focused 'university-as-knowledge businesses' that corporate interests and political leaders have been promoting" (Menzies and Newson 2005).

Time Loops of Networking and Control

What insight can we gain from these examples? First, it is important to stress that the research was not explicitly aimed at analyzing the effects of networks. It is revealing, however, that although we did not explicitly concentrate on networks, the temporal themes that emerged from the interviews underscored just how central the role of networks was in the daily lives of both executives and academics. Second, the contexts of the work in everyday terms turn out to be embedded in and imbued with "being networked" in the double sense of the concept: organizations functioning on a global scale and ICTs enabling fast and recurrent communication, which enhances the need for keeping up with developments on both local and global scales. The effects of standardization and computerization throughout the various organizations are omnipresent. And it is precisely in these effects that we should ask ourselves if it is the "network society" that acts as the driver of change or if other mechanisms should be addressed and studied when we look at contemporary organizations from a perspective of time complexity.

The top-level managers' example illustrates how it has become taken for granted that organizations are embedded in a worldwide understanding of "organizing" via rational, clock-time-based principles. Whether a major or minor player in the field of management, each acts on the perceived and felt influences of converging, standardizing ways of how organizations should act. It is a logic motivated mainly by norms regarding growth, competition, and speed, all of which are reinforced by the self-referential effect of being networked. Recurrent change of processes in their organizations is, on the one hand, indispensable for the managers to maintain their position and to symbolically confirm their significance (Koot and Sabelis 2002; Watson and Harris 1999); on the other hand, fast and recurrent changes sometimes are counterproductive for the organization as a whole and for the personal well-being of the managers in particular. Moreover, accelerated networking produces loops in the processes of planning and decision making: ICTs provoke immediacy and speed and therefore encourage fast action upon receiving "fast" information. This consecutively disperses part-decisions throughout the organization and prompts "solutions" that need "repairs" elsewhere. In the quest for efficiencies, computerization tends to produce more bureaucratic control. This causes expertise based on experience and craft to give way to virtual, standardized programs (Ybema and Sabelis 2006). Over time, the latter easily adds to alienation from the product of one's work or to a short-term task orientation that in turn gives way to new systems that promise more control again.

The workload examples make explicit how, in the assumed gain of time by application of ever-finer methods of control in organizations, time "gained" is immediately filled, either with more rules and regulations for streamlining processes of information exchange or with new tasks following the assumption that time is dear and therefore has to be productively utilized. As argued elsewhere (Paolucci 1996; Sabelis 2002), the side-effects of teleworking paradoxically show both an increased sense of autonomy for the individual and a fine-tuning of control systems for the organization. Output demands, as one of these control mechanisms, serve various goals: not only do they exercise control over the (invisible) work done during and outside regular office hours, but they also camouflage the fact that rhythmicities of different tasks (teaching, research, international networking) are reduced to measurable entities through the logic of rational calculation.

Bureaucratic systems related to the function of administration provide reliability, but over the long term they produce more intricate webs of communication and control, which eventually require more time investments. It is not just the fact that efficiency and compression enable more to be done in less time but also that the structuring devices to become more efficient are standardized according to the temporal understanding of specific groups, or subcultures, in the organization. This also applies in the managers' study: managerial understanding of the importance of time is projected onto other professions and other parts of the organization. It may be argued from the workload study especially, that the concept of time regimes has emerged as valuable. It seems useful to combine the structural elements of time use with the underlying realms of sense-making, autonomy, and creativity; it highlights the tensions between official-explicit and unofficial-implicit temporal structuring devices in processes of management and organization.

We are not simply dealing here with differences in temporal perspectives. What is happening is that certain temporal structures or institutions are considered more important, valuable, and readily applicable than others. Computerization and "being networked" are important aspects of these structures, but it is questionable whether they should be considered the triggers of, or the means for, acceleration. Temporalities, also the ones related to ICTs and globalization, seem to be embedded in and intertwined mainly with processes of organization politics and control. The working of these temporal regimes can be described as patterns of time use and time understanding that are contextualized and pervaded by values and norms that remain mostly implicit in studies of labor, organization, and management. In organizations, time regimes thus act as *zeitgeber*, or temporal markers, that conceal the inherent political character of the application of various time uses.

Time regimes become apparent in the expectations people have about the work of others. This was evident in the example of the top-level managers "expecting" that their subordinates (and families) would deal with the expanded "overflow" of time from their compression. Temporal regimes thus partly develop into basic assumptions (Schein 1985; Tennekes 1995) and become taken for granted in such a way that, for instance, people readily accept the one-best-way character of one time regime to other often more complex solutions. Some types of time regimes tend to become dominant in an organization. Either they prevent other regimes from being applied or cause mismatches in communication, policy development, and strategy design. Making time regimes explicit can reveal the diverse ways of time use and expectations about how others "manage" theirs, in short: the ways in which people make sense of (and with) their time in organizational settings and beyond and especially how time use and perception are manipulated and dealt with in the political arena in and between organizations.

The workload study provided the opportunity to uncover the effects and implications of "management" in the daily life of those who are managed in this context. Together with the studies of managers operating in various professional contexts, we can see how networking has an important impact on daily life in these organizations. Looking at the study with an eye to the embeddedness of being networked, we also see complex interconnections between work processes that lead to the conclusion that networking (as a form of globalization and computerization) puts pressure on the everyday experience of work instead of providing efficiency or time "saving." In the daily work experience, however, acceleration, compression, and speed are mainly triggered (and felt) through the dominance of one-sided temporal perspectives that are closely attached to "organizing" and control from specific organizational actors. Being networked should therefore be considered the extension of the organization's striving for control and standardization. It may even be seen as developing into a time regime itself, but more empirical research is needed to sustain this argument, especially about the changing interrelations of different regimes over time. Other time regimes, like those included in physical and psychological rhythms (deriving from the "cultural times" outlined in Figure 13.1), are largely excluded, and this seems to add to the time pressure and provoke coping mechanisms that end up requiring even more time.

By looking at the network society in this way, we can see how its quality of control does not necessarily enhance its suggested efficiency but rather produces recurrent loops that add burdens to one's everyday time experience. In that sense, being networked may be seen as another variation of the paradoxical bias in the clock-time perspective: the networking paradigm promises time saving and more control, yet it produces more work to do, which spills over into the "other times" of our lives.

Notes

1. Apart from some single studies such as those by Peter Clark (1985, 1997a, 1997b) and T. K. Das (1987, 1993, 2004) in which temporal patterns are (quantitatively and qualitatively) reviewed for their contribution to, respectively, the status quo of rewards systems and questions of strategy development, I found no other studies in which the workings of clock time per se are thoroughly analyzed in their relationship to goal orientation, long-term effects, (in)visible power structures, and patterns of norms and values as sense-making devices in management and organization.

2. The study was carried out by use of the biographical method (Becker 1970; Denzin 1989, 2000; Gullestad 1996; Stanley 1992), including the guidance of a topic list (categories: life history, views on current societal developments, insights in managerial knowledge and trends, and personal strategies to deal with the management of the organization). Fifteen top-level managers from big organizations (profit and nonprofit, all with more than one thousand employees) were interviewed at least five times, for a total of five or more hours, in their offices and in restaurants or other places of their

choice; the total time span of the research covered a period of five years (also to avoid socially desirable answers and remarks). They were observed by students (weeks); the discussions were taped and transcribed, the observation notes elaborated. All data were analyzed based on the topic clusters and insights from theories of management and organization. Data saturation occurred after two-thirds of the respondents had been interviewed. For a more elaborate overview of the applied methods see Koot and Sabelis (2002, 45–60).

3. The workload study was carried out in 2003 and 2004. It consisted of three phases: first, a survey (response = 64 percent) based on general questions taken from former research at the university level; second, focus groups for finding out about seemingly contradictory results and deepening of issues; and third, a phase of re-flexive (qualitative) analysis. The latter included in-depth interviews, combined with facts and figures of former research within the university and available statistics from, for instance, medical staff (work-related illness). The survey, the focus groups, and a first analysis were carried out by an external consultancy (Loggers Consultants, Groningen, NL); the secondary analysis was done by I. Sabelis and was interactively supervised by management of the faculty and the university's health and personnel departments.

References

Adam, Barbara. 1995. *Timewatch: The social analysis of time*. Cambridge, MA: Polity.

———. 1998. *Timescapes of modernity: The environment and invisible hazards*. London: Routledge.

———. 2004. *Time*. Cambridge, MA: Polity.

Adam, Barbara, Richard Whipp, and Ida Sabelis. 2002. Choreographing time and management, traditions, developments, and opportunities. In *Making time: Time and management in modern organizations*, ed. R. Whipp, B. Adam, and I. Sabelis, 1–28. Oxford: Oxford University Press.

Alvesson, Mats, and Kaj Sköldberg. 2000. *Reflexive methodology*. London: Sage.

AMJ. 2002. A new time. *Academy of Management Journal* 45 (Oct.), special research forum.

Becker, H. 1970. *Sociological work*. Chicago: Aldine.

Bluedorn, Allen. 2002. *The human organization of time: Temporal realities and experience*. Stanford, CA: Stanford University Press.

Clark, Peter A. 1985. A review of the theories of time and structure for organizational sociology. *Research in the Sociology of Organizations* 4:35–79.

———. 1997a. American corporate timetabling: Its past, present, and future. *Time & Society* 6 (2/3): 261–285.

———. 1997b. The duality of strategic time reckoning and the influence of national predispositions on production and inventory control systems. In *Between tradition and innovation: Time in a managerial perspective*, ed. Dawn Caseby and Gabriele Morello, 235–263. Palermo: ISIDA.

Das, T. K. 1987. Strategic planning and individual temporal orientation. *Strategic Management Journal* 8:203–209.

———. 1993. Time in management and organization studies. *Time & Society* 2 (2): 267–274.

———. 2004. Strategy and time: Really recognizing the future. In *Managing the future: Strategic foresight in the knowledge economy*, ed. Haridimos Tsoukas and Jill Shepherd, 58–74. Oxford: Blackwell.

Denzin, Norman K. 1989. *Interpretative biography*. Newbury Park, CA: Sage.

———. 2000. The practices and politics of interpretation. In *The handbook of qualitative research*, ed. N. Denzin and Y. Lincoln, 897–922. Thousand Oaks, CA: Sage.

Geertz, Clifford. 1973. *The interpretation of cultures*. New York: Basic Books.

Gell, Alfred. 1992. *The anthropology of time: Cultural constructs of temporal maps and images*. Oxford: Berg.

Gleick, James. 1999. *Faster: The acceleration of just about everything*. New York: Vintage.

Gullestad, Marianne. 1996. *Everyday life philosophers: Modernity, morality, and autobiography in Norway*. Oslo: Scandinavian University Press.

Gurvitch, Georges. 1964. *The spectrum of social time*. Dordrecht: D. Reidel.

Hall, Edward T. 1983. *The dance of life: The other dimension of time*. New York: Anchor-Doubleday.

Handy, Charles. 1990. *The age of unreason*. Boston: Harvard Business School Press.

Karsten, Luchien. 2003. Management draait om tijd [Management is all about time]. Groningen, NL: Rijksuniversiteit.

Keenoy, Tom. 1999. HRM as hologram: A polemic. *Journal of Management Studies* 36 (1): 1–23.

———. 2005. e-Scape from the castle: The ambiguous potential of e-mail. Paper presented at the 21st EGOS colloquium, "Unlocking organizations," Berlin, June 30–July 2.

Koot, Willem, and Ida Sabelis. 2002. *Beyond complexity: Paradoxes and coping strategies in managerial life*. Amsterdam: Rozenbergh.

Kümmerer, Klaus. 1996. The ecological impact of time. *Time & Society* 5 (2): 209–236.

McTaggart, John Ellis. 1908. The unreality of time. *Mind: A Quarterly Review of Psychology and Philosophy* 17:456–473. www.ditext.com/mctaggart/time.html (accessed Jan. 25, 2007).

Menzies, Heather. 2005. *No time: Stress and the crisis of modern life*. Vancouver: Douglas and McIntyre.

Menzies, Heather, and Janice Newson. 2005. Time, stress, and intellectual engagement in academic work: Exploring the gender difference. Paper presented at the 4th International Interdisciplinary Conference of Gender, Work, and Organization, University of Keele, UK, June 22–24.

Pahl, Ray. 1995. *After success: Fin-de-siècle anxiety and identity*. Cambridge, MA: Polity.

Paolucci, Gabriela. 1996. The changing dynamics of working time. *Time & Society* 5 (2): 145–168.

Parker, Martin, and D. Jary. 1995. The McUniversity: Organization, management, and academic subjectivity. *Organization* 2 (2): 319–383.

Peters, Peter F. 2005. *Time, innovation, and mobilities: Travels in technological cultures.* London: Routledge.

Rosa, Hartmut. 2002. Social acceleration: Ethical and political consequences of a de-synchronized high-speed society. Paper presented at the 15th World Congress of Sociology (ISA), Brisbane, July 4–8.

Sabelis, Ida H. J. 2002. *Managers' times: A study of times in the work and life of top managers.* Amsterdam: Bee's Books.

———. 2004a. Work and load—a study of temporal issues related to changing work conditions. Amsterdam: Faculty of Social Sciences, internal publication.

———. 2004b. Global speed—a time view on transnationality. *Culture and Organization* 10 (4): 291–302.

Schein, Edgar H. 1985. *Organizational culture and leadership: A dynamic view.* San Francisco: Jossey-Bass.

Schouteten, Roel. 2005. Werkdrukonderzoek FdM—presentation of a work load study, Dec. 21, 2005. Nijmegen: Radboud Universiteit/FdM, internal publication.

Stanley, Liz. 1992. *The auto-biographical I: The theory and practise of feminist autobiography.* Manchester: Manchester University Press.

Tennekes, J. 1995. *Organizatiecultuur. Een antropologische visie* [Organizational culture: An anthropological approach]. Leuven-Apeldoorn: Garant Uitgeverij.

Thompson, E. P. 1967. Time, work-discipline, and industrial capitalism. *Past and Present* 38 (1): 56–97.

Virilio, Paul. 2002. *Desert screen: War at the speed of light.* London: Continuum.

Watson, Tony, and Pauline Harris. 1999. *The emergent manager.* London: Sage.

Whipp, Richard. 1994. A time to be concerned: A position paper on time and management. *Time & Society* 3 (1): 99–116.

Ybema, Sierk, and Ida Sabelis. 2006. The "shop floor man": Identity struggles of lower middle managers. Paper presented at the conference "Managing identities in complex organizations," University of Lund, May 11–12.

Ylijoki, Oili-Helena, and Hans Mäntylä. 2003. Conflicting Time Perspectives in Academic Work. *Time & Society* 12 (1): 55–78.

Index